Licensing

The International Sale of
Patents and Technical Knowhow

Licensing

by

Michael Z. Brooke

and

John M. Skilbeck

———————

Gower

© Michael Z. Brooke and John M. Skilbeck 1994

All rights reserved. No part of this publication may be reproduced, stored in a retrieval system, or transmitted in any form or by any means, electronic, mechanical, photocopying, recording or otherwise without the permission of the publisher.

Published by
Gower Publishing Limited
Gower House
Croft Road
Aldershot
Hampshire GU11 3HR
England

Gower
Old Post Road
Brookfield
Vermont 05036
USA

M. Z. Brooke and J. M. Skilbeck have asserted their right under the Copyright, Designs and Patents Act 1988 to be identified as the authors of this work.

British Library Cataloguing in Publication Data
Brooke, Michael Z.
Licensing: International Sale of Patents and Technical Knowhow
I. Title II. Skilbeck, John M.
341.7586

ISBN 0-566-07461-3

Library of Congress Cataloging-in-Publication Data

Brooke, Michael Z., 1921 –
Licensing : the international sale of patents and technical knowhow / Michael Z. Brooke, John M. Skilbeck.
p.   cm.
ISBN 0-566-07461-3
1. Foreign licensing agreements. 2. Technology transfer--Law and legislation.
I. Skilbeck, John M. II. Title.
K1530.B77 1994
346.04'8--dc20
[342.648]
94-19954
CIP

Typeset in 11pt on 14pt Goudy Regular by Aitch Em Wordservice, Aylesbury, Buckinghamshire, Great Britain and printed in Great Britain by the University Press, Cambridge.

Contents

List of Tables	xi
List of Figures	xii
List of Case Examples (notes on the use of case examples in this book and where to find them)	xiii
Foreword by Sir Alastair Pilkington FRS	xv
Briefing (summary of the purpose of the book)	xvi
Service to readers (offer by authors to respond to enquiries)	xviii
How to use this book	xix
Acknowledgements	xxi
Part 1 Executive Summaries (notes and checklists for quick reference and indications of where to find further information on each topic)	1
1.1 The global sale of knowhow	3
1.1.1 Selling knowhow	5
1.1.2 Licensing agreements	8
1.2 Guidelines for licensors	11
1.2.1 Identifying the markets for licensing	11

		1.2.2 Stalking the licensee	13
		1.2.3 Negotiating the contract	14
		1.2.4 Monitoring performance	15
		1.2.5 Anticipating problems	15
		1.2.6 Finance and remuneration	17

1.3 Guidelines for licensees — 19

1.4 Guidelines for governments and international organizations — 23

1.5 Licensing agreements — 29

1.6 Background: the most common uses of intellectual property protection, some myths dispelled — 35

Part 2 Business Strategy — 43

2.1 International licensing: its relationship to other business strategies — 45
- 2.1.1 Reasons for preferring licensing — 47
- 2.1.2 Disadvantages and problems — 49
- 2.1.3 Licensing compared with other options for foreign business — 51
- 2.1.4 Taxation and the repatriation of profits — 56
- 2.1.5 Other strategic issues — 57
- Appendix to Chapter 2.1: A scheme for evaluating potential licensing agreements — 59

2.2 Licensing: the decisions — 67

2.3 Related means of selling knowledge — 83
- 2.3.1 Franchising — 83
- 2.3.2 Other knowledge agreements — 86

Part 3 Legal and Political Issues — 89

3.1 Intellectual property rights — 91
    3.1.1 The protection of industrial property — 95
    3.1.2 Copyright — 96
    3.1.3 Trademarks — 100
    3.1.4 General issues — 102

3.2 Regulations and services (government and private sector) — 117
    3.2.1 Government regulation — 117
    3.2.2 Government assistance — 118
    3.2.3 Arbitration — 119
    3.2.4 Litigation: the protection of general corporate knowledge — 128

3.3 Drafting an agreement — 131
    3.3.1 The technical and business agreements — 131
    3.3.2 Remuneration — 132
    3.3.3 Marketing and other services — 132
    3.3.4 Duration and scope — 133
    3.3.5 Review, renewal and termination — 133
    3.3.6 Provisions for the settlement of disputes — 134
    3.3.7 Insurance and liability — 134
    3.3.8 Confidentiality and the right of inspection — 134
    3.3.9 Quality — 135

3.4 The political background — 137
    3.4.1 Characteristics — 140
    3.4.2 International organizations (see also part 6) — 142
    3.4.3 Regional Trading Organizations — 143
    3.4.4 Training — 143

3.5 A typical technology transfer agreement based on knowhow and a trademark — 145

Part 4 Managing the Licensing Agreement   157

4.1 Organization and communication   159
    4.1.1 Authority and responsibility   159
    4.1.2 Organization   162
    4.1.3 Decision-making and communication   168
    4.1.4 Data transfer: machinery and process manuals   169
    4.1.5 Updating the licence   170

4.2 Planning and controlling the licensing process   173
    4.2.1 The licensing development in five stages   174
    4.2.2 The control and monitoring of the licensing stages   185

4.3 Finance, prices and costs   191
    4.3.1 Revenues and costs: the licensor's profit   191
    4.3.2 Revenues and costs: the licensee's interests   198
    4.3.3 Sources of funds   199
    4.3.4 Fees   199
    4.3.5 Taxation   203

4.4 Marketing   207
    4.4.1 The four stages   209
    4.4.2 Market research and assessment   213
    4.4.3 The marketing of technology and advertising   225
    4.4.4 Selling   226
    4.4.5 Other marketing issues   227

4.5 Personnel and other services for licensor and licensee   235
    4.5.1 Recruitment, staffing and conditions of employment   235
    4.5.2 Training   237
    4.5.3 Management services   247

4.6 The relationship between the licensor and the licensee   249

Part 5 Licensing in Specific Countries and Regions   257

5.1 The industrialized countries (including the
European Union)   261
    5.1.1 The European Union and the European
Economic Area   261
    5.1.2 Industrialized countries   269

5.2 Some regional and international organizations   281
    5.2.1 North American Free Trade Association (NAFTA)   284
    5.2.2 The Association of South East Asian Nations
(ASEAN)   285
    5.3.3 The Andean Pact (ANCOM)   286

5.3 Developing and former communist countries   287
    5.3.1 The licensor's viewpoint   288
    5.3.2 The licensee's standpoint   289
    5.3.3 The government viewpoint and compulsory licences   291
    5.3.4 Specific countries   296

**Part 6 Present and Future: The Professional Licensing
Executive**   335

6.1 The state of the art   337

6.2 Problems and errors   339
    6.2.1 Competition   339
    6.2.2 Political risk   340
    6.2.3 Differences in size and time horizons   341
    6.2.4 Liability   342
    6.2.5 Over-optimistic forecasts and inadequate
information   342
    6.2.6 Conclusion   343

6.3 Prospects   345
    6.3.1 The licensing profession   345

	6.3.2	Advantages of licensing and knowhow selling as	
		a business development strategy for the nineties	348
	6.3.3	Trends in the exploitation of intellectual property	357

Part 7 Appendices 369

7.1	Definitions		371
	7.1.1	Thesaurus	371
	7.1.2	Additional definitions	390

7.2	Publications	395

7.3	Organizations	401

Part 8 Indexes 411

8.1	Index of subjects	413

8.2	Index of names	417

List of Tables

1.3.1	Appraising the project: a licensee checklist	19
1.6.1	Patents between industrialized countries	36
1.6.2	Research and development expenditure	37
1.6.3	United Kingdom national research and development expenditure versus international knowhow receipts	38
1.6.4	Analysis of ICI's research and development expenditure and royalty income	38
1.6.5	Analysis of Pilkington's research and development expenditure and royalty income	39
2.1.1	Accumulated income (profits) to technology originator	64
3.2.1	Statistics of cases heard by the International Chamber of Commerce Court of Arbitration in 1992	123
4.1.1	Degree of delegation of work in various company resource-utilization strategies	161
4.3.1	Pricing a licensing agreement	193
4.3.2	Withholding tax on royalty income	204
4.4.1	Linear Power Ltd: Technology application matrix	216
4.4.2	Chemical and other plant construction	218
4.4.3	Linear Power Ltd: Other survey results	219
5.2.1	Membership of regional and international organizations	281

List of Figures

1.1.1	The international sale of knowhow	4
1.1.2	The options for knowhow sales	6
1.1.3	Equity in a licensing project	6
2.1.1	The place of licensing in international business	46
2.1.2	Options compared	60
2.1.3	Export marketing: diminishing returns	61
2.1.4	Cumulative profit versus sales achieved	63
2.1.5	Comparison of pre-tax income	63
4.1.1	Organization structures	163
4.1.2	Organization of senior management of Mohpam Components	165
4.4.1	Operation sequence for early innovation decisions	210

List of Case Examples

Throughout the book a number of examples are quoted which show the use of licensing under various circumstances. For the benefit of readers seeking examples relevant to their interests, these are listed below. The names of the companies have usually been disguised, as have other details, to preserve confidentiality. Note:

* those disguised are marked with an asterisk.
+ those considered especially suitable for use at a management training seminar are marked with a plus sign.

Industry Sector	Name of Licensor	Region or country of Licensor	Region or country of Licensee	Principal issues	Page
Biotechnology	National + Industrialization company	Various	Saudi Arabia	Licensing (in many sectors) and contract manufacture	330
Fashion clothing	Selina Knitwear			Piracy of copyright	96
Electrical electronics	Linear * + Power Ltd	Britain	Germany Italy	Market research and location	215
Electrical electronics	Mohpam * Components			Licensee large international components producer with inadequate design and production technology	165

xiii

Industry Sector	Name of Licensor	Region or country of Licensor	Region or country of Licensee	Principal issues	Page
Electrical electronics	Company C * +	Britain	Hungary	Licence leading to joint manufacture	315
Furniture	Lidmar * +	Britain	United States	Extend product range	73
General Manufacturing	[Company A] * +	Britain	Turkey	Development from export through licensing to investment	54
General Manufacturing	Company B * +	Britain	Poland	Approval from licensee	329
Medical	British University + *	Britain	Germany	Blood transfusion equipment	230
Transport engineering	Company A	Britain	Turkey	Change from licensee to subsidiary	274

Foreword

It is a pleasure to welcome this practical guide to licensing executives in which is distilled much experience which they will like to keep at their elbows for quick reference when required.

A major theme of the book is maintaining and enhancing the professional standing of licensing executives and this is also a significant interest of the Society which I serve as Honorary President.

Many reports tell of a rapid increase in the number of licensing projects as more companies find this a profitable way of selling their technology abroad.

Sir Alastair Pilkington FRS
Honorary President, Licensing Executives Society
(Britain and Ireland)

Briefing

This book is designed to take the reader through the maze of activities necessary for the successful selling of technical expertise internationally. Part 1 summarizes the main issues and is a quick guide for the busy executive who can refer to the more detailed information in the other parts when required.

This is a book for **managers** who have responsibility for determining and implementing international licensing; in consequence Part 2 positions licensing in a context of business strategy by demonstrating relationships with other business strategies and of methods for selecting options that are suitable for various occasions. Part 3 moves into more detail by outlining legal and political issues. Since this is not a book for lawyers, the legal issues are in the form of advice and checklists for discussion with legal advisers who must, of course, draft the agreements. This part also discusses the protection of patents and other forms of intellectual property. Part 4 deals with other management issues such as organization, planning, finance, marketing and staffing as well as relationships between licensor and licensee. Part 5 looks at agreements in specific countries and regions while Part 5 summarizes the subject and Part 7 is a series of Appendices giving sources of information.

KNOWLEDGE AGREEMENTS

Licensing is one form of knowledge agreement – the sale of expensively acquired knowhow and experience – there are many other forms. The similar technical assistance agreement is used for the transfer of unprotected (public domain) technology.

Another is **management contracts**, in which a complete management package is sold by a contractor company to a client. Yet other forms include franchising (the sale of a commercial package, usually in a service industry), turnkey projects and contract manufacture.

THE WORDS

The parties to an agreement are referred to, in this book, as licensor (or principal) and licensee (or client). They are also known as participants or partners. The pronoun used is 'it' since they are considered to be companies not individuals. These words represent a business relationship, not necessarily a legal reality. Other words like grantor or grantee are sometimes used, but not on these pages except in quotations. The information being sold is described as a patent or 'knowhow'; the latter word is not used in any other sense.

A glossary can be found at the end of the book.

Note the word **knowhow** is used here in the normal business sense of the total body of knowledge required to implement a technical transfer; this is not necessarily the legal meaning of the term.

Disclaimer: naturally every effort has been made to ensure the accuracy of the contents of this book but – equally naturally – no liability can be accepted for problems encountered by readers (although see service to readers on the next page). In such a rapidly changing subject, statements correct when they were written can be out-of-date by the time of publication. It is **essential** that expert professional advice is sought before drafting or signing an agreement.

Service to Readers

Licensing is a practical reference book, it is designed for a place on your desk to be consulted when one of the questions it considers confronts you. It is not designed to be read straight through like a novel or a textbook.

Below are notes to help readers to find their way around, but any help the authors can give will be gladly given. Write to either of them c/o the publisher, Gower Publishing Company Ltd, Gower House, Croft Road, Aldershot, Hampshire GU11 3HR, England or phone Michael Brooke on 061-746 8140 – from outside Britain: +44 61 746 8140. **Call anytime**, all enquiries welcome. Enquiries by fax should be addressed to either John Skilbeck or to Michael Brooke on +44 61 746 8132.

How to use this book

In using this book to shed light on your problems, you (the reader) have several methods of tracking down the advice you require:

1. look at the list of case examples and the column which identifies the issues to see if your problem is there; the examples include a number of small companies intended to convince you that licensing projects are successfully undertaken by firms of many different sizes;
2. look at the contents list to see if your problem rates a chapter;
3. look at the lists of figures and tables for the same reason;
4. if your problem does not find a mention in the contents, it will almost certainly find a place in the subject index at the end of the book;
5. failing that, too, give us a call.

To combine accessibility with comprehensiveness, the book is written at three levels of information.

Level 1 (Parts 1 and 6) provides a series of quick guides – briefing notes for licensors, licensees, regulators and other interested parties. Part 1 includes cross-references to later chapters where the subject is examined in more detail.

Level 2 (Parts 2 to 5) is the more detailed account, with evidence and examples, for those who want to go into the subject more thoroughly.

Level 3 (Part 7) is a series of appendices with a glossary, a reading list for those who want to examine the subject in more detail and a list of organizations whose addresses could be useful to readers.

The scheme of the book

The aim of the book is to provide a comprehensive review of licensing for the practitioner: how and where licensing is used, the kinds of business supported, the opportunities, the problems and their solutions, together with other relevant issues.

After **Part 1**, which summarizes current usage, attention is turned to examining the different aspects of the subject in greater depth. **Part 2** examines the strategic aspects of licensing as a method of operating outside the home country; the relevant decisions are listed as are other options such as investment and franchising.

In **Part 3** we turn to legal and political issues with one chapter (3.5) containing a specimen agreement. **Part 4** deals with the managerial issues expected to be of greatest interest to our readers; it looks in turn at organizing, planning, financing, marketing, staffing and other issues; the part also includes a brief concluding chapter on the vexed question of relationships between licensor and licensee.

Part 5 looks at special considerations for nations and regions (including the developing world) while **Part 6** summarizes and looks to the future. **Part 7** contains the appendices already mentioned while the final part (8) includes the subject index designed to help the reader find a specific topic and a name index to guide you to countries or organizations which feature in the book. In accordance with common custom, the subject index is selective, omitting topics that do not find a significant place in the book, while the names index is more comprehensive and lists all names where even a single reference may be valuable to the reader.

Acknowledgements

This book is a comprehensive manual for executives, engineers and administrators and has been made possible by assistance from many quarters.

One of the authors (Michael Z. Brooke) wrote a book some years ago made possible by a grant from the Leverhulme Trust. This book, too, has benefited from that grant. He would also like to thank Carl Thunman from Uppsala, Sweden, who wrote most of Chapter 4.2; Piero Telesio of Northeast Consulting Resources Inc. of Boston, Massachusetts gave generously from his knowledge of the subject. Thandi Hurworth (technology transfer consultant and editor of the *Intellectual Property Journal*) provided invaluable advice.

Finally Michael thanks his PA, Elizabeth Hickson who has worked imperturbably through continual revisions and many panics to key in (as we now have to call it) the 150 000 words of text and to design and draft the figures and tables.

John Skilbeck thanks Karen Williams for her valuable research on current licensing practices in a number of international groupings, countries and companies.

Jeffries Briginshaw, solicitor, for his able contributions and advice on a wide variety of legal topics.

Barry Quest, of M'Caw and Co., Manchester, Vice President of The Licensing Executives Society Britain and Ireland for his support and advice on numerous matters.

Tim Loxton-Vowles of The Glacier Metal Company Ltd for the benefit of his wisdom and experience, particularly concerning licensing agreements.

Ken Campbell, Wogen Technology Ltd, London, for his assistance in updating our information on the latest trading conditions in The People's Republic of China.

David Bleach for his journalistic skills in researching recent case studies.

Part 1

Executive Summaries

This book is designed as a management handbook. It is **not** meant to be read through like a textbook. Each chapter is there and each major subject is listed in the index to be used for reference when the topic appears on your agenda. As part of the scheme, Part 1 is a series of summaries and checklists based on what is to follow. There are frequent cross-references to chapters in which the summary statement is expanded – summaries do not usually include the underlying reasoning nor the ifs and buts.

After a brief outline of the theme of the book in Chapter 1.1, the rest of this part summarizes the issues as they especially affect licensors, licensees, governments and regulatory bodies along with the other topics examined in more detail later. The final Chapter (1.6) provides a background to what is to follow.

Figure 2.1.1 (in Part 2) should be consulted now for an overview of the options open to the international business.

1

1.1 The global sale of knowhow

At the end of the century, the whole nature of trade has changed amazingly. Merchants are as likely to be offering the way to make things as the things themselves. Increasingly, products are made locally and not shipped round the world; but the ability to make them may still depend on technology patented elsewhere or techniques laboriously acquired in another country. Business people are not addicted to reinventing the wheel with the result that they are prepared to buy in knowledge they require and find this the most cost effective way of developing a new business.

SELLING KNOWLEDGE

Numerous methods are available for selling a body of knowledge or expertise that has commercial value. This book concentrates on technical knowhow (see Chapter 2.1) in contrast to commercial knowhow, the sale of which is the subject of a **franchising** agreement, or a general package (including, when relevant, technical, commercial and management knowledge) known as a **management contract**. The word licensing is frequently applied to the other two methods as well, but not in this book – except that the distinctions are blurred in many projects.

Technical knowhow includes, for the purposes of this book, documentary records but is not confined to these. Also included are training programmes and the development of skills in using the equipment to be licensed as well as an understanding of the market into which it will be sold. When a company buys a licence, the principal object it sees itself buying is the ability to manufacture a product or to use a saleable piece of equipment, in either case safeguarded by a patent which it would otherwise be illegal to use. The protection of trademarks (although frequently important in licensing agreements) is addressed in passing.

Executive Summaries

MOVING KNOWHOW AND GOODS

Current technology makes the movement of knowledge around the world easier and much faster than the movement of goods. Devices from the telephone to the on-line link and to the fax machine facilitate the movement of knowledge. Data does not have to come packaged in bundles of paper although even these can be air-freighted more easily than most goods.

Current politics – which includes protectionism as well as the problems of overcoming it represented in the General Agreement on Tariffs and Trade – also hinders the movement of goods, at least across regional boundaries, where knowledge usually passes unimpeded. The only serious obstacle to the flow of knowledge and information – censorship, including prejudice against certain ideas – is not usually successful for long.

Figure 1.1.1 The international sale of knowhow

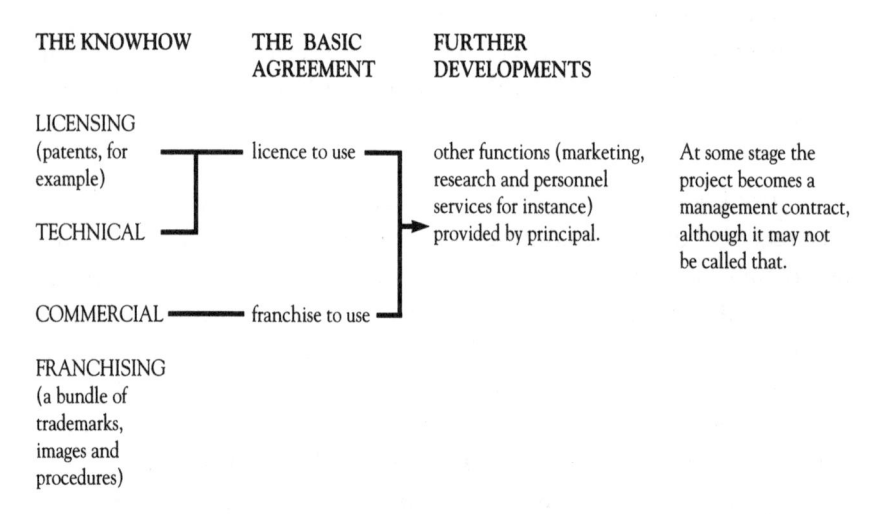

THE KNOWHOW	THE BASIC AGREEMENT	FURTHER DEVELOPMENTS	
LICENSING (patents, for example)	licence to use	other functions (marketing, research and personnel services for instance) provided by principal.	At some stage the project becomes a management contract, although it may not be called that.
TECHNICAL			
COMMERCIAL	franchise to use		
FRANCHISING (a bundle of trademarks, images and procedures)			

At any stage the process may turn into an investment project – if, for instance, the principal buys the client company.

1

1.1.1 SELLING KNOWHOW

The possibilities for licensing have long been recognised and its use is now becoming more common – although still accounting for only about ten per cent of world trade, whose total volume is increasing rapidly. Figure 1.1.1 illustrates the usual processes in a licensing project.

Licensing and franchising, the two major methods for the sale of knowhow, are shown on the Figure. Both have a **basic** (sometimes called 'pure') form in which a vendor (the **licensor** or **franchisor**) agrees to sell trade secrets to a buyer (the licensee or franchisee).

In neither case does the basic form usually prove permanently satisfactory and other functions or facilities are added, sometimes in the original agreement. If, as is common, the licensor is a larger company than the licensee, it may want to inject the skills of its central services in marketing, finance, research or personnel (including training) or other functions. There may be difficulties in obtaining payment for these services and a revised agreement is likely to become necessary.

With the addition of management services, a licensing or franchising project becomes (in fact, although usually not in name) a management contract – an agreement to sell management as well as technical or commercial expertise.

APPROACHES TO THE SALE OF KNOWHOW

Licensor companies adopt a number of approaches to the activity, including the following.

1. Protecting the business, defending the technology (see Chapter 1.6).
2. Earning more revenue on the strength of expensively acquired knowledge and expertise (see Part 2).
3. Entering new markets (see Part 2).

Executive Summaries

THE BASICS OF KNOWLEDGE AGREEMENTS

Figures 1.1.1 and 1.1.2 illustrate the basics of knowledge agreements. Figure 1.1.1 shows how they can develop from the germ of an idea towards a full-blown investment project, while Figure 1.1.2 identifies the main actors.

Figure 1.1.2 The options for knowhow sales

Option	Principal	Client
Licensing	Licensor	Licensee
Franchising	Franchisor	Franchisee
Management contracts	Contractor	Contract venture
Contract manufacturing and other similar arrangements	Contractor company	Client company

The knowledge that is being sold includes the commercial skill to sell it profitably, hence the word knowhow used throughout this book in the normal business sense (of knowledge and skill combined) and not in any of the technical meanings employed in law or engineering.

Figure 1.1.3 Equity in a licensing project

Phase 1	Phase 2	Phase 3	Phase 4
a small amount of equity to establish the project	a larger amount of equity aimed at either rescuing or enlarging the project	a still larger amount turning the project into a joint venture	100% turning the project into a wholly-owned subsidiary

1

Figure 1.1.3 lists various proportions of equity; these vary so greatly between projects that it is impossible to insert percentages except in phase 4 which brings total ownership. These phases do not represent a common progression – each may be dispensed with; once some equity is committed there does seem to be a likelihood of more to follow, but phases 1 (the token amount) and 4 (the total ownership) may never occur.

Some companies enter only phase 2; in this phase funds are injected into the licensee to improve its debt:equity ratio, to help over a critical period or to promote a restructuring or enlargement.

Phases 3 and 4 – the joint venture and the wholly owned subsidiary – are usually regarded as alternatives (either:or) with a preference these days for a joint venture in which both parties are committed and can share the benefits.

Other methods of selling knowhow are listed in Chapter 2.3. These include: **contract manufacture**, the sale of technical knowhow for a specific purpose which may or may not be accompanied by a licensing agreement (although it normally will); and **turnkey agreements**, a form of short-term management contract in which a project, such as a new plant, is built and begins operating before its handover to the client.

OTHER OPTIONS (SEE CHAPTER 2.1)

There are two principal means besides knowledge agreements of conducting international business.

1. Export. Providing exports are possible by using existing facilities and resources, then this will normally be the most profitable route abroad unless tariffs, transport costs or other restraints make it uneconomic.
   Licensing will normally be undertaken where constraints or customer resistance make export uneconomic or where the company lacks

Executive Summaries

the resources for promotion and distribution abroad.
2 Investment (either through a joint venture or a wholly owned subsidiary). Investment is the high cost, high risk route that is expected to generate high returns.

1.1.2 LICENSING AGREEMENTS

This book is a guide to the most common form of knowledge agreement: licensing. Other forms are frequently called 'licensing' as a generic name for all.

Licensing itself is a highly professional activity and supporting this professionalism is a major theme of the book. From inception to development, a licensing project passes through the following stages (see Chapter 4.2):

1 pre-negotiation,
2 negotiation,
3 knowledge transfer,
4 manufacturing start-up, and
5 long-term development.

At any stage in the development of a project, starting with the basic agreement, the licensor may decide to inject some equity because:

1 it immediately adds to the licensee's profitability or,
2 in the longer term, it ensures revenue from the licensee's success or,
3 for a number of other reasons (see Chapter 4.3).

If equity is inserted (and this is unlikely especially if one of the licensor's motives is shortage of capital), then a fresh chain of events is started. The process of change is illustrated in Figure 1.1.3.

Licensing people are likely to be especially interested in the protection of intellectual property now provided by a number of international treaties as well as most national governments.

One problem is that the countries which do not offer the protection are also the ones most suitable for licensing projects if only on the grounds that they are unsuitable for investment.

International protection is explained in Chapter 3.1; the addresses of the organizations can be found in an Appendix (7.3). The principal international organization is the World Intellectual Property Organization (WIPO).

In Chapter 4.2, the following five stages in the development of a licensing agreement are identified and explained.

1. Pre-negotiation.
2. Negotiation.
3. Knowledge transfer.
4. Manufacturing start-up.
5. Long-term development.

1.2 Guidelines for licensors

Licensing arrangements can be used to satisfy corporate objectives – a cost effective route to expansion and the servicing of new markets as well as a means of safeguarding patents. The types of strategy can be either:

1. defensive, safeguarding existing markets or technology;
2. aggressive – the search for new opportunities; or
3. responsive, when the licensor enters a deal in response to approaches from would-be licensees. This is not necessarily inconsistent with the other two types of strategy but care is needed. Accepting an unrefusable offer which is inconsistent with other strategies has often proved a trap in the longer term.

The following is a checklist of points which are considered later in the book.

1.2.1 IDENTIFYING THE MARKETS FOR LICENSING

The following considerations are important for spotting markets.

1. Either:
   (a) those most suitable for developing a business (especially small businesses with saleable technology);
   (b) those most unsuitable for export or investment; or
   (c) those where protection for existing business is required.
   Which of these alternatives dominates the decision-making will depend upon the size and global strategies of the licensor.
2. The decision in either case needs to be supported by market research (4.4.2).
3. Likely and unlikely countries can be identified (Part 5) as follows:
   (a) those that need protection; or
   (b) those most suitable for developing the business (if a small company searching for immediate outlets); or
   (c) those most unsuitable for export or investment (if a large company).

Executive Summaries

4 Monitor the proposals and projects of international organizations especially the World Bank, the regional development banks and the United Nations Industrial Development Organization. Opportunities for licensing schemes are likely to develop from these proposals (3.4.2).

MARKETING LICENSING PROJECTS

Many would-be licensors do not need to market the project; once they have built up a reputation, eager partners approach them. If they do not have a reputation, it will be difficult to find satisfactory licensees who are likely to be much concerned with the skills and reliability of the licensor. If a marketing programme is required it should be set up along the following lines.

1 Work hard on the company's image and reputation.
2 Ensure that the company is geared up for the project, and that the expertise and the facilities are available.
3 Select country (see above) and get to know it, together with its language and culture, thoroughly.
4 Select companies in relevant industry sectors and target those with known track records.
5 Develop a specification, as a negotiating stance, which brings together the essential issues to be matched in the project.

Be prepared for the four stages in marketing (identified in Chapter 4.4).

1 Innovation (a crucial stage when the product idea is adopted commercially).
2 Market research (including the assessment, but going into greater detail).
3 Marketing thrust (including promotion).
4 Selling (opening up negotiations with potential licensees).

In spite of the strains on its management system, the licensor needs to sell licences in as many markets as possible to produce a satisfactory return.

1.2.2 STALKING THE LICENSEE (CHAPTER 2.2, DECISION 6)

A number of warnings and pieces of advice are applicable to the search for licensees.

1 Beware of lists of potential licensees which many organizations offer. There is so much demand for good licensees that anyone who is any good will be snapped up before the list is printed. Treat other people's lists as a last resort.
2 Compile your own list. This can only be done when someone from the licensor company or a trusted representative visits the country and discovers a company that is capable of manufacturing the product under licence, whether or not it is actively seeking to become a licensee. Once a company is known to be seeking licensees, it is likely to be inundated with offers which can then be evaluated by the trusted representative.
3 Evaluate the potential licensee:
   (a) track record;
   (b) examine finances;
   (c) examine corporate strengths and policies;
   (d) availability of staff and ability to communicate;
   (e) familiarity with target market.
4 Set out key issues to be incorporated in the agreement:
   (a) division of responsibilities;
   (b) liabilities;
   (c) pricing policies including royalties;
   (d) marketing policies including sales areas;
   (e) settlement of disputes;
   (f) dates for renewal or termination.

Executive Summaries

1.2.3 NEGOTIATING THE CONTRACT

The following issues must be taken into account.

OBJECTIVES

The licensor needs to enter the negotiations with a clear idea of what it intends to obtain from them. Essentials are:

1 an adequate return on the investment of knowledge and skilled personnel;
2 commercial benefits in home, host and third-country markets.

NEGOTIATIONS WITH LICENSEES

The licensor will aim to make the best possible use of these advantages.

The licensor will also wish to ensure that the nature of the technology is fully understood along with its purposes and uses.

So long as the objectives are clear, the licensor should hold most of the trumps when it comes to negotiation, provided the technology is sufficiently advanced and relevant, the presentation and the customer orientation are right and the price is not too high.

NEGOTIATIONS WITH GOVERNMENT

A licensor attempts to establish a system in which statutory dealings with foreign governments are in the hands of the licensee; a minor motive for preferring a licensing project, after all, is to ensure that local business is conducted locally and is not a concern of head office. Nevertheless, the licensor company may wish to become involved when delicate negotiations are involved, especially when tax and the transfer of funds are at stake.

Occasionally, also, the licensor may wish to rebut an attempt to claim liability either for an employment or for a product claim. In spite of great care in ensuring that there can be no liability, attempts can be made.

CONTACTS

The licensor will also want to use its worldwide contacts (if they exist) to negotiate for advantageous terms. Among the 'advantageous terms' is likely to be the ability to change the licensee if targets are not achieved. This is part of risk minimization, a significant aim of the negotiating process. The licensor will also need to be assured of direct access to the market. If the agreement denies this, the market may not be available for any purposes.

1.2.4 MONITORING PERFORMANCE

A normal aim of licensors is to ensure that the project brings in the forecast revenue with a minimum demand on head office management, thus avoiding high hidden and overhead costs. This is best ensured by establishing an effective control system. The system itself will not differ from that set up for any other foreign operation. It will include establishing and operating regular contacts between the two companies, establishing a standard agenda which will ensure that the key issues are aired at each meeting, and producing reports, at monthly intervals, of operating figures for the licensed project.

A list of questions that the reports will be designed to answer can be found at the end of Chapter 4.2.

1.2.5 ANTICIPATING PROBLEMS

A number of problems inevitably accompany licensing initiatives (see Chapter 6.2).

Executive Summaries

COMPETITION

The most widely anticipated, if not the most dangerous, problem is that a licensing agreement can establish a competitor. Also problematic is the changing competitive situation – especially in countries or regions that are adopting legislation to prevent restraints of trade.

POLITICAL RISK

A licensing project may be put in place either where political risk is low and the economy of the host country can be expected to support a viable business, or where political risk is too high to justify direct investment but the market is considered promising for the local opportunities that licensing could top.

DIFFERENCES IN SIZE AND TIME HORIZONS

These are frequently the cause of problems. If there is a difference in size, the problem is to ensure that the big company systems of the licensor can be made to work satisfactorily along with the more haphazard methods of the licensee.

LIABILITY (BOTH PRODUCT AND PERSONAL)

This is of special concern to the licensor; it may indeed be the clinching argument in a decision to proceed by a licence, and must be the responsibility of the licensee as far as possible.

OVER-OPTIMISTIC FORECASTING AND INADEQUATE INFORMATION

These can both lead to disappointment with the project and a sense of its failure.

1.2.6 FINANCE AND REMUNERATION

COST

The licensor has to take into account the costs of developing the technology and the direct and indirect costs of transferring it along with opportunity and the dissipation costs. Be wary of proceeding unless all these costs (many of them hidden) are fully met.

REMUNERATION

The licensor can expect to be paid by a number of means.

1. Dividends (if any equity is included).
2. Royalties for the use of the patent; these may be compounded by a lump sum or a percentage or both. The percentage itself is sometimes based on the number of products, sometimes on the value of sales and sometimes on profits. Some lump sum, as an upfront payment, is essential unless the product is regarded as totally risk-free, which is unlikely.
3. Countertrade is increasingly used. Among the current systems are payment by products of the licensed machinery or payments by other products or services. In either case, the licensor forced into this method of remuneration will also be forced into lengthy consideration of the best method of disposing of the fruits of the countertrade. If they are products sold by the licensor, great discretion will be needed to avoid damaging existing markets. For other products, a firm specializing in moving the fruits of countertrade is recommended.

1.3 Guidelines for licensees

The licensee may be the sought after party which the licensor approaches after going through the process of selection described elsewhere, but negotiations may start the other way round. Many licensees, especially in developing countries, operate the other way round. They seek foreign technology on which to build their businesses. Whichever way the project develops, the licensee will face the issues outlined in this Chapter beginning with the checklist in Table 1.3.1. The table provides a means of assessing a project.

Table 1.3.1 Appraising the project: a licensee checklist

	Decision	Priority Code	Is monitoring required?	Is to be included in agreement?	Role of licensor	Comments
1. ORGANIZATION 1.1 New company? 1.2 New department? 1.3 Appointment of staff 1.4 Training						
2. PLANNING 2.1 Long-range 2.2 Immediate plans 2.3 Arrangements that will continue after agreement expires						
3. FINANCE 3.1 Budgets 3.2 Borrowing 3.3 Equity 3.4 Royalties 3.5 Credit 3.6 Expenditure 3.7 Revenue 3.8 Pricing 3.9 Insurance						

Executive Summaries

Table 1.3.1 continued

	Decision	Priority Code	Is monitoring required?	Is to be included in agreement?	Role of licensor	Comments
4. CONTROL 4.1 Control systems 4.2 Accounting procedures						
5. MARKETING 5.1 Promotion 5.2 Sales 5.3 Distribution 5.4 Pricing 5.5 Product decisions 5.6 Competition						
6. PRODUCTION 6.1 Planning 6.2 Production control 6.3 Production planning						
7. OTHER SERVICES 7.1 Purchasing 7.2 Computer services 7.3 Other services						
8. THE AGREEMENT 8.1 Duration 8.2 Review 8.3 Renewal 8.4 Renegotiation 8.5 Conflict resolution 8.6 Termination						

THE DEFINITION OF OBJECTIVES AND STRATEGIES

These will be of three types according to the nature of the firm.

SMALL SCALE

The licensee company is normally planning on a smaller scale than the licensor; its ambition is for the development of a viable business in a local market although plans may already exist for a global reach; in some industries this will certainly be the case, but not too overtly at this stage otherwise the licensor might look elsewhere, fearing competition.

LARGER SCALE

If there are international ambitions, they may be limited to a region in which fresh business is emerging as industrialization takes place. The licensee may be seen as taking a first step towards the big league.

RAPID PROGRESS

The licensee is also likely to be a company in a hurry looking for quick results on capital that has been hard to raise. The difference in time scale is seen as a common cause of conflict between the two parties (see Chapter 6.3).

1

1.4 Guidelines for governments and international organizations

> Under the craft system, the average consumer bought a good made by a craftsman of average ability. Under mass production, every consumer could buy from the best designers in the world, provided that their government did not interfere with international trade in goods and the free flow of direct foreign investment.' (Romer, P. 'Ideas and things', *The Economist* September 11-17, 1993, p. 87.)

The quotation neatly sums up the benefits of technology transfer of which licensing is one method, although usually regarded as second best to 'direct foreign investment'.

Unless national security or secret technologies are involved the licensor's government is unlikely to be concerned with outward licensing. Nevertheless trade follows a licence; fellow-countrymen of the licensor (even the licensor itself) may well find themselves in a position to supply materials or components to the licensee. This possibility should form part of a government's long-term industrial strategy. It is also in the interests of governments to promote licensing to countries to which exports (otherwise considered to contribute more to a country's balance of trade) are improbable.

But the licensee's government is almost sure to be involved in ways that affect the licence arrangement. These are considered in the course of these pages and can be summed up as follows.

1 Tax. Some countries levy a withholding tax on royalty payments, but many do not (see 4.3.5).
2 Grants may be available if the licensee is establishing a new enterprise especially in a geographical or a product area to which the government is giving priority. Equally:
3 Prohibitions. In developing countries the government may decide which are desirable products for national development.
4 Product regulations. Health and safety and other regulations may determine the form that the product takes before manufacture.

Executive Summaries

5 Competition policies prevent licensors placing undue restrictions on licensees. Control of prices and sales areas are likely to be challenged. These policies are specific to certain regions (see Part 5). All licensing agreements impose some restraints on trade and merit examination.
6 Currency regulations. Most developing countries have non-convertible currencies and restrictions on taking money out of the country. These regulations often favour licensing projects but the implications still need to be studied carefully. If the over-riding object is to promote industrialization, the tax system must not prevent this. In the long term, the licensees' tax payments – and those of its employees – will more than compensate for taxes foregone on the royalties, hard as it may seem to allow these to be paid in another country; frequently a double taxation agreement takes care of anomalies.

Licensing policies

Where a need for licensing policies is felt, the following issues are included (see Chapter 3.4).

1 Decision-making: national needs and national capabilities.
2 Appraisal and monitoring:
   (a) checking on the employment opportunities and the stimulus to employment provided by licensing projects;
   (b) checking on the additional income generated through tax revenues.

Advantages of inward licensing

The advantages a country can expect to gain from inward licensing (see 5.3.2) include:

1 growth of the economy and with it jobs;
2 transfer of technology;

3 acquisition of technology;
4 ability to profit from a licensor's reputation and expertise;
5 training, both technical and for management, provided by the licensor;
6 reduced need for costly research and development; and (for developing countries)
7 the benefits can be gained without appearing to compromise a country's independence.

Cross licensing, on the other hand, can be a problem; it can effectively close markets.

There are also problems from the developing country's point of view:

1 stimulating local licensees in a country where there is no tradition of interest in science and technology; and
2 discouragements to business during periods of military government resulting in transfers of funds abroad.

Less developed countries use regulations on the transfer of technology to promote competition and development.

A recurring dilemma of government is to regulate without driving away. This dilemma has been a stimulus to the emergence of regional groupings. A common form of moderate intervention, on the part of otherwise liberal regimes, is the use of guidelines or codes of conduct for licensing projects.

COMPULSORY LICENSING

One question for an official in a trade or industry department to ask is: are this country's patent laws being used to restrict the emergence of a national industry here? If so the country is likely to consider compulsory licensing. As an alternative, a condition may be applied to the issue of a patent that ensures its use.

Executive Summaries

Fixing priorities

To assist or restrict licensing projects in such a way that they make a satisfactory contribution to national objectives, the following issues need to be on the administrator's agenda.

1. Jobs. A successful licensing project will promote employment and bring other benefits such as boosting morale in the business community and improving the level of its activity. Failure will not only have the opposite effect, a succession of failures can be devastating. It is therefore worthwhile, especially for a developing country looking for rapid industrialization, to foster licensing projects to reduce the risks of failure to a minimum.
2. Balance of payments. Licensing does not bring in funds, for this purpose direct foreign investment is to be preferred. Either method can be expected to boost exports.
3. Industrialization (transfer of technology). Licensing brings a transfer of technology more cost effectively than imports but no more so than direct investment.
4. Economic growth and independence. Licensing promotes growth without compromising a nation's independence, although it is important for regulators to ensure that too high a price is not being paid and that licensees select from licensors and suppliers in many industrial centres so as not to become over-dependent on any one. The imposition of undesirable restrictions, such as limited trading areas, needs to be watched, as do any attempts by the licensor to enforce long-term employment of its resources.
5. Taxation (see Chapter 4.3). Withholding taxes on remittances are a form of revenue for the government, but these are often conceded away in taxation agreements. A larger source of revenue is likely to come from the licensee's corporate taxes and the personal taxes of its employees. For a country that levies sales' taxes (such as VAT) there is also revenue from that source resulting from the raised level of business.
6. Commitment. A country which sees foreign expertise and management as a long-term means to economic growth will probably favour foreign investment. The investor, whatever the legends

about footloose companies, is only likely to withdraw as a result of a critical situation; the loss involved will deter haphazard disinvestment. The management contract can provide a similar, but less convincing, security if backed by some equity from the licensor. Otherwise this method is not designed to provide permanence; on the contrary one of the advantages for all parties is that the arrangement can be reconsidered at the end of a defined period. The commitment of the licensor company is to its reputation.
7 Monitoring. The licensee's government, as well as the partners, may wish to watch progress if only to develop guidelines for future projects. If the licensee has benefited from investment grants, the monitoring will be designed to ensure that the conditions of the grants are observed.
8 Other national interests. Employer and labour organizations are likely to prefer a licensing project to foreign investment as it brings an organization that can play its part in the national business and industrial relations scenes uninfluenced by policies determined in another country.

INTERNATIONAL ORGANIZATIONS

There are a number of international organizations which can provide services, facilities and advice for those involved in licensing projects. The most important are listed under the following headings.

INFORMATION AND ADVICE

World Intellectual Property Organization (WIPO) which oversees international treaties on the protection of patents, trademarks, copyright and a number of other issues of interest to licensing people (see Chapter 3.1).

The United Nations Centre on Transnational Corporations. Through its series of publications and through the provision of consultancy services to developing country governments, the Centre strengthens

Executive Summaries

the bargaining positions of licensees. The headquarters of this Centre in New York has now been closed and some of the work transferred to UNCTAD (the United Nations Conference on Trade and Development) in Geneva.

ARBITRATION

A number of international organizations offer conciliation and arbitration services for the settlement of disputes. If these are to be used (and they are easier to operate than national arbitration schemes and much less costly than litigation) a provision is required in the contract in all cases. See 3.2.3 for further details about the following providers of arbitration services.

International Centre for Settlement of Investment Disputes a World Bank affiliate which provides arbitration for disputes between the public and the private sectors.

The International Chamber of Commerce provides a long-established conciliation and arbitration service.

London Court of International Arbitration

All of these organizations provide arbitration tribunals in various parts of the world; the skill and impartiality of all three is beyond question.

1.5 Licensing agreements

Company A (the licensor, principal or contractor) undertakes to sell to company B in another country (the licensee or client) the right to manufacture a device protected by patent in both countries. Both parties recognize that the document lodged with the patent application will not be sufficient to set company B up in business. There have to be other documents (such as blueprints) but these will also be inadequate by themselves and personal contact to explain how to use the information, along with the body of knowledge that goes with it, will be required.

A licence is required for the use of the patent. Normally the use of the relevant knowhow accompanies the licence; but if the knowhow alone is being sold, a licence would not be required. It is protected (patented) information that is being licensed.

Before beginning the search for a licensee, the principal will need to think out carefully the whats and the whys of the project:

1 the technology,
2 the knowhow, and
3 the purposes:
   (a) to protect an existing business;
   (b) to expand into a new market.

An agreement, perhaps thrashed out over many months, will be designed for the contractor company to derive further income from its technology and for the licensee to establish a business.

The following is a checklist of items that need to be considered in discussing an agreement.

1 Particulars of parties. Names of parties: clarifying the licensee if it is a division of a large company, if registered and principal addresses of the parties.
2 Definitions of territory, scope and patents to be licensed.
3 Obligations of the parties.

Executive Summaries

4   Nature of agreement:
    (a) licence;
    (b) agreement to grant a licence;
    (c) knowhow agreement;
    (d) assignment of rights;
    (e) limitations on use by the licensee.
5   Nature of property:
    (a) invention;
    (b) design;
    (c) knowhow;
    (d) copyright.
6   Property to be licensed or assigned or the subject of the agreement:
    (a) patent application;
    (b) design application;
    (c) letters patent;
    (d) registered design or trademark;
    (e) knowhow;
    (f) written information.
7   Ownership of property:
    (a) Who is the owner of the property which is the subject of the agreement?
    (b) Who is the owner of the beneficial interest in the property which is the subject of the agreement?
    (c) What is the nature of the licensor's right in the property which is the subject of the agreement, including the right to grant licences or other rights?
8   If the licensor is the owner of the beneficial interest and is not the legal proprietor of the property which is the subject of the agreement, identify the instrument giving licensor the right to grant a licence or other right thereunder.
9   Specify what is to happen, if anything, with regard to future patents, designs, inventions, technical information, knowhow, or improvements to any of the foregoing to which:
    (a) the licensor obtains rights;
    (b) the licensee obtains rights.
10 Nature and extent of rights; is the party being granted:
    (a) exclusive;

(b) sole; or
(c) non-exclusive rights?
(d) A combination of any of them for different purposes or different territories?
11 Nature of rights granted:
(a) manufacture;
(b) use;
(c) sale;
(d) lease;
(e) territories in which rights are granted;
(f) identification of nature of rights granted for different territories.
12 Is technical assistance to be given?
13 If an agreement to grant a licence, specify the form of licence which may be registered at the Patent Office.
14 In the absence of any patent or registered design, authority to the licensee to exercise rights granted in respect of the property which is the subject of agreement. (This arises with knowhow, technical aid, copyright, inventions or designs when industrial property protection has not been granted for any reason, for example, a patent application.)
15 Has either party the right to assign the agreement or benefits?
16 What is the position of subsidiaries of the licensee under the agreement?
17 What is the right of the licensee to grant sub-licences in respect of licensed property?
18 What is to be the form of sub-licence?
19 What is the licensee's responsibility for acts of the sub-licensee?
20 What is the licensee's responsibility for maintenance of confidentiality with respect to knowhow?
21 Is the licensee to have the right to sub-contract manufacture of articles derived from licensed property (the so-called derived articles)?
22 Payments and royalties:
(a) Is a down payment to be made and, if so, is it to be set off against royalties or other receipts deriving from the agreement?
(b) What is the royalty rate to be paid in respect of the **derived articles**?

Executive Summaries

(c) Is a minimum royalty to be paid certain; if not, is there to be a right of determination of the agreement if minimum payment is not made?
23 Is there to be an arm's length provision in the event of sales of derived articles by the licensee to its subsidiaries or associates?
24 What royalty rate is to be paid when derived articles form part of a larger product?
25 Are payments other than royalty to be made by the licensee to the licensor?
26 Specify currency in which all payments are to be made, and dates at which rates of exchange are to apply.
27 Is the licensee to keep records of:
   (a) amount of derived articles dealt in;
   (b) sales or other commercial dealings;
   (c) receipts in respect of commercial dealings in the derived articles?
28 What are the rights of inspection of records by the licensor?
29 What provisions are to be made for the marking of articles the subject of patent or design protection.
30 What provision is to be made for indemnity by the licensee in respect of failure to comply with marking provisions?
31 What provision is to be made for preservation of copyright?
32 What is to be the date of commencement of the agreement?
33 What is to be the duration of the agreement?
34 What are to be the rights of determination by the licensor and the licensee?
35 Provision for determination on breach of the agreement on insolvency and change of management or control of the licensor or the licensee.
36 Does licensee retain any rights in the event of termination?
37 Provision for the licensee to respect validity of industrial property right the subject of the agreement?
38 Exclusion of warranty by the licensor that licensed property does not infringe rights held by another?
39 What is to happen in the event of failure of the property that is the subject of agreement?
40 Provision for certificates of renewal of industrial property.

41 Provision for the licensee to make endeavours to create a market for and to sell derived articles.
42 Provision for the licensee to take such action as may be necessary to avoid a compulsory licence being granted in respect of industrial property.
43 What is to happen in the event of infringement of industrial property the subject of the agreement?
44 Provision as to service of notices.
45 List of licensed property.
46 Confidentiality.

1.6 Background: the most common uses of intellectual property protection – some myths dispelled

For most companies and individuals, the protection of intellectual property is a strategy for the defence of existing or future business opportunities, rather than a means of obtaining additional income. It is extremely difficult to obtain accurate figures about the number of licence agreements in force in any country, but a United Kingdom survey by one of the authors indicates that only about six per cent of United Kingdom patents are used for licensing purposes. Only one sixth of patents granted run their full life, which would again indicate that after ten years or so, the remaining five sixths progressively cease to offer any significant protection or earnings potential.

The market also recognizes the protection offered by trade and service marks which, in contrast to patent protection, is not limited in time. While some 22 000 patent specifications a year were published in the United Kingdom in 1990 and 1991, some 30 000 trademarks and 6500 service marks were filed in each of the same years. At the same time, these figures reflect the increasing role of distribution and service industries in the United Kingdom economy, also illustrated in the increasing role of franchising as a means of exploiting intellectual property.

Likewise, design registrations are on the increase, and over 9000 designs were registered in the United Kingdom in 1990, over twice the number registered in 1982.

Further evidence on the protective use of patents and trademarks is given by the number of patents registered by foreign owners in the United Kingdom. In 1991, 8277 out of 27 587 patent applications (30 per cent) of applications were made from abroad (including the Channel Islands and the Isle of Man). Although seven per cent of patent applications came from the United States, patents were applied for on behalf of firms in countries such as Bahrain, Cyprus, Kenya and Nigeria. The evidence is that many of these registrations by foreign companies are to protect potential exports to the United Kingdom,

Executive Summaries

rather than to form the basis of licence agreements.

This conclusion is more strongly supported by the examination of the 28 639 trademark applications made in the same year: no less than 16 064 (56 per cent) of the applications came from abroad.

The ten patent applications from the Netherlands Antilles indicate the use of an off-shore base by multinational companies, which are more likely to have licensing implications.

Similar trends apply in other countries. Table 1.6.1 shows the detailed figures for a limited number of industrialized countries' patent applications granted in the United Kingdom and Germany in recent years.

Table 1.6.1 Patents between industrialized countries

Patents granted in the United Kingdom in 1991		
Country of origin	**No.**	**% of total**
France	183	2
Germany	994	11
Japan	1879	20
United States	1718	18
United Kingdom	3307	35
United Kingdom total	9346	
Patents granted in Germany in 1998		
Country of origin	**No.**	**% of total**
France	532	3
Germany	11480	57
Japan	3043	15
United States	273	1
German total	20141	

The defensive role of patent and trademark registrations is further evidenced by the published figures on the technological balance of payments of OECD countries. Few countries, other than the United States, were net earners in payments resulting from various types of technology transfer.

RETURN ON RESEARCH AND DEVELOPMENT EXPENDITURE

One argument for licensing and knowhow selling frequently adduced by its proponents is the funding of research and development expenditure. In fact on a national scale, the income from royalties as such is relatively small compared with expenditure on research and development.

Table 1.6.2 shows the expenditure of seven OECD member countries on government funded research and development for civil and defence objectives, compared with business enterprise research and development.

Table 1.6.2 Research and development expenditure as a percentage of gross domestic product for seven Organisation for Economic Co-operation and Development member countries for 1990

Country	Government funded R & D as a % of GDP			Business enterprise R & D as a % of GDP	Total as a % of GDP
	Civil	Defence	Government Total		
France	0.85	0.57	1.42	1.40	2.82
Germany	0.90	0.14	1.04	2.00	3.04
Italy	0.70	0.05	0.75	0.70	1.45
Japan	0.43	0.02	0.45	2.10	2.55
Sweden*	0.93	0.29	1.22	1.70	2.92
USA	0.44	0.74	1.18	1.90	3.08
UK 1990	0.51	0.40	0.91	1.40	2.31

* Business enterprise figure is from 1989

Executive Summaries

Table 1.6.3   United Kingdom national research and development expenditure versus international knowhow receipts for 1985 and 1990 in £ million

	GDP	R & D Expenditure	As a % of GDP	Knowhow Receipts	As a % of GDP
1985	305895	8014	2.62	809	0.26
1990	479452	11075	2.31	1264	0.26

As a nation, the United Kingdom has been spending about 2.5 per cent (see table 1.6.3) of its gross domestic product on domestic research and development and recovering 0.26 per cent in the form of knowhow receipts from abroad. Even assuming that the income generated by royalties within the country were the same as that from abroad (which is unlikely), this gives an upper limit of 0.5 to 0.6 per cent of the gross domestic product as royalty income, which is only around 25 per cent of domestic research and development expenditure. As far as one can gather, the expenditure on international research and development is additional to the domestic expenditure, so that the United Kingdom spends about 2.88 per cent of its gross domestic product and recovers no more than 0.5 per cent in knowhow related payments.

Table 1.6.4   Analysis of ICI's research and development expenditure and royalty income in 1992

	£ million	% of turnover	% of profit
Sales	12,061.0	–	–
Trading profit	735.0	6.2	–
Expenditure on research and development and technical service	721.0	6.0	98.0
Royalty income	57.0	0.5	8.0

Source: ICI Annual Report 1992

In comparison, ICI (as it then was), one of Britain's most successful exploiters of knowhow, spent six per cent of its sales on research and development in 1992. Its declared royalty income was just under 0.5 per cent of sales and 7.2 per cent of its research expenditure but made a contribution of eight per cent to the group's profits. It should be noted that the figure for royalty income does not appear to include income from knowhow and management fees. The figures are in Table 1.6.4.

Pilkington Plc, another highly successful exploiter of knowhow, shows in its accounts for the year ended 31 March 1993 that it recoups nearly 33 per cent of its research and development expenditure and makes 20 per cent of its profits from licensing income, as shown in Table 1.6.5.

Table 1.6.5   Analysis of Pilkington's research and development expenditure and royalty income in 1992/3

	£ million	% of turnover	% of profit	% of R & D spent
Sales	2572.5	–	–	–
Trading profit	88.0	3.42	–	–
Expenditure on research and development	53.2	2.07	60.45	–
Licensing income	17.5	0.68	19.89	32.89

Source: Annual Report for 1992/3

There are of course companies with exceptionally high knowhow earnings; Texas Instruments, the United States manufacturing company, recently reported that revenues from patent royalties are greater than its revenue from manufacturing.

FINANCIAL STRATEGIES

From the figures published annually by the United Kingdom Government it can be seen that the majority of licensing and knowhow

Executive Summaries

payments are actually transfers between related companies; in these cases there is a strong element of financial policy concerned with the transfer of profits or dividends.

The inclusion of film royalties, and especially mineral royalties, swings the balance of trade from negative to positive, but what is most remarkable is the percentage of the royalties and knowhow fees paid to related concerns. In 1990, 65 per cent of United Kingdom knowhow receipts and 85 per cent of expenditure were paid to related concerns.

This is not to imply that there is anything illegal in this tactic: it shows that licensing and knowhow contracts relating to the exploitation of various forms of protected information can strengthen a company's power to take cash out of foreign subsidiaries, and that in terms of the volume of trade, this is the main use of licensing agreements.

This shows why, in practice, there are two main forms of licence agreements: those between unrelated concerns (or even competitors), where great emphasis is placed on getting the two parties to fulfil their obligations, and on the remedies if they fail to do so; and those between related concerns, in which conflicts can be resolved at the group headquarters. This also indicates why it is valuable to have provisions in an agreement between related concerns to cover remedies for non-fulfilment in case one of the parties leaves the common group. In other cases, a change in shareholding triggers the renegotiation of certain aspects of the agreement.

As a comparison, the income from other knowhow services in the form of technical consultancy activities is shown; this, in 1990, reached over 50 per cent of the receipts from licensing and knowhow contracts. In general, consultancy would be in the form of unprotected advice, supported by documentation or software subject to copyright. Although it is not made clear in the United Kingdom figures, one should not forget that a substantial portion of these consultancy fees is likely to be between different parts of related concerns.

Hence, while it is an attractive and romantic idea that licensing agreements allow an inventor to make money by sharing with the world at large the fruits of his intellect, the highest amounts of money are actually earned by parent companies gaining a return from their investments in foreign subsidiaries. Nevertheless, even between related concerns, it is attractive to transfer money within the protective wall of patents, trademarks, designs and secret knowhow.

Part 2

Business Strategy

An international licensing arrangement will stem from the strategies of both the licensor and the licensee. The former will have determined that this is the route to expansion in certain markets. The licensee will have decided that its business needs foreign technology to grow. Strategy is all about objectives and, in both cases, these are for expansion of an existing business. This is the identity of interest the partners need to establish before an agreement is negotiated.

Part 2 examines the process of determining when licensing is the correct strategy and outlines some of the preliminary decisions that need to be taken in implementing the strategy.

2

2.1 International licensing: its relationship to other business strategies

This chapter, following on from the executive summaries, forms an introduction to and a general review of the subject.

Company x has a superb invention. A new peripheral for personal computers that solves a long-recognized problem; it has to be a world beater. There is just one snag: company x cannot manufacture and distribute this invention throughout the world – it lacks the resources. For a high technology company with a small capital base (less than £10m), the route to world markets is through licensing.

For the purposes of this book, **licensing** is an arrangement between independent organizations for the sale of the use of technology protected by patents, trademarks or other legal forms of monopoly between a principal (licensor) and a client (licensee) which are usually in different countries. Licensing agreements also occur between different units of a company or a joint venture but, for the purposes of this book, investment is treated as a separate option. Pure licensing agreements, in the sense employed here, do not include any equity from the licensor.

In their coverage of technology protected by patent, licensing agreements contrast with **franchising** (the sale of commercial knowhow – including trademarks – that are sometimes protected by copyright but in which other business assets do not have legal protection) and **management contracts** (the sale of total business packages). The difference between these arrangements may be small, in fact they shade into one another, and the same words are often used for all the business methods; the concept is illustrated in Figure 2.1.1.

The force of the word 'shade' is that licensing arrangements frequently require additional management services until they become (in fact if not in name) management contracts. An article in *Communications* (February 1989) took this a stage further by explaining how licensees for specialized mobile radio systems can choose a third party management company. This 'shading' can also operate in the opposite

Business Strategy

direction to that shown in Figure 2.1.1 when a licensing agreement expands its forms to become a management contract which then needs re-financing. If both parties inject equity capital, it becomes a joint venture.

Figure 2.1.1 The place of licensing in international business

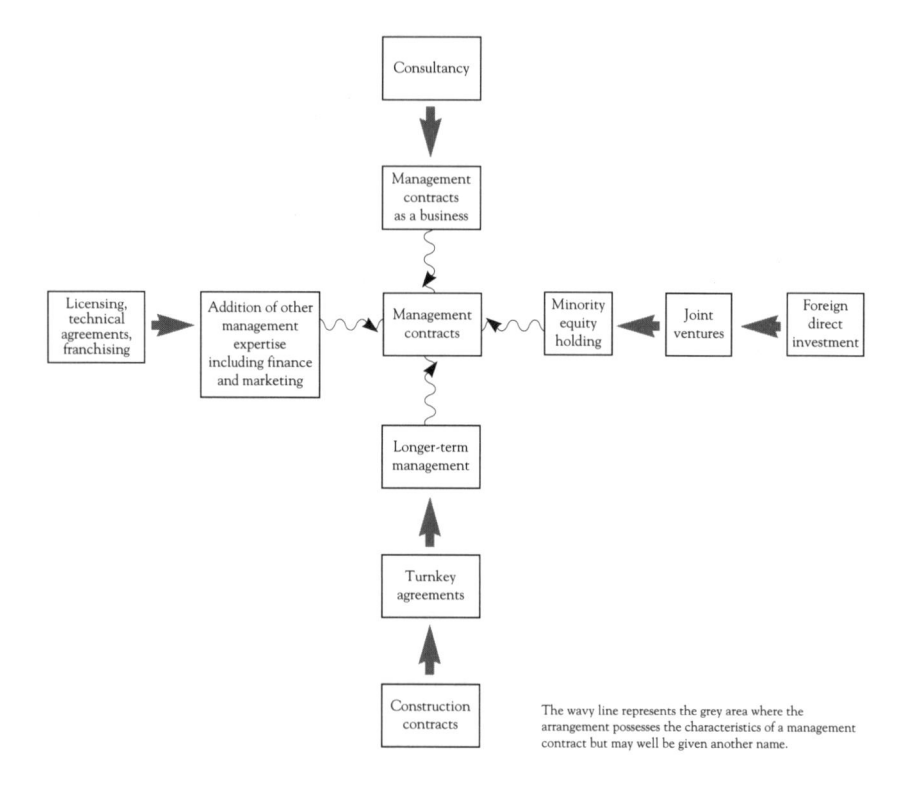

```
                         ┌─────────────┐
                         │ Consultancy │
                         └──────┬──────┘
                                ▼
                         ┌─────────────┐
                         │ Management  │
                         │ contracts   │
                         │ as a business│
                         └──────┬──────┘
                                ∫
                                ▼
┌──────────┐   ┌───────────┐  ┌──────────┐   ┌──────────┐   ┌──────────┐   ┌──────────┐
│Licensing,│   │Addition of│  │Management│   │ Minority │   │  Joint   │   │ Foreign  │
│technical │ ▶ │  other    │∽▶│ contracts│◀∽│  equity  │ ◀ │ ventures │ ◀ │  direct  │
│agreements│   │management │  │          │   │ holding  │   │          │   │investment│
│franchising│  │ expertise │  │          │   │          │   │          │   │          │
│          │   │including  │  │          │   │          │   │          │   │          │
│          │   │finance and│  │          │   │          │   │          │   │          │
│          │   │ marketing │  │          │   │          │   │          │   │          │
└──────────┘   └───────────┘  └──────────┘   └──────────┘   └──────────┘   └──────────┘
                                ∫
                                ▼
                         ┌─────────────┐
                         │ Longer-term │
                         │ management  │
                         └─────────────┘
                                ▲
                         ┌─────────────┐
                         │  Turnkey    │
                         │ agreements  │
                         └─────────────┘
                                ▲
                         ┌─────────────┐
                         │Construction │
                         │ contracts   │
                         └─────────────┘
```

The wavy line represents the grey area where the arrangement possesses the characteristics of a management contract but may well be given another name.

Reproduced from Brooke, M.Z. (1985). *Selling Management Services Contracts in International Business*, Holt, Rinehart and Winston.

The left hand end of the line in the figure – a so-called 'pure' licensing agreement in which the licensor provides nothing more than the stipulated information – is a licensor's dream but is rare in practice. Normally, additional services and demands of the licensor's management are required for the success of the project.

2

At the heart of a licensing arrangement is a contract: a legal document which will be drafted by lawyers; but this is a book for business people not lawyers and is designed to demonstrate the business considerations of which the legal experts must take account as well as some legal issues of which the business executive should be aware (see Part 3).

2.1.1 REASONS FOR PREFERRING LICENSING

One of today's leading academic experts on international business, asserts that: 'theoretically [licensing] is best since an income – royalties – is received with few resources expended'. (See Peter Buckley (1992), *Studies in International Business*, St Martin's Press.)

Licensing is a strategy for business development both for the licensor and for the licensee. For the former, it means a viable way of entering or holding markets; for the licensee, it means the opportunity to develop a business without the costs associated with developing the technology. In many a developing country, licensing is the only route for the ambitious entrepreneur to enter world markets.

Above all, licensing provides a locally manufactured product which has its own impact on the market for that reason.

One authority (Telesio, see reading list at the end of the book) asserts that firms who already manufacture abroad are less likely to go in for licensing than those which do not. He also reports one firm which always considers licensing as a first step. The same author advises that very large companies and those with low levels of diversification rarely go in for licensing projects. Would-be licensees are therefore advised to avoid these companies.

On the other hand licensing can be an easy route to diversification for a company that finds itself saddled with a dangerously low growth core activity.

Business Strategy

THE LICENSOR'S POINT OF VIEW

One reason for the licensor to prefer licensing has already been mentioned: lack of resources to operate any other way – that is by direct export or local manufacture through a subsidiary (take another look at Figure 2.1.1, the options are clearly set out there). 'Lack of resources' can imply a number of considerations including: an inability to fund a subsidiary, a shortage of management to establish a new venture and a lack of adequate knowledge of the market.

Shortage of resources is a reason which operates especially powerfully with universities and research institutions which do not possess their own manufacturing or marketing facilities but it also applies to inventors in general and especially to small, entrepreneurial high technology firms, none of which is meant to imply that larger firms may not wish to deploy their resources in other ways.

There are also more positive reasons for preferring licensing. It may, for instance, be the most profitable use of existing resources. The choice of licensing will be conditioned by the capacity of existing manufacturing plant. If so, it will form a part of a global strategy and the licensor will make efforts (which may be frustrated) to limit the licensee's markets.

If a domestic plant is reaching the limits of its capacity, a company has the opportunity of scanning the world to determine a site for its new facilities. After the scan, a cost-benefit analysis may show a certain country to be the best site – labour is available with the required skills at low cost while the industrial infrastructure is in place – but the country is unsuitable for investment.

If political and economic uncertainties suggest that the risks of investment are too high, licensing is likely to be the preferred option because it provides a means of establishing the facility without an investment recorded on the balance sheet. Very competitive markets also rate as high risk and large companies may record their first presence on some markets through licensing even though they intend to invest later.

Other uncertainties, like the possibility of tariffs being introduced, may be met by a licensing agreement which can also be used as a form of test marketing. This widely canvassed advantage must be treated with caution. Licensing, in any case, involves a greater commitment on the part of the licensor than that of the licensee while its success depends on the effectiveness of the latter and on the relationship between the two. This relationship will not be improved if the licensor's commitment is limited to test marketing since it implies a view that the project can be abandoned as a result of teething troubles, at the first sign that success is uncertain.

Other advantages of licensing include circumstances in which the costs of export add materially to the price (see appendix to this chapter) when, for instance, transport costs or agent's commissions are high or transport delays may lead to a loss of market share.

Licensing further enables a company to jump cultural and other barriers to operating with confidence in a difficult business environment.

The licensor may well expect to increase its income through sales of components, machinery, training and other incidentals to the licence. To add to the advantages of licensing may be government pressure towards this means of operation (which can include government nomination of and support for a licensee) as well as the difficulty of entering a market due to strong local competition.

From the licensor's point of view, also, licensing can make possible a rapid penetration of new markets before competitors get in on the act. There can also be valuable spin off if other products or components are sold to the licensee.

2.1.2 Disadvantages and problems

A main source of difficulties arises from disputes and misunderstandings between the two parties to the agreement while incompatible objectives cause most problems. The licensee company is likely to be

Business Strategy

much more reliant on the agreement either as a route into a business or as a major step forward in an existing enterprise. It will be looking for rapid progress and growth in profitability in the reasonably short term. The licensor, on the other hand, is likely to be less dependent on the project which will be another step in an international strategy. A failure in one country can be retrieved by success in another. A licensor's investment is under-written in a way that a licensee's is not and these differences will produce different approaches to business decisions. The licensor is likely to look to the long-term establishment of the business, while at the same time being liable to threaten withdrawal if progress appears too slow.

Another disadvantage often cited is that of establishing a competitor to the licensor. Once possessed of the technology, a licensee can soon find a means of developing a world business. There are forms of contract designed to prevent this happening, but the only effective answer is for the licensor to keep developing new technology which will ensure that the licensee remains dependent. The licensor is also faced with the rapidly emerging international legislation, designed to promote free trade, that forbids the limitation of export markets.

This risk is minimized in two ways:

1. when the licensor company continues with high level research and development to ensure that the licensee's business remains dependent;
2. specific points at which licensees are known to break free – such as the development of new uses for the technology – are carefully monitored by the licensor.

In any case, licensing is often regarded as a means of entering a market at an acceptable risk.

Other common causes of problems are covered in Chapter 6.2.

Cost and income comparisons are a necessary part of the licensing decision, especially comparisons with other methods of conducting business.

2.1.3 LICENSING COMPARED WITH OTHER OPTIONS FOR FOREIGN BUSINESS

EXPORTING

The cheapest way to sell in an export market is to obtain free publicity by means of press releases in technical journals, and wait for results. But, as so often, a method that appears cheap at first proves ineffective in the long run. The technique may not promote a satisfactory description of the product, or overcome people's suspicion of something devised for a market in a different culture, and further money has to be spent on promotion before success is achieved. Nor does it provide for a learning process in the market. Another way is to send a sales representative into the territory after advertising or attending exhibitions in order to locate potential customers. This provides a company with knowledge about the market but, after a certain point, travelling costs and the strain on the home system will stall further progress.

The next option is to come to terms with the cultural barrier and opt for a local agent. An agent company will already be selling other products and may well place restrictions on the proportion of its time devoted to a new principal's business. This difficulty can be overcome by setting up an agent specially for the purpose and providing most of its business. Commissions on offer make agency agreements an expensive arrangement in Europe and even more so in the United States; confidence in the market is needed before being assured that such an agency is going to be cost effective unless it is possible to find a partner.

The choice between the export options will be determined by an assessment of the resources to be placed at risk and the possible returns. For export, an agent not tied to the principal is usually adopted. For a long-term business this generally turns out to be an effective option. However export may cease to be cost effective when certain expenses price the product out of the market. Typically these can include:

Business Strategy

1 packing and transport: three per cent addition to costs;
2 customs duties: ten per cent (although not for trade within the European Union);
3 agent's commission: five to ten per cent (see appendix to this chapter).

As against the cost advantages of licensing, some developing countries restrict royalty rates and apply high taxes on remitted royalties. There may also be payment delays due to balance of payments difficulties. Even so, in areas of political instability and currency risk, a licence (with an option to invest) is often as profitable a venture as any: one is earning a limited income without risking a large investment. In fact, compared with a joint venture or an overseas subsidiary, capital employed and negative cash-flow are negligible. Other benefits, such as sales to the licensee company, can be attractive. The licensor may also use the licensee as a cheap source of products or raw materials. In the case of Coca-Cola, these are the chief benefits in addition to the franchise income. Knowhow selling is equally important on the home market, especially for research organizations, who often sell their expertise to companies in their own country – the United Kingdom Atomic Energy Authority has been very successful in this respect.

Direct investment options: joint ventures

One way of financing a project which might otherwise be the subject of a licensing agreement is a joint venture. The licensee company may, for instance, offer equity as part payment of the fees for knowhow and possibly for equipment. A joint venture can be highly profitable, but there are some problems. The withholding tax on dividends is often higher than that on royalties, and the income may be lower unless the venture is very successful.

Cooperation agreements (especially with those countries suffering from balance of payments problems) give opportunities for a specialized form of joint venture. Instead of shares in the recipient, the knowhow seller is paid in the form of the goods produced by using its knowhow (which might otherwise be surplus, in the sense that they are not earning revenue); the goods themselves can then be sold at a profit.

Alternatively, the licensor may insist on some payment in cash. Some industries, however, find it difficult to absorb this kind of barter deal. In former Yugoslavia, Romania and other once socialist countries, joint ventures involving shareholdings on a more westernized basis have become accepted. A banker in Yugoslavia (as it then was) once argued that some investment ensured that a foreign company was more committed to a venture.

The relationship between licensing and investment is complex. Dissatisfaction with a licensing agreement frequently leads to direct investment (either by means of a joint venture or a wholly owned subsidiary) and vice versa, when an investment comes unstuck a company is liable to opt for a licensing agreement. Another example of a relationship between the two methods of servicing a market is when a government is a main customer, in arms deals for example. In such a case local manufacture may be a requirement and this may be met – depending on other circumstances – by either licensing or investment. The point has been made that strong competition in a particular market is likely to reduce prices and thus make investment less attractive. Under these circumstances licensing will be preferred as a means of market entry.

INVESTMENT OPTIONS: THE WHOLLY-OWNED SUBSIDIARY

An overseas subsidiary involves the greatest investment and risk but does not necessarily show the best return – especially if remittances are blocked. One advantage is that profits can be ploughed back towards the day when conditions change or invested in other companies in the country concerned. Alternatively, a subsidiary can be used as a source of cheap products for the parent company's own markets as the Japanese have done extensively in South-East Asia. There are risks arising from unfamiliar politics, laws, currency exchange and high

Business Strategy

taxation on exported dividends – a factor which applies less widely than in the past. The foreign subsidiary also suffers from a cultural risk, that of being expected to recreate a miniature twin of the parent company in a country where standards of behaviour, ethics, etiquette and efficiency are judged from different standpoints from those in the country of the parent. Such operations may place a strain on the resources of the parent company and on those of the subsidiary; this strain involves the total management of the parent company, questioning its sense of human values.

These cultural risks are demonstrated by the difficulty of conducting international market research. When smaller sums are risked in sales agencies, there is room for error; but the difficulties of researching one's home market are compounded when dealing with different cultures in order to set up local investment in a foreign country. No more than a small minority of the world's business is conducted between independent companies by licensing agreement; but the revenue generated is vital to the companies concerned which could not make profitable use of expensively acquired technology by other means.

From the point of view of the recipient country, buying in knowhow can be a cheap way to success – as was often claimed for Japan and West Germany in the 1960s.

However, for less developed countries, any form of local manufacture for sophisticated industrial goods can be less economical than importing unless the process is labour intensive. Under the circumstances, it may not be profitable for a manufacturer to produce locally unless the local government prohibits imports or subsidises exports.

CASE EXAMPLE: FROM EXPORT THROUGH LICENSING TO INVESTMENT

A private Turkish company had imported products from Company A for over 19 years and the relationship had proved to be very successful.

Company A were very happy with the Turkish company and the relationship which they had developed, and identified the Turkish company as a key strategic player in their Mediterranean marketing plan. In addition, Company A also thought that, in the long term, the Turkish company would make a good subsidiary. This had been raised with the Turkish company which had not pursued the idea further.

The Turkish company subsequently decided to become involved in manufacturing. However it had virtually no experience in this, so it was decided to licence one of Company A's products which it had sold and which had demonstrated a high level of sales.

Licensing negotiations were undertaken with relative ease on both sides, assisted greatly by the discussions and cooperation which took place between engineers from each of the companies. These engineers were the product champions and although the initial drive originated from Company A's engineer, it was quickly matched by that of the Turkish company. Both were committed to making the relationship work and succeeded in doing so, despite the fact that conditions in the Turkish manufacturing industry were primitive at the time.

The licence itself was structured to allow the Turkish company to enter the manufacturing of the product in various stages from importing full assemblies down to eventually manufacturing their own die-castings and most other parts.

Several years, and a successful licence relationship, later the Turkish company did indeed became a full subsidiary of Company A.

This case example was supplied by the Licensing Centre Ltd, Glasgow.

An overall view

The non-commercial constraints of politics and of customs duties are more significant in marketing abroad than constraints like distance and time. A product, however bulky, can be brought to a market in a reasonable time and at a fair cost. From the point of view of many developing countries (as we shall see in Chapter 5.3), a licensing agreement appears to have the advantage of bringing foreign technology without the much feared threat of continuing dependence on foreign concerns; for the licensor, there is also the assurance of safe entry into countries for which security is a serious consideration. After considering the other options, licensing may turn out to be the only one that is feasible.

In fact, from the point of view of less developed countries, licensees or subsidiaries which assemble or import semi-finished products are likely to prove the most profitable ways of serving home demand. Often expensive plants are set up, using foreign aid, in the hope that more foreign earnings will be generated by exports of surplus production. This can be a mistaken assumption in these days of anti-dumping legislation, even assuming that the goods are competitive on international markets in quality and in price. For many markets, especially where demand is small, local agents or distributors are the preferred method of overseas selling, since they require less investment than an overseas marketing subsidiary and often produce comparable returns. A limited licence, or joint venture, based on imported semi-finished products, is often the second preference since the parent company receives profit on the direct sales of semi-finished products in addition to licensing income; the licensee or subsidiary does not have such a large investment in plant. The long-term weakness is that the licensee may be able to buy alternative semi-finished products unprotected by patent or trademark.

There is yet another complicating factor: the consequences of tax in a foreign country.

2.1.4 Taxation and the Repatriation of Profits

The profits from direct export are earned in the home country and are, therefore, subject only to its own taxation.

However, royalties, dividends and (in some cases) knowhow fees are usually taxed at source. Dividends, which still find themselves regarded as the unworthy gains of capitalist exploitation, are sometimes taxed at up to 55 per cent where royalties are taxed at up to 45 per cent at the most; in some countries they are not taxed at all. Unless the home country has a double taxation agreement with the country in which it is intended to set up a licensee or subsidiary, taxation can seriously influence the profitability of a venture. It can also lead to the choice of a licensee rather than a subsidiary or joint venture. This is why some international companies charge subsidiaries a management or consultancy fee, which may be treated separately from royalties or dividends for tax purposes. Taxation and licensing is dealt with in Chapter 4.3.

When taxation is taken into account, the return on investment can be poor if the dividends are returned to the home country. As a result some international companies buy goods from subsidiaries at reduced prices or rent production plant rather than setting up a foreign subsidiary to earn high profits which are then eaten up in taxation. Multinational companies can succeed in setting up subsidiaries in different countries in order to move goods and dividends or royalties from one to another, taking advantage of taxation or trading agreements between the various countries. Once a company becomes involved on a systematic basis, licensing must take place within the total investment policy of the company. The three routes to foreign markets – export, investment or knowledge agreements – each have their place in an overall strategic approach. None excludes the others and each is used under relevant conditions.

In sum, then, licensing is to be regarded as a low risk, although sometimes low return, method of servicing a market which might otherwise not be entered at all. The various considerations proposed in this chapter make the licensing decision a strategic issue which requires oversight at top management level. Other decisions, once licensing has become a selected strategy, are examined in the next chapter.

2.1.5 OTHER STRATEGIC ISSUES

Licensing can form an integral part of a strategy of international

Business Strategy

production so long as there is also a tactic of a less controlled operation in some markets. If, on the other hand, corporate policies call for tightly controlled production facilities everywhere, licensing a third party will not be used.

For smaller companies, on the other hand, licensing can provide a means of making money out of an invention which they cannot market profitably themselves.

2

Appendix to Chapter 2.1: A scheme for evaluating potential licensing agreements

This scheme has been tested and used in a company with extensive licensing experience.

Figure 2.1.2(a) shows a graph of the percentage of identical items in a standard range of goods which are normally sold at a given price. Cost is the addition of material and labour costs for a fixed quantity of products (marginal costing is ignored for the purposes of this example).

Figure 2.1.2(b) shows that the most profit comes from the range of products sold at above the modal price (or, at least, not below it – see the broken line marked 'mode' on the figure).

Figure 2.1.2(c) shows the percentage of the market which could be captured if a manufacturing company was prepared to reduce its price indefinitely. Note the dotted curve on 2.1.2c; in most markets, the majority of buyers become suspicious if the product is offered at too low a price, while anti-dumping reactions may be triggered.

Taking these three graphs together it is clear that, in a case where the costs of exporting are high, the price at which the goods are sold on the export market will also be high: points x1 (home) and x2 (export) on Figure 2.1.2(a). The number sold at that price will be low – points z1 and z2 on Figure 2.1.2(c) – and the profit obtained could well be lower than that from similar items sold in comparable quantities in the home market: points y1 and y2 on Figure 2.1.2(b).

The conclusion is that once the small demand for a product at a high-price is saturated, exporting becomes unprofitable unless viewed on a marginal cost basis and that this is only relevant if the domestic plant has spare capacity. In addition to considering the resources available and the plant capacity, the options for foreign market penetration will be examined.

A graph of market penetration against profits gained on a venture is

Business Strategy

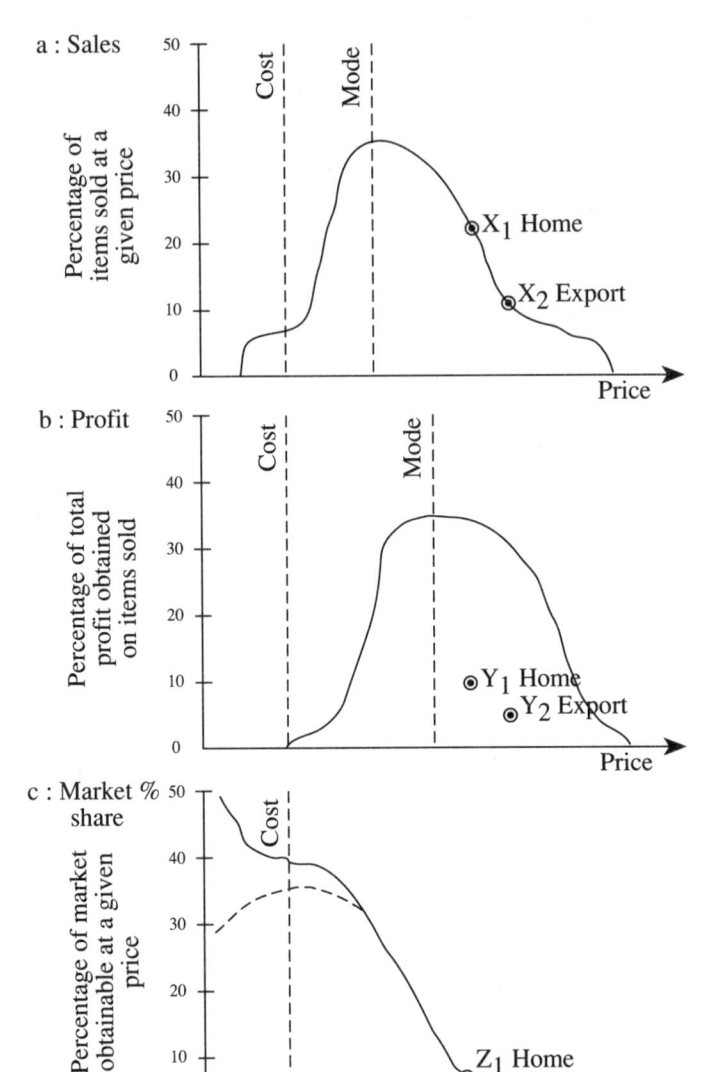

Figure 2.1.2 Options compared

a : Sales

b : Profit

c : Market % share

shown in approximate terms in the graph in Figure 2.1.3(A). After a time, it is possible to continue spending money on any method of marketing, but this will not improve profitability unless the product can bear the increased costs.

Figure 2.1.3(B) shows that a full time representative can produce a negative cash-flow before making a profit, and even a company's own representatives must make a few trips before they start earning their keep.

Figure 2.1.3   Export marketing: diminishing returns

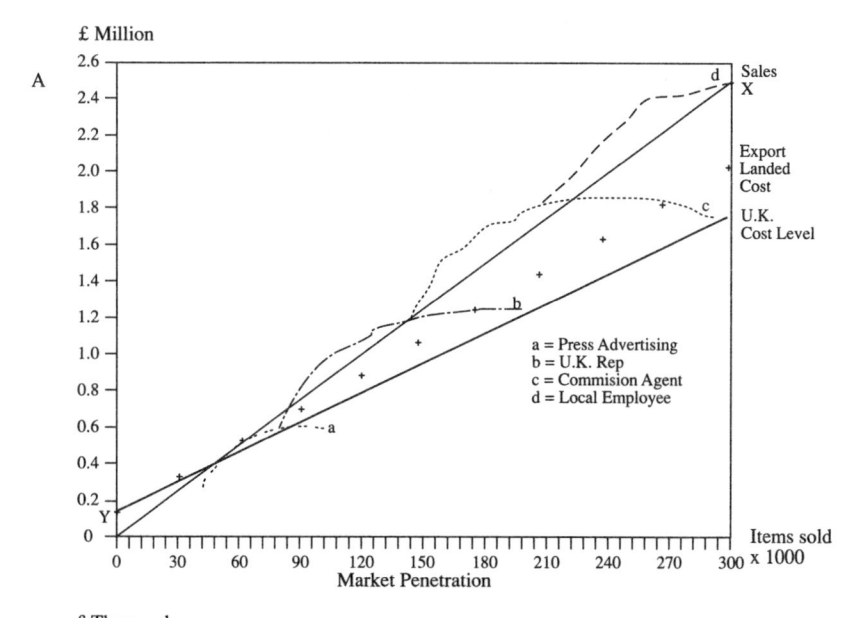

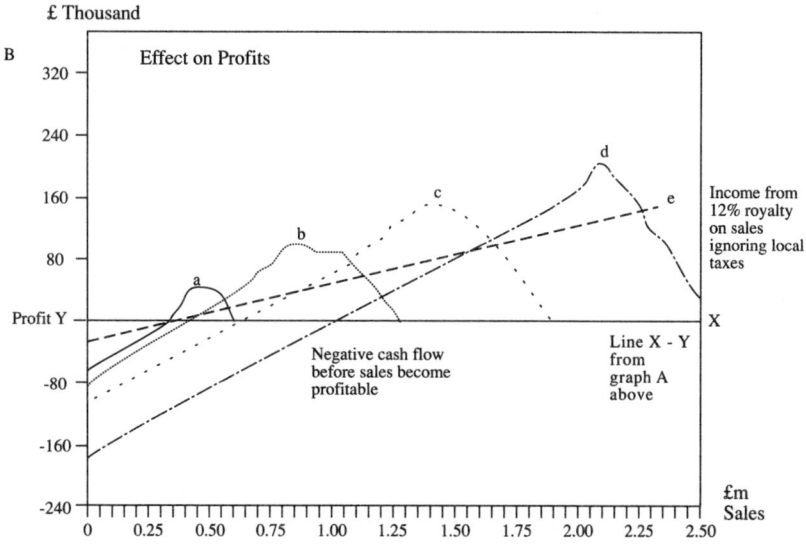

Business Strategy

Figure 2.1.3 demonstrates that, if a licensee can win a 50 per cent market share, a 12 per cent royalty is required to generate the same income as can be obtained by direct export. This is shown by the dotted line (e) on the figure.

Knowhow selling is not always the most profitable way of exploiting the market. It is only used **in the first instance** when constraints of capacity – distance, time, bulk or the relationship between price and volume – make it impossible to earn enough by exporting to a given market. In Figure 2.1.3(B) curves a,b,c and d can be seen to be more profitable than licensing for low market penetration. The constraints of distance and time led to the franchising of fast food chains like Kentucky Fried Chicken. The effects of cost and volume also influence the decision whether or not to franchise. Other constraints – like bulk, cost and volume – influenced two agreements that were once the subject of much publicity: Dexion's licensing deals for warehouse packing systems and Pilkington's float glass licences (other considerations enter into this latter example as well).

Second-order, localizing, factors are also reasons for licensing, especially in the case of Japan and Korea (culture, language, distance) when viewed from Europe or America.

Import duties and taxes are among the most significant hurdles and are especially prevalent in South America and parts of Asia (such as Pakistan); but even France and Australia have forms of protection for local manufacturers; in the case of France restrictions only officially apply to countries outside the European Union.

The relative profitability of a licensee, a joint venture or an overseas subsidiary is shown in Figure 2.1.4. If there is capacity, and the overseas market is not large enough to support a foreign plant while export prospects are good, a licensee or joint venture or subsidiary should be considered secondarily.

The potential for different returns from various means of operating in foreign markets is shown in Figure 2.1.5.

2

Figure 2.1.4 Graph of cumulative profit versus sales achieved

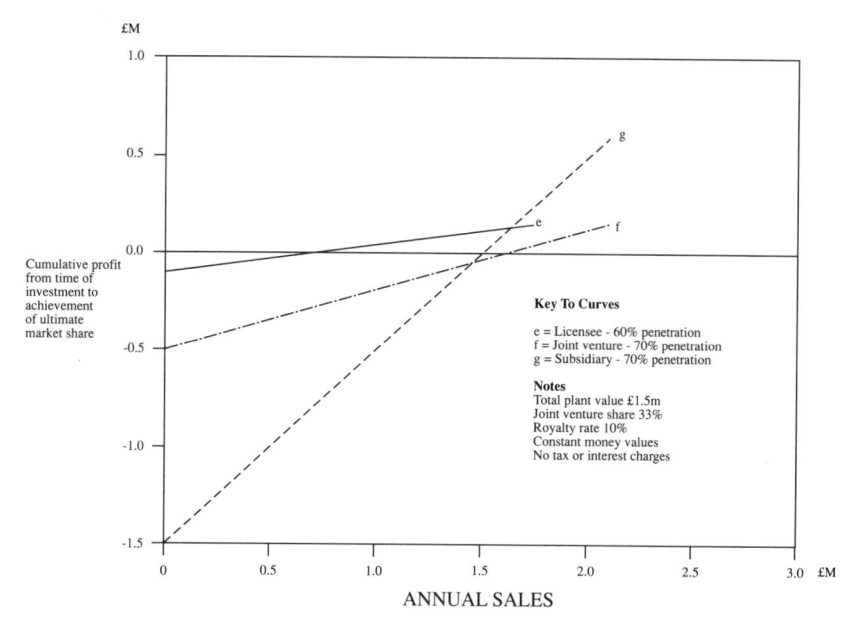

Cumulative profit from time of investment to achievement of ultimate market share

Key To Curves
e = Licensee - 60% penetration
f = Joint venture - 70% penetration
g = Subsidiary - 70% penetration

Notes
Total plant value £1.5m
Joint venture share 33%
Royalty rate 10%
Constant money values
No tax or interest charges

ANNUAL SALES

Figure 2.1.5 Comparison of pre-tax income for 5 years

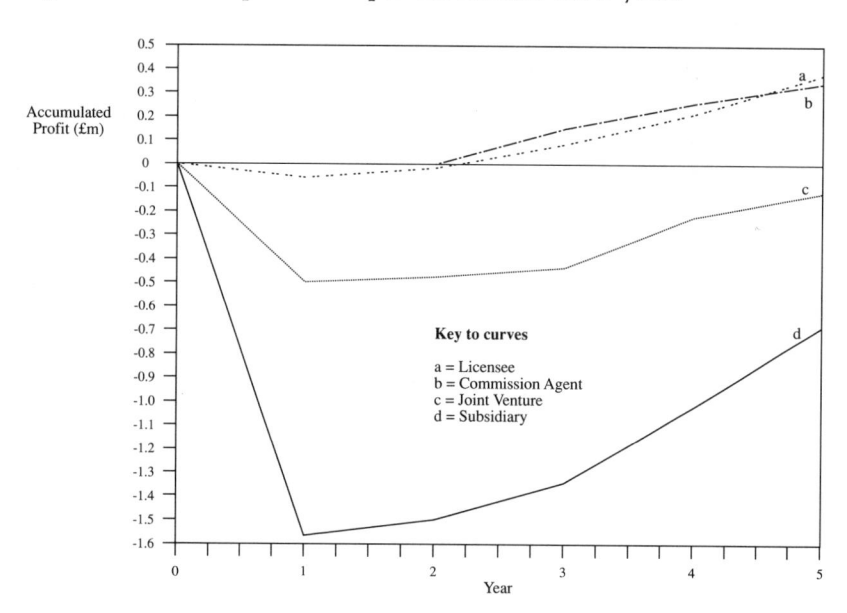

Accumulated Profit (£m)

Key to curves
a = Licensee
b = Commission Agent
c = Joint Venture
d = Subsidiary

Year

63

Business Strategy

For long-term results, when market size warrants, the wholly-owned manufacturing subsidiary is to be preferred; but with the difficulties of market research, risks of political instability, currency risk and the attitudes of some overseas governments towards the repatriation of profits, this form of venture needs thorough preparation. For products with a life-cycle longer than the licence period (say ten years) some form of investment should be considered in order to continue to enjoy the fruits of the venture in its later stages: alternatively provision should be made for the renewal of the licence. The cash-flows from typical versions of these options are shown in Figure 2.1.5 which supplements the simplified view of Figure 2.1.4. It can be seen that interest charges on investment delay pay-back, but constant money values will still be used, and a static market will be assumed. Also, a more realistic royalty rate of 7.5 per cent will be used, along with a cost for setting up the licensee not covered by the down payment. Maximum market-share is obtained in three to four years. The accumulated profit for ten years is shown in Table 2.1.1.

Table 2.1.1

(A) Accumulated income (profits) to technology originator working on same basis as Figure 2.1.4

Foreign marketing method	Accumulated Profit £	Maximum Market share %
Direct sales	382500	10
Part-time UK rep.	606000	20
Commission agent	830500	30
Local rep.	897000	45
Licensee	1068750	60
Joint venture	577000	70
JV + export	842000	70
100% subsidiary	1320000	70

(B) Accumulated income (profits) to technology originator corrected for local taxation of 20% on royalties and 30% on dividends from investment

Foreign marketing method	Accumulated Profit £	Maximum Market share %
Direct sales	382500	10
Part-time UK rep.	606000	20
Commission agent	830500	30
Local rep.	897000	45
Licensee	858000	60
Joint venture	403900	70
JV + export	668900	70
100% subsidiary	924000	70

A main fact to emerge from this discussion is that licensing increases income and hence return on capital employed for the licensor. The expenses of the licensor will be entered as revenue expenses. The money is not earned entirely without risk: what is risked is a valuable company asset – the potential for the sale of its knowhow.

2.2 Licensing: the decisions

Once a licensing policy has been decided, sub-options become available and a number of decisions have to be taken.

Decision 1: to explore the project further (to undertake a feasibility study and to draft a confidentiality agreement).

Even before other preliminary steps (such as market research) have been taken the would-be licensor and licensee will carry out a review of the market; round figures for possible revenues and costs including financing will be worked out. During this process, the licensee may acquire valuable information and be asked to sign a **confidentiality agreement** to prevent disclosure or control the use of the information received, should the main agreement not be concluded.

A major element in the feasibility study, for the licensee, will be to assess the **credibility** of the project. This will be increased if the licensor company is using the patent or franchised system itself and is a well-known promoter of successful innovation. From the licensor's point of view, the feasibility study will assess the risk to ensure that possible losses (especially when guarantees are required) will not exceed anticipated profits. The terms of the feasibility study will depend on the industry sector. For projects demanding long time lags and large amounts of capital, as with pharmaceuticals, more detailed investigations will be required including a study of financing problems during the process of winning acceptance.

Decision 2: the extent of the project. A company can decide to limit the arrangement to a sale of technical information. Most licensors find a pure licensing agreement unsatisfactory. Their client companies (the licensees) may not have the knowledge or skill required to interpret the information and translate it into saleable products. In this case technical back up will be required. Another common requirement is for marketing assistance. A licensee, with the technical and financial backing necessary to attract the licence, may not have the in-depth

Business Strategy

knowledge needed to promote the particular product successfully. Other forms of assistance or training may be required by the licensee as well as production and marketing. A problem is to agree a formula with a client that ensures adequate remuneration for these extra services.

The agreement may need to cover the supply of raw materials, semi-finished products or production equipment.

Decision 3: finance. Another decision is about the financing of the project. This will not arise if the licensee company has been chosen for its financial strength. If this has not proved possible, a number of questions have to be answered, such as: will the extra finance be injected by loan (either from the licensor or from outside sources which may be in the country of the licensee, that of the licensor or a third country) or by equity? If the latter, does the licensor see an advantage in putting equity into the project? Are there any grants or concessionary loans available either within the licensee's country or from an international organization? Additional finance will depend on the answers to these questions.

Decision 4: use of intermediaries. The next decision is about the use of intermediaries, the answer to the question: will the licensor manage the project directly or will that be subcontracted to a licensing specialist? Most companies will choose the direct management option, but some will consider their resources inadequate in spite of their technical expertise; such companies will prefer to pay fees to an intermediary.

Decision 5: cross-licensing. Many companies adopt policies of both buying and selling licences with compatible foreign enterprises. Such policies involve cultivating a special relationship between the relevant departments in the companies that enables a difficult series of business arrangements to work.

The producer networks which have become standard in some sectors (including vehicles and electronics) are likely to be sustained by cross-licensing.

The desire for a cross-licence is likely to make the negotiations easier – both parties will be that much more eager for an agreement – and it will also mean that proposals will be scrutinized more closely.

Decision 6: choice of partner. It may be banal to say that the choice of partner is **the** crucial decision, but it remains true – a truth that no amount of optimism or faith in training programmes can change. This implies that the selection process needs careful planning and preparation, and this is carried out in the following stages.

Stage 1: preparing a short list. Various organizations (government departments, chambers of commerce, banks, consultants and others) produce lists, but the accepted wisdom is that few worthwhile names appear on these lists. If a satisfactory licensor or licensee is in the market, it will be snapped up in less time than it takes to print a list; a successful company in an advanced technology would not need the publicity.

For a licensor, the most effective method of finding a licensee is to station an executive, or to appoint an agent, in a market to list suitable companies – high performing local concerns already operating in relevant technologies. A national search for a licensee in an industrialized country might start with a list of all firms in the same or a closely related technology or the choice could be limited to those which were wanting to expand. The search for a licensor might be conducted by the same method, compiling a list of firms in a country known to possess the required expertise.

Apart from track record, the criteria for inclusion in a short list will include an examination of the financial strengths of the proposed partner. Once this is established, the back-up services that the strengths can support need examining. There needs to be staff capable of communicating between the partners along the routes outlined in the chapters on organization (Part 4). The licensor will also be interested to know how familiar the licensee is with the target market, especially if its motive is to service a market for which export or direct investment is not considered cost effective.

Business Strategy

Stage 2: negotiation and contract. The licensor company will bargain for a return on its expertise without which the deal is pointless. The licensee will seek concessions on the basis of its equally important understanding of the market. Both will have fallback positions. The licensor will need an agreement which provides enough revenue to cover the expenses of the project – including possible costs for training or product modification, and some unanticipated expenses that are bound to arise – as well as making an adequate contribution to operating income; its ambitions may be restricted by local legislation. The licensee will be looking for an income which enables it to build a substantial and viable business; this requirement will provide its fallback position.

Negotiating the agreement will provide both parties with an opportunity to re-examine their essential requirements.

Decision 7: ultimate objectives. The negotiating positions of the licensor will be coloured by its long-term plans. If investment is ultimately intended, a partner will be sought which might be purchased. If a sustained development of a large market is planned, the licensor must be large enough to undertake this or, at least, be capable of expansion. If a more modest project – virtually a test market – is anticipated, the contract will need to allow for easy termination. The licensee's interests are likely to be the reverse of these; its emphasis is likely to be on longer term plans in its search for a permanent business, but it may hope ultimately to emancipate itself from the licensor and press for easy termination as a result.

Decision 8: the amount of discretion granted to the licensee. On principle licensing agreements permit maximum discretion to the licensee. Subject to stipulations about quality and markets, the licensor is usually anxious to limit the amount of management time spent in supervision and regrets the fact that this is not always possible in practice. A reason is the gap in size and business experience that often exists between the two parties, not to mention the gap in experience in the licensed activity which is bound to exist. These gaps give rise to a need to provide other services for the use of the licensee.

That this need may occur is not always foreseen or included in the agreement, but the limits of discretion will normally depend on the competence of the licensee. Where discretion limits are included in the agreement, there will usually be a penalty for failure to conform. This issue is considered further in Part 3.

Decision 9: who shall negotiate the deal? It is all too easy to give the task of negotiating the agreement to the most obvious person, always with a plausible reason, for instance:

1 the research and development manager because the agreement is to do with exploiting a piece of technology;
2 the sales manager because he or she is good at negotiating;
3 the legal adviser because he or she is normally used to dealing with legal matters.

Any one of these individuals could be ideal for the job, but could equally be disastrous. The company lawyer may lack technical and commercial expertise; the sales director may not understand some of the legal complexities. The answer may indeed lie in a team – one skilled negotiator, and one or two advisors who can supply knowledge outside their own fields on technical or legal matters.

If a single negotiator is to represent the company, the negotiator must be fully briefed by the manager and colleagues, and given clear instructions about the points on which independent decisions may be made and those on which contact with head office is required. As a negotiating tactic, it is often a good move for negotiators or the team to have one or two points on which they cannot give way without further reference. In any case, it is also best to agree on the main terms of the agreement and to leave the legal experts to finalize the precise terminology. The lawyers should also be experienced in the field of knowhow transfer, as the legal problems are very different from the normal concerns of company law or contracts of sale.

In all these matters it may be wise to retain the services of a licensing or franchising consultant who has worked in a similar field before.

Business Strategy

Some smaller companies may feel it is too expensive to pay for such advice. In such a case, they should either try to finance the advice through the early benefits of the deal, or seriously ask themselves whether they should be making the deal in the first place. As in all transactions between business partners, there is ample scope in know-how transfer agreements for one party to impose unfair or onerous terms on a weak or unwitting partner.

An additional option, sometimes available, is the patent pool; in this the group of companies who form the pool have free access to the patents held there regardless of individual contributions.

PREPARING FOR A LICENSING AGREEMENT

This heading covers the following series of questions which need to be answered before the negotiations begin, even though it is recognized that they may be modified later.

1 Is the company ready to take part in a licensing partnership? This is largely a matter of attitude and commitment which needs to be built up at all levels.
2 Are the resources available? Failure to answer this question lies behind some notable failures. Also, a perceived lack of resource on the part of the other party has been a reason for the ending of negotiations.
3 Has a satisfactory cost-benefit analysis been carried out? It has been demonstrated that a lack of adequate cost-benefit analysis can seriously affect the quality of decision-making on licensing.
4 Is the organization right and is there some person of sufficient seniority responsible for the project? (See Chapter 4.1.)
5 In which country is the training to take place? (See 4.5.3.)
6 What is to be the language of the agreement? (See 3.4.9.)

2

Case example: Motives for negotiating a licence agreement

Lidmar Designs Ltd with Winsco Ltd

[1] Background

Lidmar Designs has been contacted by Winsco Ltd, who state that Winsco in the United States wish to manufacture under licence custom made office furniture for Winsco. The office furniture was designed specially for Winsco, and is already made by Lidmar for the European market. Winsco Ltd has 100 people but Lidmar do not have any further information about the size of Winsco (US).

Action: Lidmar to check on the size and activities of Winsco (US).

It is far from obvious why Winsco, as manufacturers of high class domestic furniture want to get involved in the manufacture of relatively unsophisticated office furniture.

[2] The knowhow selling strategy

[2.1] Partners

Lidmar is a relatively small company and Winsco is of a more substantial size. The problem which can arise in such cases is that the larger partner completely overwhelms the smaller in terms of negotiating power and quality of legal advice. It would take typically six to 18 months to negotiate a suitable agreement and move into production.

Business Strategy

[2.2] UNITED STATES MARKET

The demand from the United States would double Lidmar's sales overnight, which would create problems of capacity and finance. Prices in the United States are low, for items of similar quality, as evidenced by mail order catalogues, although Lidmar have little direct experience of the American market and the price structure.

Winsco (US) would like to buy at a target cost of $85 per unit, compared with the current European wholesale price of $132 (£82.50). Winsco intend to sell the furniture as an own brand accessory. It is not clear whether the target cost is the cost at which Winsco could make the furniture, or the cost at which they would like to buy in order to be able to retail the furniture at a particular price.

Lidmar would not be able to achieve enough margin at these target prices, and feel that the low cost quoted by Winsco may be artificially low as the cost ceases to fall when certain volume breaks have been exceeded. It is also doubtful whether the overall increased volume at radically lower margins would improve Lidmar's overall profitability. It may be that components could be purchased more cheaply by manufacture in the United States.

Lidmar wants to look at the United States and Canadian markets in due course, and offer its standard range of office furniture under the Lidmar name.

Action: Before going any further, Lidmar must estimate the likely sales which could be made in the States, preferably not based solely on what Winsco says.

[2.3] RISKS OF KNOWHOW SELLING

Since it is unlikely that Lidmar can obtain a sufficiently strong form of design protection in the United States, there might be a risk that a licensee could copy and sell other designs of Lidmar; in addition sales might be conducted in other countries, such as Europe. The Lidmar view is that the battle against the competition is always a question of quality, price, marketing and service.

A knowhow agreement will take a lot of energy to negotiate as well as involving costs for legal advice. It will probably need up-to-date drawings of the products, lists of components, training visits to the United States, and represents a quantifiable commitment of time and resources. In future, Lidmar may have to have a small department devoted solely to licensing matters. Can it afford the cost?

[2.4] OPPORTUNITIES FOR KNOWHOW SELLING

It may be that Lidmar has no choice about whether or not to make a knowhow and marketing agreement with Winsco. Lidmar do not have the financial or personnel resources at present to double capacity, and do not have the sales resources to sell direct into the United States at this stage. Executives might be fooling themselves if they thought they could cope with the American market at such an early period in their development. The agreement would give them time to establish a firm home market base before venturing into very large volumes, with long supply lines. It might be better to use all their means to gain ground in France and Germany and guard their own back yard.

In addition to this, once Lidmar started selling to the United States at low prices, the European subsidiaries of Winsco would expect to buy from Lidmar at the same price eroding margins all round. At least the licence would increase the minimum European price by the cost of transport from the United States.

The manufacturing agreement in the United States would be a way for Lidmar to gain penetration in the American market without having to take its attention off Europe. In addition, any income from the sale of knowhow would be a welcome supplement to the financing of Lidmar's other activities especially during a period of rapid growth.

Business Strategy

[2.5] INVENTORY OF SALEABLE RIGHTS AND KNOWHOW

A licence agreement depends on rights under which the owner company can stop other people using its designs or knowhow.

Lidmar has no patents or trademarks in the United States, although it does have a registered design in the United Kingdom relating to the appearance of the furniture.

Action: Lidmar to check on whether any protection may be obtained in the United States based on the United Kingdom registered design. In any case, Lidmar should try to register its trademark in the United States as soon as possible.

Action: Lidmar should consider the Winsco design, and itemize what knowledge, production expertise, jigs and fixtures, **showhow**, purchasing and quality specifications or cost information is possessed and which represent a saleable commodity and answer the question: how much will it cost to get all this into an easily communicated form?

While discussing the whole question of product identity, it was suggested that Lidmar mark a number of components used in their furniture with their company logo. For example, it could be stamped on metal legs and other components, much as Ford mark many of the components used in their cars. It could be used like a franchise mark.

The logo could be registered as a trademark in a large number of countries, and used to show the authenticity of the Lidmar designs. Since it would not be in the form of words, Lidmar could also use the stamp on products sold under the brands of customers, and could likewise insist that its licensees used the mark.

If the stamp were used on the products of licensees, it would help Lidmar to market in the United States at a later date, as it could point to products designed by the company which had already served in the United States market.

Action: Lidmar to assess the implications of the stamping idea.

[2.6] ASSESSMENT OF OPPORTUNITY VERSUS RISK

On the face of it, it looks as though Lidmar should seriously consider a licence or knowhow agreement, providing the intentions of Winsco are honourable.

Action: What Lidmar should now do is to weigh up the pros and cons from all sides – personnel, financial, marketing and so on.

Action: They should also work out a minimum amount of money which they must get out of the deal for it to be worthwhile, bearing in mind the above commitment of resources, and answer the question: what is the minimum income at which they should walk away from the deal?

Although licensing and knowhow selling have been called profit without investment, the buyer of knowhow wants value for money and the documentation, training and service involved all cost time and money.

[3] MAIN ISSUES FOR NEGOTIATION

The agreement grants rights from Lidmar to the user, allowing it to manufacture and sell a specific product in a specific territory.

In this case it should be clearly stated that only the particular Winsco design can be made and sold in the United States and Canada, and nowhere else.

Note that once Winsco has sold the product legitimately in the United States, Lidmar cannot stop someone else selling it into other markets. If Winsco insists on exporting, the markets should be more precisely defined. Try for a higher royalty on exports to certain countries or see

Business Strategy

if Winsco can be persuaded to export only via Lidmar. This is a thorny question which requires discussion with legal experts as national laws frequently change.

The agreement should not permit Winsco to let anyone else make the products – not even subcontractors – without the written permission and approval of Lidmar.

Winsco should not be allowed to change or modify the design, without the approval and permission of Lidmar. Arrangements could be made for Lidmar to provide improvements or new designs on agreed terms.

In general, Lidmar should set and maintain worldwide standards for its products; otherwise at some later date there will be expensive problems concerned with rationalizing the product range and sorting out squabbles between licensees making to different standards. Differences in quality might also prevent Lidmar sourcing from certain licensees for supply to third markets.

Normally, any improvements made or suggested by Winsco would be made available to Lidmar free of charge.

The agreement should last for the duration of any protected rights but in general for at least as long as the product life of the product concerned.

Ten years would be a good period in this case, with the parties meeting to review it one year before it ends to see if there are ways of continuing the relationship.

Lidmar should get the right to purchase a given volume of goods from Winsco on an agreed price basis. This might help Lidmar to cope with market fluctuations in Europe.

Lidmar should supply as many products and components to Winsco as possible – for example complete x units in the first six months, while Winsco are building up experience; and complete y units in knocked down form for the next six months, to ensure proper lines of supply. The quality of all components should be approved by Lidmar.

Even later in the agreement, Lidmar should encourage Winsco to buy certain components from Lidmar as this may allow Lidmar to negotiate very low prices for their own requirements due to increased volume.

Winsco must identify in their accounts all the products subject to the agreement, and allow an auditor appointed by Lidmar to look at the accounts, stocks and production facilities. They should make monthly statements of production and sales, and pay fees quarterly.

[3.1] FEE LEVELS AND OTHER REMUNERATION

In this type of agreement, a ten per cent royalty would be satisfactory, five per cent fairly usual, and one per cent too low. Lidmar needs to examine the margins in their products if made in the United States and consider what would be a fair split of the margins between itself and the partner.

It is necessary to clarify the basis of the fee, for example: Winsco's net invoiced selling price, excluding sales tax. Would the fee be reduced if Winsco gave discounts?

Whatever happens, Lidmar must make sure it is fully paid for any costs associated with the agreement, such as patent costs or patent maintenance.

Once a sum of money has been calculated from the assumed sales pattern, efforts should be made to get 30 to 50 per cent in the form of a down-payment, especially if the agreement is based on unprotected knowhow – once Lidmar lets the cat out of the bag, it will be difficult to stop the partner from producing; the on-going percentage fee could be reduced accordingly.

Some companies even charge disclosure payments for showing the

Business Strategy

prospective partner limited amounts of information before the main agreement is made.

It should also be decided what amounts can be invoiced from the United Kingdom as training fees or payments for drawings and other requirements. (See Taxation.)

If Lidmar staff go to the States to give training, their hotel and travel costs should be paid by Winsco.

[3.2] OTHER POINTS TO BEAR IN MIND

[3.2.1] **Taxation** Royalties under a patent licence are usually taxable at source. Other payments under a licence or knowhow agreement should be examined with a tax expert – for example drawings supplied from, or training given in, the United Kingdom could be invoiced from the United Kingdom as normal goods and services. The main criterion is usually: in which country was the service performed? The expert will be able to advise on the double taxation agreement between the United States and Britain. The question of value added tax on goods and services supplied in the United Kingdom also requires examination.

[3.2.2] **Product liability** If Lidmar sells into the United States and there is a problem with the product leading to a claim for damages, the company will be in the front line and will bear the brunt of the claim. If the product is made under a knowhow agreement or a licence, the local manufacturer will bear the brunt of the claim, unless it can be shown that the Lidmar design was inherently faulty or Lidmar had advised the partner incorrectly.

Action: Lidmar to check its position with product liability insurance in general and with the United States in particular. It might be better to cover risks only in Europe and 'go naked' in America since product liability insurance for the United States can be expensive.

[4] CONCLUSIONS

The following recommendations were made by consultants; readers should develop their own views on each.

Before taking the matter further, Lidmar needs to know more about the United States market and the intentions of Winsco (US). Direct contact should be made with the American staff at the earliest opportunity.

Advisers should not make operating decisions for a company and Lidmar must assess the pros and cons of licensing in the United States bearing in mind other issues such as product liability, taxation, and the effect on the European market.

In any case, Lidmar might do well to strengthen its registered rights in the United States and other countries, and the idea of the Lidmar authenticity stamp should be followed up.

When all is clear, one negotiator should be given terms of reference and sent to the United States to discuss the deal with Winsco; for this purpose United States advisers should be sought.

2.3 Related means of selling knowledge

Most business deals include some sale of knowledge. Licensing is different from others because knowledge is the product being sold. There are several other methods for selling knowledge both nationally and internationally. All are designed to provide the seller with other benefits from the sale. Most of them are **packages** in which different forms of knowledge are wrapped together to make deals which are attractive to the client and profitable to the principal. The most common are: franchising, management contracts, construction contracts, turnkey arrangements, contract manufacture and technical assistance agreements. Most have similar objectives, opportunities and problems. Management contracts are examined in detail in a reference guide by one of the present authors (see Brooke, M.Z. (1985), *Selling Management Services Contracts in International Business*, Holt, Rinehart and Winston, now distributed by Cassell). Franchising will be considered here.

All knowledge agreements work on the principle that it is possible to operate in another country without substantial investment there by the owner of the knowledge.

2.3.1 FRANCHISING

Franchising is a similar device to licensing and the two words are often used interchangeably. In this chapter franchising is used of projects in which one partner (the franchisor) permits a franchisee to use trademarks and a total business package which includes an image, a marketing framework and a set of procedures as well as usually a mandatory system for recruiting and training. This is a commercial system in contrast to the technical system of licensing.

Whereas licensing deals associated with patents depend on knowledge **published** in the claims of a patent, franchising deals frequently depend on **trade secrets**.

Business Strategy

This means that the whole question of secrecy and disclosure has to be treated differently. A patent owner has the right to stop improper use of the terms of a patent, whereas it is very difficult to stop someone using an unpatented recipe or a business method. This is why franchise agreements are often associated with licensable rights such as trade marks, copyright or registered designs. These provide the owner of the idea with at least some control over the use of his or her business formula.

The strategies of franchising operate as with licensing. The franchisor usually intends an arms-length relationship but frequently discovers that this does not always work and hence ends up with a closer relationship than originally intended perhaps including an investment. In this case the franchisee becomes a subsidiary which takes the project outside the definition of franchising or of licensing used here. In any case, the franchisor is usually perceived to have more to safeguard than the licensor. There are sufficient problems in protecting a patent, there are many more in protecting an image as well as a trademark and a business system. At the same time there are numerous incentives for the franchisee to remain loyal such as worldwide publicity and considerable supportive services.

The essence of franchising is the sale of a successful business method and its associated trade secrets together with the information needed to run the business in the form of operating and training manuals which provide quality instructions and safeguards. There may be additional assistance such as the supply of raw materials, equipment, accessories, staff training, marketing and even the design of forms and stationery. In the case of international franchising, the company name and image are usually promoted worldwide and are often household words. Both domestically and internationally, franchising provides a route to establishing a new business for ambitious entrepreneurs. The method is usually used in service industries, most commonly in retailing, hotels, food, car rental, car repair and similar businesses. It has also been extended to accountants and recruitment agencies. Where relevant the franchisor gives advice on issues like siting, layout of premises, recipes and formulae. A distinctive house style and heavy advertising makes piracy of a franchisor's secrets as difficult as possible.

A FEW EXAMPLES OF INTERNATIONAL FRANCHISES

Among the best known examples internationally are Hertz and Avis car rental, most major hotel chains and fast food chains like McDonald's and Kentucky Fried Chicken.

Another example of a food franchise is Mrs Field's Cookies. The franchise covers the design and siting of the shop among other instructions, an example of a franchising principal investing its total experience in the project and (hopefully) applying that experience internationally.

Mail order catalogues are also the subject of franchising agreements; in one case the deal covered the design and production of the catalogues, the supply of the goods, advice on advertising and direct marketing as well as the supply of computer systems to run the business and assistance with staff training.

As with licensing, many franchising companies adopt whichever method is regarded as practical or which promises the highest returns under current circumstances. Many franchisors, like Holiday Inns, also use management contracts and direct investments. The contract clients and subsidiaries are naturally required to sign agreements franchising the use of the business systems.

A number of problems have to be overcome in franchising projects. As with licensing, quality control heads the list. Another problem is that a range of skills have to be built up quickly if (as is sometimes the case in catering, accommodation or retailing franchising) the franchisee has limited business skills. Some franchises, such as those for mass production soft drinks like Pepsi Cola, are normally awarded to existing and large companies which can enter manufacture immediately on the basis of an existing track record.

One main strength of franchising is also a common cause of problems

Business Strategy

– that of a product package which has universal appeal. The universality may be restricted in its scope as Pepsi discovered when an advertising slogan did not adapt to some languages (the phrase Come Alive with Pepsi was somehow associated with The Resurrection) and strict adherence to layout rules by a hotel chain did not fit local hotels and building regulations in some countries. In Pepsi Cola, too, the franchisor built a global advertising campaign around a well-known pop-star; the campaign came to an end when the star was thought to have fallen from grace.

2.3.2 OTHER KNOWLEDGE AGREEMENTS

Sales of knowledge are normally between two parties, one of them is a principal (a contractor, licensor, franchisor) and the other a client (a partner, licensee or franchisee). But many are not as simple as this and include complex agreements with many partners, some of them highly specialized. The ability to bring together complex consortia for achieving complex aims is becoming an increasingly valuable negotiating skill. All knowledge agreements operate on the principle that it is possible to operate – to provide a service or to manufacture – in another country without substantial investment there. The investment has to be made at home to ensure that the **knowledge** which is being sold is updated regularly.

In addition to licensing, franchising and management contracts, there are construction contracts and other major projects set up by international consortia. There is also contract manufacture whereby a company provides for a production shortfall by a temporary arrangement for manufacture under contract. In addition there are various forms of technical assistance agreement, although these are similar to if not part of licensing arrangements.

The best known form of knowledge sale apart from licensing or franchising is the turnkey contract, the agreement to hand over a new plant in operating order – usually after it has been running for long enough to sort out the problems appearing after it started up. This contract is almost invariably attached to major construction contracts, although it may also be attached to the smaller projects that are becoming more common.

Company X, a firm of consultants specializing in steel plants, undertook the planning of a turnkey operation in West Africa as the concluding part of a construction project which had attracted international aid finance. An operating steel works was eventually handed over to the client company a year after it had begun to operate.

Part 3

Legal and Political Issues

Licensing arrangements have several political implications – a fact sometimes overlooked during negotiations – and these are explored in this part. The interests of governments, concerned with the costs and benefits to their countries, are outlined as well as the activities of international organizations.

Legislation, providing both incentives and constraints, will influence the framing of the contract in ways listed in Chapter 3.4 and a specimen contract is provided in Chapter 3.5.

3

3.1 Intellectual property rights

Intellectual property in the broadest sense is understood as a right to control the use of the technology (including a design, an invention or some knowhow), trademarks and business names. It includes industrial property, computers and information technology, literary and artistic matters, entertainment, trademarks, patents, design rights. At another simpler level it is the 'property' that one has in an idea and its exploitation.

The increasing globalization of business has brought the protection of trade marks and patents (as well as other forms of intellectual property) more prominently onto the business agenda. Knowledge (research and development) has become a major cost in modern businesses which thrive on innovation, a development which adds to the importance of intellectual property. The protection provided varies considerably; in some countries there is no protection and in some the patent law is selective. Even when there is apparently strong protection, there may be discrimination against operators from abroad. Detailed information is required on a particular market before approaching it. Large markets with minimal protection can be devastating for companies with major research and development costs but, on the whole, legislation tends to follow a country's changing economic status. Part 5 identifies some characteristics of national systems.

When a country begins to develop its own technology, it is likely to enact patent protection for foreign innovation in return for similar protection abroad. As in so much trade regulation there is an element of reciprocity. South Korea, for instance, has introduced patent protection while India – previously known for its lack of support for foreign patents – has begun to strengthen its own legislation. The developing countries have accepted, although not unreservedly, the inclusion of intellectual property rights on the agenda of the General Agreement on Tariffs and Trade (GATT).

There is a considerable body of opinion that intellectual property rights should be regarded as an issue whose time has come. In the

Legal and Political Issues

1990s this issue has reached the agenda of top management and, as a result, it appears more insistently in government discussions. One writer (Robert H. Mallott, himself chief executive of a substantial chemical corporation) quoted an estimate in *Les Nouvelles* (issue 244, December 1989, pages 149-153) that violations of intellectual property rights cost United States' companies from $40bn to $60bn a year. He added a quotation from Carla Hills – then United States' trade representative – asserting that more than a quarter of the country's exports are made up of articles that depend on intellectual property protection. That country's international trade commission has extended the reach of national legislation considerably.

International bodies have been attempting to develop more stringent codes but one of the relevant facts is that most countries do not have strong protection for patents and licences and often little means of enforcing the protection that does exist. This enforcement is often weakened still further by a nationalistic bias in local courts and it has been noted that countries begin to take the subject more seriously only when they themselves have technical knowledge to export. Moves towards greater protection are reinforced when countries like the United States include it as an article when negotiating a bilateral trade agreement. The protection issue, which used to be mainly concerned with restraints on obvious copying in certain countries, is now extended to the promotion of worldwide codes. These have been especially prominent in the GATT negotiations.

The negotiations have been particularly concerned with trade related aspects of intellectual property rights (commonly known as TRIPS); at the time of writing it is not clear what the outcome will be.

Intellectual property rights, so crucial to developers of advanced technology, are safeguarded by their own international institution: **The World Intellectual Property Organization (WIPO).**

The World Intellectual Property Organization (WIPO) and its affiliated organizations

The World Intellectual Property Organization had 139 member countries in June 1993. A specialist agency of the United Nations since 1974, WIPO is an institution which has taken under its umbrella two groups of earlier treaties which cover:

1 the protection of industrial property including inventions, trademarks, industrial designs and appellations of origin. The protection stems from the Paris Convention originally signed in 1883; and
2 copyright which has been internationally protected since 1886 by the Berne Convention.

A booklet describing the work of WIPO explains that the protection is not an end in itself, but a means to encourage creative activity, industrialization, investment and honest trade. It also warns that there is no universally accepted definition of expressions like 'inventions' and 'trademarks' and that the definitions and the legal protection provided vary from country to country, since each nation has developed its own approach.

There are, however, exceptions to the rule that protection is only provided through offices of individual nations; these exceptions, which will be important to some readers, include:

1 For members of the European Union, there is also a **European patent office** in Munich (Erhardtstrasse 27, D-8000 Munchen 2) which provides a European registration for members and some other European countries. The European Patent Office, established by the Munich Convention in 1977, has taken over the patenting requirements of the European Union and other subscribing countries; the office grants patents that are effective in 17 countries (including all the members of the European Union). The Convention now contains a provision that enables a patent to be extended beyond the twenty years which is the normal period in some member countries including Britain.

Legal and Political Issues

2 The **Patent Cooperation Treaty** (PCT) as a result of which patent protection can be sought in up to 59 countries through one centralized international application. Under this treaty, the 52 members undertake to provide a simple system for registering patents in their countries if they are already registered in another. Apart from this arrangement there are no 'world patents' as is claimed by some manufacturers, each patent has to be registered in each country – often a long and expensive process. The World Intellectual Property Organization facilitates registrations of patents between member countries.
3 The **Madrid Agreement** for international trademark registration which protects trademarks regulated in any of the 35 member countries.
4 The **Hague Agreement** for the protection of industrial designs which protects industrial designs registered in any one of the 21 member states in that state and in all the others.

Both patents and designs are protected in the 11 countries which subscribe to the **African Regional Industrial Property Organization (ARIPO)**.

There is also an **African Intellectual Property Organization (OAPI)** with 14 members and similar objectives.

Each of the African organizations includes different countries on the continent from The Sudan in the north to Lesotho and Botswana in the south.

Executives who believe themselves to have problems under the headings of industrial property or copyright are recommended to make contact with the WIPO (address: 34 chemin des Colombettes, 1211 Geneva 20, Switzerland, phone 022 730 9111, fax 022 733 5428). Unfair competitive practices are taken under the WIPO wing as are the safeguarding of the written word, patents and ensigns.

Besides the Paris Convention and the Berne Convention, numerous other treaties dealing with specialist aspects of intellectual property internationally have been signed and now come under the WIPO umbrella. These complete a pattern of protection which is enforced by their member countries. Normally a member country undertakes to extend the same protection to other members as to its own nationals.

3.1.1 THE PROTECTION OF INDUSTRIAL PROPERTY

In the case of **industrial property** (patents and industrial designs) the member countries of the **Paris Convention** undertake to modify any legislation they have that is notably hostile to foreign companies especially those from other member countries. For instance, if a country will not protect a patent that is not being used within its boundaries, the Convention commits it at least to giving reasonable notice of cancellation of the patent and to permitting the owner company to justify its inaction. International patent searches are carried out under the terms of yet another WIPO-affiliated organization – the **Patent Cooperation Treaty (PCT)** detailed above.

Another affiliate of more modern establishment is the Budapest Treaty of 1977 'on the International Recognition of the Deposit of Microorganisms for the Purpose of Patent Procedure'.

Trademarks are safeguarded by a Madrid Agreement by which registration in the country of origin can be followed by international registration (for one fee and in one language) in all other member countries. The European Union operates a similar system for its members.

A more limited number of countries have signed the Lisbon Agreement which protects 'Appellations of Origin' and provides a means for registering them internationally. Also limited is the number of states that have signed other agreements for the classification of patents, designs and trademarks although many countries that are not signatories adhere to them. These agreements do not sound so interesting but are, in fact, vital when it is necessary to trace existing patents or designs. Lists of member countries can be found in a booklet entitled

Legal and Political Issues

WIPO (subtitle: World Intellectual Property Organization General Information; latest edition published by WIPO, Geneva 1993). This booklet tells you which countries have signed the various agreements – most of them have limited membership and therefore applicability.

3.1.2 COPYRIGHT

The other main topic which is covered by WIPO is copyright. The **Berne Convention** for the protection of literary and artistic works takes under its wing all forms of writing, music and art both published and unpublished. 'Literary works' include technical manuals, handbooks and leaflets. As with patent protection, copyright is the subject of legislation in individual countries but the Berne Convention sets standards which are widely incorporated into national laws such as protection during the lifetime of the author and for fifty years afterwards. If an author was an employee, the employer is normally entitled to claim copyright.

Copyright usually applies to the author's country alone and confers two rights – an economic right by which authors (or copyright owners) are entitled to be paid for the use of their work and a moral right by which they are entitled to ensure that any use of their work is faithful to the original. These rights are also safeguarded by the Berne Convention in other countries that are signatories to that Convention.

Other Conventions (Rome, Geneva and Brussels) extend protection to businesses that make disks, cassettes, broadcasts or films.

CASE EXAMPLE: PIRACY OF COPYRIGHT

In the past, it has been difficult for small companies to stop either large corporations or fly-by-night operators from copying their ideas. However, times are changing. In the United Kingdom the 1988 Copyright, Designs and Patent Act enables the company which believes it is being copied to take the copiers to a magistrates court thus avoiding a long and costly civil action.

On the international front things are also changing, as is shown by the example of Selina Knitwear who took on a major United States retailer in the American courts.

In the following account, the word **copyright** is used to mean copyright in the terms of registered industrial designs. Here is a good example of why a smaller company should not hesitate to take legal action over the commercial giant. In March 1992 Norwich-based Selina Knitwear served a case against the US Shoe Corporation, concerning copyright infringement. Selina had discovered that the Casual Corner division of the US Shoe Corporation had infringed copyright on two of its designs registered in the country. Selina designs, knits and sells hand-knitted sweaters, an expensive process. Its sweaters are sold in the United States from prestigious stores such as Nordstrom, retailing at $375 upwards. Casual Corner's copies of their designs retailed at a much more affordable $74.18. Allen Senel, Selina's managing director, stated most succinctly how Casual Corner's lax, copy-cat attitude must have affected his company's American business: 'Our business in the United States had been virtually destroyed as a result of Casual Corner's infringement, and we believe it will take another five years to re-establish at considerable expense.'

The US Shoe Corporation has admitted infringement and Selina has won the case. The total amount of damages, however, remains to be seen. During litigation it emerged that three more designs had been copied, and further court actions are likely to follow. Even copyright experts disagree on the total amount of damages the case could bring – estimates have varied from two to five million dollars.

What makes Selina's victory even more astounding is that they have beaten the American giant on its own territory – the case was heard in the United States courts. Having insured their individual rights through international copyright law, Selina can now happily sit back and watch the US Shoe Corporation squirm.

Legal and Political Issues

If Selina's case is a testament to how copyright can protect the small company from the commercial giant, then Monsoon's recent and ruthless legal campaign is a shining example of how to deal with the cut-price fashion pirate.

This campaign, which has brought financial success to Monsoon and misery to its plagiarisers, can be put down to the no nonsense attitude of the company's managing director, Peter Simon. 'You steal our designs and your importers will get injunctions, we will put your distributors in the dock and summons every shop and street trader we can find.'

Many companies have already felt the severity of this warning. Most recently Top Shop capitulated on the eve of High Court action, agreeing to destroy thousands of copied garments, and pay damages which are thought to approach six figures. In early October 1993 Hennes chain made an out of court settlement as Monsoon's lawyers completed paper work for a criminal prosecution. The New Look discount chain did go to court, to discover that it had to pay £10 000 in fines and return 1097 copied garments.

However, it must be remembered that Mr Simon is not doing this merely to see how effectively he can damage his competitors, but to protect the long and expensive design process his company has invested in: 'We have had cases where every one of the fifteen colours in a print design has been copied almost exactly and then appeared in someone else's window.'

Fashion, being the fast and flexible industry that it is, is not unused to having its ideas stolen. Robin Fry of copyright lawyers Stephens Innocent had this to say on the positive side of what Peter Simon's legal battles might bring: 'The history of the fashion industry in this country is of companies that have gone bankrupt or into liquidation. Some of them would have survived if the copyright laws had been enforced.'

If there is one factor which unites both Selina Knitwear's and Monsoon's victories in the courts it is their managing director's determination to see justice done, and halt the copiers. Facing very different enemies, they still approached their foe with a remarkably similar attitude: Allen Senel on the US Shoe Corporation – 'The company's attitude has been very arrogant, and it has tried to walk all over us because we are small. We want the British knitwear industry to know what is going on.' Managing director of Monsoon, Peter Simon, is just as adamant: 'We have kept fighting and we have won. No company, no matter how big, is going to pirate our designs.'

Much like any kind of insurance, money spent on the registration of designs and the upholding of copyright can be looked upon as a gamble. The key to the usefulness of such expenses is an early assessment of the likely profitability of each design. Let us say that a new company, with high overheads, decides that it cannot afford the price of legal action to support its copyrights. After all, the product might be a complete failure, and then having to pay the legal fees would be throwing good money after bad. The shrewd business person would never be faced with such a scenario. After carrying out market research, he or she will have an idea which designs will be successful and are worth protecting, and will then proceed to invest in as much copyright protection as he needs. These examples show (encouragingly) that relatively small companies can successfully defend their interests in their home markets and abroad.

Copyright protection normally lasts for the life of the author plus 50 years, irrespective of who owns the copyright (this will be extended to 70 years if a European Union directive is adopted). There are important exceptions: where an **artistic** work has been industrially exploited and marketed under the licence of its owner, protection will then be limited to 25 years from the date of first marketing. Copyright protection for computer generated works extends 50 years from the end of the year the work was made, and for anonymous works for 50 years from the end of the year in which a work was first made available to the public.

Legal and Political Issues

3.1.3 TRADEMARKS

A **trademark** for goods, or a **service mark** for services provided, is a **point of identification** enabling a purchaser to distinguish between one trader's goods and another's. A trademark may take many forms. It may be one or any combination of a device, brand, heading, label, ticket, name, signature, word, letter or numeral.

Registration of trademarks at the Trademarks Registry in Britain is not compulsory but a successful registration, quite apart from giving the right to use the symbol R on notepaper and packaging and the right to exclusive use of the trademark in relation to goods for which it is registered, provides two important advantages in protecting the distinctiveness a trademark owner cultivates in his product. First, registration gives a right of action for infringement of the trademark; production of the certificate of registration and proof of infringement will entitle the trademark owner to an injunction to prevent further use of the infringing mark and to damages for any loss suffered. In Britain the owner of an unregistered trademark can only bring an action for **passing off** (see Glossary, Part 7) and will have to prove more to get the remedies available to the registered trademark owner. The unregistered trademark owner will also have to establish a reputation in a mark and also that the use complained of would be likely to confuse or deceive the public. Secondly, registration acts as a badge, its presence on the register serving as notice to others that the proprietor has an interest in the trademark.

PRACTICAL CONSIDERATIONS

A trademark application in Britain is likely to take about two years from the date of filing to registration. Although the whole process can be conducted by the trader or prospective proprietor it is more common that a trademark agent will be instructed to pursue the application as the agent will be familiar and able to cope with the types of problems which often arise. Of course the instruction of an agent will increase costs and add an amount – difficult to predict, but for an uncomplicated application possibly in the region of £500 – to the bare fees payable to the Registry for registration.

In licensing, the licensee's use is deemed to be its own. This has the effect that the trademark, registered on the basis of the licensor's own use will not be liable to be expunged for non-use. Also, in a passing-off action, the licensee's use will be imputed to the licensor to prove the latter's reputation in a trademark.

For a licensee, a registered user, one advantage of a licence is the right (which can be excluded by agreement) to call upon a proprietor of a patent or trademark to take action for infringement against a third party. If the proprietor fails to do so within two months, the user has the right to take proceedings and to join the proprietor as a defendant.

INTERNATIONAL PROTECTION

A trademark awarded in any country does not provide protection abroad. It will be necessary to apply for a registration separately in each country in which protection is required. The creation of a portfolio of registrations may go some way to preventing competitors from exporting goods, for which they would otherwise have legitimately obtained the same mark for the same use in their home market, into the proprietors' market. Thought too should be given to obtaining an international registration under the provisions of the Madrid Convention.

An inventor is under no obligation to apply for a patent in respect of his invention. Unless someone else already has a patent for the same thing the inventor cannot be prevented from carrying out the invention irrespective of patent protection. A 'patent' is nothing more than an invention to which the state has lent its protection in the form of a monopoly right to the manufacture, use or sale for which it has been granted. A patent owner, the 'patentee,' is given the right to take legal action to prevent other people from exploiting the patented invention without consent.

Legal and Political Issues

The requirement of newness (in much patent law) is that the invention must never have been disclosed publicly in any way, anywhere, before the date on which the application is filed. Disclosure includes word of mouth, demonstration of a model, an article in a journal, or any advertisement. As a preliminary measure, a patent applicant should undertake surveys of relevant trade or technical magazines, text books or reference books before proceeding to file. A comprehensive search carried out by a patent agent may, in certain circumstances, also be appropriate.

3.1.4 GENERAL ISSUES

Some issues cut across those identified in this chapter, for instance the servicing of the international operations and the assistance WIPO is expected to provide to developing countries which are framing laws to safeguard intellectual property.

THE INTERNATIONAL BUREAU

Most of the staff (68 per cent) of the secretariat of WIPO, the International Bureau, are occupied servicing the five international operations which cover the main concerns of the Organization – patent cooperation, registration of trademarks, deposit of industrial designs, registration of appellations of origin, film registers.

Three new activities have already started.

1 Preparing new treaties on harmonizing patents and trademarks; these treaties are intended to supplement the Paris Convention.
2 Additions to the Berne Convention to take account of new technology and, in particular, to increase protection in connection with phonograms (disks and cassettes).
3 Preparing a new treaty on the settlement of disputes between countries over intellectual property issues.

LICENSING IN DEVELOPING COUNTRIES

As a major part of its work, WIPO is concerned with promoting licensing agreements in developing countries to provide them with a quick route to industrialization. To this end the Organization has published a manual of advice on setting up agreements: (*Licensing Guide for Developing Countries*, World Intellectual Property Organization 1977, drafted by G.A. Ledakis). The purposes of the Organization are set out in the following terms:

> to encourage and increase, in quantity and quality, the creation of patentable inventions;
> to improve the conditions of acquisition of foreign patented technology ..., making those conditions more favourable to them than they are today;
> to increase their competitiveness in international trade through a better protection of the trademarks and service marks of relevance in such trade;
> to facilitate their access to the technological information contained in patent documents.

In order to achieve those objectives, most developing countries are in need of creating or modernizing domestic legislation and governmental institutions, acceding to international treaties, having more specialists in government, in industry and in the legal professions, and acquiring more patent documents and better methods for using their contents.

The manual explains the problems that developing countries perceive in licensing arrangements including the danger of over-dependence on a particular technology or economy and that of paying too much for an unwanted technology. Part II of the manual goes into considerable detail in filling a need that is often referred to – the need to improve negotiating abilities on the part of officials and licensees in developing countries. Affirming that a minimum period for negotiating an agreement is six months and that this can extend to two or three years, the manual points out that a series of inter-related legal documents may be

Legal and Political Issues

required; the number depends partly on the extent of the knowhow to be included and partly on the laws of the licensee country.

One comment in the document is for the benefit of both parties, that is an assertion that success depends on their compatibility in the first place. Some examples of the business backgrounds of the participants in Part III adds clarity to the advice on compatibility. Clauses likely to be used are then dissected and explained – a feature of the manual that is as relevant to licensors as it is to licensees. The following are the main types of clause identified:

1   preliminary and definitional;
2   scope, covering four topics:
    (a) the basic technology,
    (b) its uses,
    (c) the geographical area covered,
    (d) and the use of competing technologies;
3   'special aspects concerning patents';
4   technological advances;
5   technical information;
6   technical assistance;
7   supplies;
8   production;
9   trademarks;
10 marketing;
11 management services;*
12 remuneration;
13 settlement of payment;
14 most favourable terms and conditions;
15 rights of related enterprises;
16 liability and insurance;
17 default;
18 duration;
19 approval of government;
20 settlement of disputes;
21 concluding notes and signatures.

* Note that if many management services are included in the agreement, it becomes in effect a **management contract** although it may still be called a licensing agreement.

The current priorities of WIPO

In addition to its regular activities, the following items are high on the agenda of the World Intellectual Property Organization.

1 The supplementing of the Paris Convention on industrial property to facilitate trade.
2 Increasing worldwide compatibility among the patent systems of member countries.
3 Rendering cheaper and more effective the means of obtaining industrial property protection in more than one country through international filing and registration procedures under the Patent Cooperation Treaty (PCT), the Madrid system for the international registration of marks and the Hague system for the international registration of industrial designs.

Interaction between different forms of protection of intellectual property

As the pieces on a chess board each have a different value and power and must be moved in a coordinated manner in order to optimize the players' attacking and defensive strategies, so the various forms of protection of intellectual property should ideally be used in conjunction with one another in order to optimize the commercial position of the creator or exploiter of a particular new concept. As in the game of chess, the pieces may even have a different value at a different time in the game. In this book, much discussion is given over to patent licensing, although a patent currently has a life of 20 years. A trademark in constant use has no limitation of validity and, in most cases, becomes stronger the longer it is in existence so long as it is carefully safeguarded as a trade mark and does not come to be regarded as a

Legal and Political Issues

generic term (as in the case of thermos). Many creators or exploiters of intellectual property overlook the opportunities for strengthening their long-term position by using the whole range of the protective armoury. In advising the inventor to take such a broad view, the author may be accused of involving him or her in potentially expensive forms of protection, some of which may need to be discussed with advisers and registered at the patent office in the home country, or even in a number of foreign countries. In the case of a relatively simple invention of limited applicability, such an approach can lead to a high expenditure on protecting the idea which might only have the effect of starving the project of development or marketing funds.

On the other hand, taking a broad view at the outset may well prevent a number of errors which might later become sources of considerable problems.

Supposing someone invented a new kind of cutting mechanism for garden secateurs. The first mistake commonly made is to draft the patent claims in too specific a manner so that the patent would apply to garden secateurs, but might not apply to industrial applications in hand tools or machines such as those for cutting strip metals. It is therefore best to talk to a patent agent to have the claims of the patent drafted in as broad a sense as possible in order to cover the exercise of the patent in other fields. Even if the inventor only intended himself to use the idea for garden secateurs, it might be possible to licence the principle to machine toolmakers for use in other fields. At this stage, it would also be well to consider in what other countries the patent should be registered. This choice involves the inventor in very difficult decisions about the use of resources; should the company pay over $50 000 to have the patent registered in a few key countries or should it use the $50 000 to fund initial prototypes or start an advertising campaign? Perhaps, even at this early stage, the company should find a backer who would provide finance for the protection and subsequent development of the idea.

At this stage, the inventor might also think of a name for the secateurs – something like 'Eezicut'. Although such a name gives the purchaser an immediate insight into the advantages of the product, it is descriptive and would be difficult to register in most countries. There are well-known products on the market which do have descriptive names, but most of these were developed many years ago and have built up a value by widespread use over the years. In general it is becoming increasingly difficult to gain any useful protection from descriptive marks and it is almost impossible to obtain protection for marks based on names such as those of people and places.

The advantage of finding a good trademark under which to sell something like secateurs is that the name would become well established during the twenty years of patent life so that, even after expiry of the patent when potential copiers were able to produce a similar product, it would take them some years to build up a name and reputation in the field.

Once a trademark has been established with respect to secateurs, it might be capable of expansion to cover other groups of garden products, thereby giving further opportunity for business development. If the patent for the secateurs covered not the cutting method used by the secateurs but a method of producing the secateurs themselves, it might also be advisable to register the design covering the aesthetic appearance of the product if it were sufficiently distinctive. This would prevent potential copiers from using different manufacturing techniques to produce an item of similar outward appearance.

One could think of other cases in which various forms of intellectual property protection were used to optimize the income from an investment over time. These techniques are well understood by the pharmaceutical industry which, in addition to obtaining patents covering the composition or manufacturing process of a new drug, also seek to make it immediately identifiable to the public by choosing a suitable name. It is an interesting characteristic of many trademarks in the English language, that they are increasingly using consonants such as q, x and z, which have a low frequency of use in the common vocabulary of English. One must also marvel at the linguistic ingenuity of Japanese car manufacturers, who have succeeded in generating a

Legal and Political Issues

number of trademarks consisting of English-sounding names with no dictionary meaning.

A consideration of the protective strategies available would not be complete without mentioning two very cheap techniques with differing effects: secrecy and restricted publication.

If a bicycle manufacturer invented a clever way of making some component for a sealed gearing system, it might be better to use the improvement, but not to tell anyone in the outside world about it. The essence of a patent is controlled publication and, since many companies make constant searches of patent literature, the publication of a patent for a relatively minor component might only attract the attention of competitors. Would it really be worth patenting the minor component in countries such as India or the People's Republic of China? There are often arguments for keeping minor inventions and improvements as part of the secret knowhow of a company. In the case of foodstuffs, drinks and perfumes, such secret formulae have acquired an enormous value over the years and, so long as the secret is successfully kept, its period of value is potentially without limit.

In the strategy of controlled publication, companies seek to publish minor inventions in an inconspicuous manner in some publication in such a way as to prevent competitors from patenting a similar invention. Although the inventor may not wish to exploit an invention at that particular moment this technique at least prevents a competitor from later closing that possibility. If the vehicle for publication is carefully chosen, it will be sufficiently public to count as publication in a court of law but would be of sufficiently restricted circulation to make it unlikely that a competitor would come across it. House magazines, or the journals of small professional groups, are sometimes used for this purpose.

As we see from the intellectual property strategies of giant companies in the electronics, computer and pharmaceutical fields, there is probably no such thing as watertight protection; all defences can be breached if sufficient ingenuity or resources are expended for the purpose. On the other hand, the value of good policy on the protection of intellectual property is shown by the judgment in favour of Polaroid against Kodak in the United States, which recently enforced a permanent injunction against Kodak attempting to compete in Polaroid's principal area of business, and awarded Polaroid over $800m damages in cash.

An area of great complexity is the degree to which senior and lower level employees may take knowhow with them on changing companies. Although manuals on personnel contracts often contain secrecy clauses, purporting to restrict employees at all levels to maintaining the confidentiality of in-house knowhow and trade secrets, there is a counter-movement in industrialized democracies to regard the knowledge of an employee as his chief means of earning a living. Hence, whatever conditions may be stipulated in his service contract, there are now many judgments in the courts in Europe whereby an employer may not make such stringent restrictions on the employee as to prevent him supporting himself. Alternatively, the employer may have to pay the employee compensation for reducing his earnings potential for a certain period during which confidential information in the memory of the employee is deemed to be of use to a competitor. This problem is likely to increase as more staff move across frontiers. A safeguard will be through the various organizations affiliated to the World Intellectual Property Organization.

In the United States there is a body of law which holds the officers and directors of companies personally liable for breaches of copyright or patent infringements by their companies – they may render themselves open to criminal penalties such as imprisonment and civil penalties including triple damages.

In chess, it is well to check regularly all pieces on the board during the progress of the game, since the evolution of play brings threats from unexpected quarters. As a company develops its strategy for increasing its earnings from its assets in intellectual property, all aspects of its activities – research, personnel, marketing, electronic data processing and even its financial and organizational structure – will be affected

Legal and Political Issues

sooner or later, and each aspect of the business should be checked for possible inadequacies with respect to the protection of intellectual property.

CURRENT DEVELOPMENTS IN THE UNITED KINGDOM PATENT SYSTEM SEEN IN THE INTERNATIONAL CONTEXT

INCREASED ACCESSIBILITY TO THE PROTECTION OF INTELLECTUAL PROPERTY

While the legal establishment and the many international treaties on intellectual property seem to be making the field increasingly complex, it is noticeable that the governments of several member countries of the Organisation for Economic Cooperation and Development are recognizing increasingly the important part of the national patrimony represented by intellectual property. This leads to a counter-movement in which governments are trying to make the protection of intellectual property more accessible to lay inventors and small businesses.

In most countries, the cost of filing an initial application for the protection of a patent or trademark and the subsequent search and examination fees are kept as low as possible, and are to some extent subsidized by the renewal fees, which tend to be higher, and indeed in the United Kingdom increase on a sliding scale for the first few years of the patent's life. In the United States in the past, the work of the Patent Office has been subsidized from federal funds, but there are currently pressures to make its activities self financing.

In the United Kingdom, the Patent Office has set up a marketing department, and issues a series of useful pamphlets (see Sources of Information, Part 7) to guide newcomers through the complexities of registering the different forms of international patents. It also makes regional presentations to groups of interested parties in an effort to demystify the processes of intellectual property protection. A similar movement is also taking place in Sweden.

Patent examiners try to help novices through the problems of applying for protection. This is not to say that the Patent Office is trying to reduce the role of the patent or trademark agent but, by making the initial steps less arcane, it is hoped that more use will be made of the system.

The patent system also represents a valuable data base for those who are interested in a particular field of activity, and the United Kingdom Patent Office offers a search and advisory service on a fee-paying basis.

NEW TECHNIQUES

The world patent authorities are having to consider new situations arising from new technologies. At the beginning of 1993, the European Community introduced supplementary protection certificates (under Article 11) for pharmaceutical products which, while not actually lengthening the period of validity of the patent concerned, extend a period of protection of the use of a particular medically active ingredient for up to five years to account for the lengthy market approval procedures required. The extension of protection is based on the time which elapses between filing data for a pharmaceutical patent and the date of approval for marketing the resulting medical product. A similar procedure is under discussion for agro-chemical products.

Other questions arise in research-based industries. Basically, scientific knowledge is not patentable in its own right but the difficulties arise in distinguishing between a scientific principle and its application, particularly in biotechnology and computing.

Although biological agents such as brewer's yeast have been known for centuries, much study is now devoted to the patent system as it should apply to biotechnology and genetic engineering.

One important problem arises when the subject of a patent is able to reproduce itself. How can one prevent the further distribution of a self-multiplying organism? There is a European Union directive under

Legal and Political Issues

discussion (Article 11) to cover the legitimate first purchase and subsequent use of such living organisms where it would not be permitted to sell on the product for the fulfilment of the patented objective, although it could be sold for a different, non-patented, purpose. For instance, a patented yeast could not be sold to start up new breweries, although it might be sold as a vitamin supplement for animal feeds.

Computer programmes are not patentable, but may be subject to copyright. A movement is developing which holds that if the application of scientific principles to material objects is patentable, the same should apply to the processing of information. Computer programmes may be covered as part of a larger system, as when a special programme is used to control a production plant. However, it is not clear whether an infringement would take place if someone operated a similar programme using a different coding system or computer language.

INTERNATIONAL TRENDS IN THE PROTECTION OF INTELLECTUAL PROPERTY

Like all other fields of economic activity, intellectual property is exposed to opposing developments: at a time when many organizations are trying to standardize and internationalize the protection of intellectual property, some states which have evolved out of the former Soviet Union, Czechoslovakia or Yugoslavia, are establishing their own local patent offices.

With the European Union, the road towards unification is also proving far from easy although the European Patent Office has been operating for over 15 years. In the Union patent system, a single application is made, which may then become the basis for patents in 17 countries. However, these are still national patents, renewal fees are paid in each country and national courts are used for attacking and defending the patent. To simplify the procedure, the claims of the patent must be translated into all the official languages used, though the descriptions may be in the original language only.

The European Patent is single and unitary; it will cover all member countries of the Union and will be valid as a national patent in other signatories to the agreement such as Sweden and Switzerland. So far (1993) only four countries have ratified the new agreement. One difficulty is that under the influence of some countries such as Spain and France, which wish to defend the use of their own language, the whole of the patent claims and descriptions must be translated into all the official languages. This represents a considerable cost and militates against the aim of simplifying protection within the European Union. In addition, inventors claim that the renewal fees (which are currently split equally between the European Patent Office and the individual member states) are very high compared with those in the United States, another area of large economic potential but where the system is not complicated by translation costs and where there is a single patent office. It is hoped that after a few decades, when the volume of European Patents has increased, the economics of making applications may swing back in favour of the unitary European Patent.

In terms of the promotion of free trade, there is always a conflict between anti-trust law and the protection of intellectual property. The European Union is working on a new version of the block exemptions under Article 85 of the Treaty of Rome to permit patent and trademark licences. The new Commission Regulation (EEC) No 2349/84 will probably be similar to the existing law.

As a result of a United States initiative in the Uruguay round of the GATT talks, discussions are continuing on TRIPS (Trade Related Aspects of Intellectual Property) whereby a linkage is being made between a country having an international standard of intellectual property regulation and its acceptance in the world trading community. Taiwan, which was formerly notorious for the illicit copying of ideas from other countries is now beginning to build up its own body of intellectual property as its own companies begin to develop technologies in their own right.

At the same time the international community is working on a 'Treaty on the harmonization of Patent Laws', to supplement the Paris Convention and which is intended to cover the whole world. One of

Legal and Political Issues

the chief changes would be that the United States might abandon its present principle of 'first to invent' in favour of the principle of 'first to file' which is the basis of patent law in most other countries. This might be matched by the introduction of a grace period to cover disclosure by the inventor. At present, if an inventor published details of a device in a scientific paper at a conference and subsequently wished to patent it, he would have severely limited his chances by this, perhaps inadvertent, publication. A similar problem arises when inventors have to have test samples produced and evaluated by third parties before they decide to patent their ideas. The availability of ideas to outsiders could in some cases prevent them obtaining patent protection.

PROTECTION MEASURES IN THE UNITED KINGDOM

There are three kinds of **orders** which are operated in the British legal system for the protection of intellectual, especially industrial, property. Although specific to Britain they have implications elsewhere and offer some means of tracking down offenders. The types of order grow more draconic as you move from one to another; they are listed below.

Anton Piller orders A plaintiff who suspects that infringing goods are being held on an infringer's premises may apply for an order that those premises be searched and any infringing items found seized. The application to the court for such an order is normally made in the absence of the defendant.

In particular, the Anton Piller order has been the subject of considerable comment in the press as well as the courts. A plaintiff can apply in the defendant's absence to gain access to the premises which could include his private dwelling in so far as infringing items may be stored there.

It has been pointed out that, apart from a search by the Customs and Excise, there are few procedures which give the authorities such wide-ranging powers with so little possibility of defence. The writ is applied for by one party only.

Anton Piller orders have been used especially in copyright cases, such as occur when videos are pirated, although such an order could be granted in other cases of suspected infringement of intellectual property rights.

The plaintiff has to persuade a judge that the defendant may try to destroy the evidence of infringement if he is approached in the normal way. Hence solicitors acting for the plaintiff use the writ to look for infringing items such as pirated videos or invoices, computer files, correspondence and others which might incriminate the plaintiff.

Although the plaintiff may have his own solicitor present during the search, and should agree the list of items taken as evidence, the search is very wide-ranging and is open to abuse. In particular, the plaintiff's solicitors may take more than is absolutely necessary, since at the moment when the search is being carried out it is not always possible to distinguish an incriminating tape or document from bona fide items.

The opponents of the order point out that the disturbance to the plaintiff's business is considerable, and object to the inherent assumption of guilt.

Some very reputable companies have had to undergo what amounted to a general trawl of their offices and resent the access which strangers and potential competitors have thus gained to confidential information.

Although there is no doubt that an Anton Piller order is a powerful weapon when used properly, there is a strong feeling that it should only be used sparingly and as a last resort.

Mareva order A Mareva order has the effect of freezing all of a defendant's assets and prevents him from removing those assets from the United Kingdom. A British court will, in certain circumstances, grant a Mareva order to have worldwide effect.

Bayer order In extreme circumstances a personal order may be made

Legal and Political Issues

by a court against a director of a company infringing another's intellectual property rights. The order will require the director to hand over documents in relation to particular activities; it will freeze bank accounts in England and abroad and require the director to surrender his or her passport.

3.2 Regulations and services (government and private sector)

Decisions about licensing arrangements are influenced by many pieces of government legislation – patent, copyright, competition, taxation and technology transfer as well as licensing agreements themselves along with company and contract legislation. In some (mostly developing) countries licensing plays a significant part in the national economy and is likely to be more subject to regulation on those grounds. Restrictions are mentioned in other chapters (mostly in Part 5) and this chapter outlines some of the topics on which legislation can be helpful to licensors, including arbitration (3.2.3).

Payments for licensing agreements are usually treated as either exports or imports. Sales of knowhow to foreign licensees are usually encouraged, so long as they do not transfer secret or sensitive technology, and government services may be available to assist. If licences are bought from abroad, payments may be taxed, but not always and sometimes lightly. One of the advantages of licensing agreements is that many governments favour the import of knowhow and do not impose heavy tax burdens on it. Some examples can be found in Part 5. Where a particular government does not support licensing, it may be because it has become convinced that foreign companies are over-charging for their knowhow. Official intervention, then, takes two forms: regulation and support.

3.2.1 GOVERNMENT REGULATION

PROTECTION

Much regulation is, in fact, a support for intellectual property. Most countries, but not all, have provisions – either in civil or criminal codes, sometimes in both – for the enforcement of rights in valuable technical information. Sometimes patents are only enforceable by companies from within a country and only then when they are themselves exercising the patent. One motive for a licensing agreement

Legal and Political Issues

(or a subsidiary) is to safeguard a patent. Details can be found in Chapter 3.1 under intellectual property.

A strong relationship between protection and innovation is frequently remarked. If a change in legislation or a court case in a particular country points to stronger protection, companies in that country are seen to spend more on research and development.

TAXATION

Withholding taxes are frequently levied on payments of royalties to foreign companies. The different rates of tax, as already suggested, depend on a government assessment of the value of the foreign knowhow and whether reasonable prices are being charged. The effects of the withholding tax are usually minimized if there is a double taxation agreement between the countries concerned.

One reason for withholding taxes and other constraints on the payment of royalties has been that licenses have been treated as a means of moving money out of a country subject to balance of payments problems. As a further justification, a royalty payment is likely to be treated as an import for tax purposes. A further discussion on taxation can be found in Chapter 4.3.

Where there are exchange control problems, licensing issues are likely to be referred to a high political level with the intention that the rival costs and benefits to the economy are thoroughly examined.

3.2.2 GOVERNMENT ASSISTANCE

Government departments dedicated to promoting trade (like the Department of Trade and Industry in Britain, the Department of Commerce in the United States and the Ministry of International Trade and Industry in Japan) normally provide assistance in promoting national knowhow abroad and in helping to match would-be licensees or licensors in their own countries with foreign partners. A government department may also be active in identifying technical and geographical areas in which knowhow sales can be expected as well as in negotiating technical collaboration agreements. In Japan, the famous MITI (Ministry of International Trade and Industry) provides an object lesson in the role of a powerful government department in negotiating agreements. The MITI contributed to the early economic growth of the country by promoting the import of knowhow. Similar government organizations have been at work in Korea and India as well as Malaysia and Singapore.

Other types of assistance include assistance with market intelligence, with credit insurance and with publicity for national expertise. Some industrial country governments, including the British, do not undertake a full-scale licensing service; this is left to professional associations.

3.2.3 ARBITRATION

Arrangements for the settlement of disputes are not likely to be different for licensing than they are for other commercial conflicts; arbitration can be sought within both national and international institutions. Arbitration has increased in popularity. Its usage has increased by a third in the late 1980s according to one source; this is natural as it is a simpler and much cheaper way of settling disputes than through commercial or civil courts. Official provision for arbitration can be by both national and international systems while private and public sector institutions have grown to meet the need. Some examples of their work are outlined later in this chapter.

To avoid problems in which one party may refuse to implement the results of arbitration, it is usual to include a clause in the agreement under which both parties agree that the decision of an arbitration by the agreed method will be final and binding. This clause has the effect that the decision is immediately enforceable in the courts of the countries of the parties. Agreed damages in the event of certain forms of breach of contract may also be awarded as a result of the action.

Legal and Political Issues

Most countries have some system of commercial courts which provide arbitration arrangements; some of the regional organizations, like the European Union, are moving in this direction too. There are also private sector organizations which provide facilities. The American Arbitration Association is one. Nevertheless licensors sometimes find that procedures that are normal in their home countries are not permitted elsewhere.

One private sector institution – nationally based, but international in its operations – is the hundred year old **London Court of International Arbitration**. Claiming to be the 'oldest arbitral body in the world', the Court has 26 arbitrators (including a president and three vice-presidents) from 17 nationalities; cases can be heard anywhere, not only at the Court's London base.

If a licensing dispute is to be arbitrated through the London Court, the following clause needs to be part of the agreement.

> Any dispute arising out of or in connection with this contract, including any question regarding its existence, validity or termination, shall be referred to and finally resolved by arbitration under the Rules of the London Court of International Arbitration, which Rules are deemed to be incorporated by reference into this clause.

The normal number of arbitrators for a case is one, but can be three at the request of the parties. Fees are based on the time taken not on the amount of money at stake.

To ensure that the Court meets the needs of its international clients, there are regional centres (known as Users' Councils) in Europe, North America, Asia (and the Pacific rim) and sub-Saharan Africa.

The Court deals with about 70 cases a year (the number is steadily increasing) of which some are disputes concerned with licensing agreements.

Note: The **London Court of International Arbitration (LCIA)**

publishes a number of booklets to describe its work. These can be obtained from The Executive Director, The London Court of International Arbitration, 2-5 Minories, London EC3N 1BJ (tel: 071-702 9599, fax: 071-702 9797).

The **International Chamber of Commerce** is another private sector organization that provides an arbitration system. According to a booklet published by the Chamber in 1983 (*Guide to Arbitration*) the inclusion of the following clause in agreements is recommended.

> All disputes arising in connection with the present contract shall be finally settled under the Rules of Conciliation and Arbitration of the International Chamber of Commerce by one or more arbitrators appointed with the said Rules.

There is also a recommended clause for the appointment of arbitrators, but more important is a provision for conciliation (which is much less expensive) before a dispute goes to arbitration.

Indeed the conciliation procedure forms a three-tier system in which the levels of formality and expense increase with each tier. At first there is conciliation, but if this fails – which, in the experience of the Chamber, it often does – arbitration is available, provided the accused party agrees. If both fail, the aggrieved party can still resort to the more onerous route of litigation within the legal system of the country stipulated in the contract.

The Chamber offers conciliation as a first stage; it appoints the sole conciliator who has wide discretion but operates within predetermined and limited deadlines; the process does not proceed if one party declines or fails to agree within 15 days. The independence of the conciliator is safeguarded and he(she) is not allowed to act in a judicial capacity in a subsequent arbitration, nor can the views or suggestions put forward at the conciliation be used later before an arbitration tribunal.

The arbitration is a more formal affair but every effort is made in this commercial system to meet the wishes of the participants. A notable

Legal and Political Issues

feature of the Chamber's procedures is the distinction between the **Court** (the **International Court of Arbitration**) and the **Tribunal** (the **Arbitral Tribunal**). The former is a supervisory body which establishes the Tribunal after listening to the views of the participants and ensures that the arbitration is carried out. The parties present their cases in writing to the Court but are not permitted to attend its meetings. The Court also advises the Tribunal and exercises supervision while ensuring and smoothing the continuity at each stage of the process; it also establishes terms of reference for the arbitration which make for a common understanding of the process by all those concerned and are held to be able to 'eliminate defects in the original arbitration clause and [to] constitute an enforceable agreement to arbitrate even in those countries of the Middle East and Latin America where an agreement to arbitrate a future dispute is not considered valid'. The procedure can only be invoked if provided for in the original contract and where both parties have agreed to abide by the results.

Among the issues on which the parties are normally asked to agree is the number of arbitrators. Only one arbitrator is required but three provide a greater range of skills especially for complicated cases. In this case one of the three could be a scientist or engineer, one an economist or business executive and one a lawyer.

The advantages of the extra skills provided by three arbitrators have to be weighed against the additional costs and possible delays – and this applies to all arbitration arrangements. Any one of the three arbitrators can hold up a settlement and involve the parties in escalating fees. The rules of the International Chamber of Commerce have been framed so as to minimize the delays but time can equal a lot of money.

The flexibility on which the Chamber prides itself is further enhanced by the ability to establish a tribunal in any country which is signatory to the New York agreement which set up the procedure; this arrangement has the additional advantage that the award can be made within a jurisdiction which will ensure that its enforcement is as easy as possible.

Note: The **International Chamber of Commerce** (ICC) publishes a number of booklets which describe the procedures of its arbitration facility and these are updated when necessary. See especially: *ICC Rules of Conciliation and Arbitration*, a 40-page leaflet setting out the rules.

The International Chamber has had considerable experience in international arbitration; as a result it has built up a body of procedures and regulations. The structure is a **court** which supervises the arbitration process. The court consists of a chairman, vice-chairman, technical advisers and about thirty members. These are unpaid volunteers who meet only when the court is in session. The court is serviced by a secretariat employed by the International Chamber including counsels, assistants and administrative staff.

Since it was set up with the object of promoting free trade (it was the source of the **Incoterms** which constantly command the attention of exporters and importers), the Chamber brought into being the Court in the 1920s as a further means of servicing its clients. The Chamber takes on 300 new cases a year and usually has over 700 in process at any one time. Of these about ten per cent concern licensing agreements. Table 3.2.1 gives the statistics of cases considered by the Court of Arbitration in one recent year (1992).

Table 3.2.1 Statistics of cases heard by the International Chamber of Commerce Court of Arbitration in 1992

Number of cases registered:	337
Number of cases pending at year end:	747
Number of countries involved in ICC arbitration:	93
of which 61 are developing countries = 65.6%	
Number of parties involved:	844
of which 188 are from developing countries	
(22.3%: 86 claimants and 102 defendants)	
Government organization was party to an ICC arbitration	
procedure – 4.8% of the requests introduced in 1992	
Arbitrators appointed or confirmed by ICC	
International Court of Arbitration:	536
from 47 different countries	
of which 23 are developing countries = 48.9%	
Places of arbitration	
in 25 countries of which 7 are developing countries = 28%	

Legal and Political Issues

Table 3.2.1 continued

Amounts in dispute				
Order	US$ 50,000			5.6%
Between	US$ 50,000	and	US$200,000	12.1%
Between	US$200,000	and	US$500,000	10%
Between	US$500,000	and	US$1M	9.6%
Between	US$1M	and	US$10M	87%
Between	US$10M	and	US$50M	16.5%
Between	US$50M	and	US$100M	1.6%
Between	US$100M	and	US$1BN	1.8%
Over US$1BN				0%
Not quantified				5%

Distribution by economic activities in 1992	
Foreign trade Agency Transport Distributorship	41.9%
Constructions and engineering Joint ventures	13.7%
Licence Transfer of Technology High Tech Technical Assistance/knowhow	23.6%
Finance Maintenance Consultancy Management Services	8.8%
Insurance Aquisition and mergers Company law Marketing Patent and trademarks Maritime Employment law Environment Others: Film production	12%
	100%

In addition to supervising the arrangements for and the carrying out of the arbitration process, the court confirms the appointment of the arbitrators, sets their terms of reference and fixes the time limits to which they must work. The main principle in the appointment of arbitrators is to follow the wishes of the parties whose proposals are usually adopted unless special circumstances suggest otherwise. The place of arbitration is not limited to the Paris headquarters of the Chamber, but has been in many different countries (including Argentina, Australia, Belgium, Canada, Colombia, Egypt, France, Ivory Coast, Jordan, Philippines, Spain, Switzerland, Syria, Tunisia and the United Kingdom). The Chamber gives advice on a suitable location and on other matters that may affect the enforceability of the arbitration. Providing the procedures have been correctly observed, and the arbitrator has stated the reasons for his decision, the award will be binding in most countries. Expenses (including the arbitrators' fees) are calculated according to the size of the sum in dispute. Contact can usually be made with the International Chamber through a national office in the applicant's country; the address can be obtained from the International Chamber of Commerce, 38 cours Albert premier, 75008 Paris, France.

An offshoot of the United Nations – the **International Council for the Settlement of Industrial Disputes** – is a public sector organization which offers an arbitration service. It was set up by the World Bank to arbitrate (or, when possible, conciliate) disputes between private companies and foreign governments, both of which are in countries which are signatories to the Convention (the Washington Convention of 1965) that set up the Centre as an integral part of the World Bank under whose authority it operates. The policy of the World Bank is to settle disputes by conciliation or arbitration when possible. Article 26 of the Washington Convention provides that consent to arbitration under the covenant once undertaken excludes other remedies, although local actions will usually have been tried first. An award is by a majority of members of the Tribunal and must give reasons. Individual members are permitted to attach their opinions, but need not do so. The Centre may not publish the award without the consent of the parties but the decisions are usually made public.

Legal and Political Issues

The constitution of the Centre provides for an Administrative Council (whose Chairman is the President of the World Bank). This Council provides a general oversight of the work of the Centre. The work is carried out by a secretariat headed by the secretary general; it is funded by the member states. Its jurisdiction is limited to disputes between member governments and private companies, from other member states but this has now been extended.

The constitution provides for a conciliation procedure where this is possible, but arbitration if not. The arbitral tribunal can consist of any odd number of arbitrators and, once established, the tribunal decides its own competence to arbitrate the dispute. If it proceeds, the decision is by a majority vote. The parties meet the cost of the proceedings which can be held at any place agreed between the parties and the secretary general. Any country that is a member of the World Bank can join the Centre and become a contracting state; disputes between states are referred to the International Court of Justice.

Most of the cases handled by the ICSID Court of Arbitration are naturally concerned with investment projects and many with management contracts. One licensing case in 1984 was 'Colt Industries Operating Corporation Firearms Division v. Government of the Republic of Korea' (Case No. ARB/84/2, reported in *ICSID Cases*, published by ICSID, 1991). Most business disputes concerned with licensing can be taken to the court.

One advantage of international arbitration is that it reduces the costs and uncertainties about enforcement of legal action in a foreign country.

ALTERNATIVE DISPUTE RESOLUTION

Alternative dispute resolution is a mechanism for solving disputes without resorting to litigation or to an arbitration. Instead, two parties who find themselves in dispute arising, for example, from a licence agreement between them both agree to put their dispute to alternative dispute resolution. This will typically involve either mediation with the help of a mediator, trained for the purpose, or the making of a presentation before a tribunal made up of agreed representatives (normally one person capable of entering into a binding agreement on behalf of each of the parties and a chairperson adviser to these two). While alternative dispute resolution is not as formal a process as proceedings before a court or an arbitration it is likely that much of the argument will be of a legal nature and that the involvement of the parties' lawyers will in most cases be appropriate. The alternative dispute resolution should be conducted on a without prejudice basis so that if it should fail the arguments put forward and any concessions offered would not form any part of proceedings before a court or in an arbitration.

Alternative dispute resolution offers significant potential for time and costs savings and for simplicity and privacy. Some practitioners though will caution that all too often it can become bogged down in disputes about terms of reference or procedure to be adopted. The process may in the end serve only to clarify the issues in dispute rather than to solve them.

Alternative dispute resolution is most likely to succeed where there is a real possibility or wish that the parties should remain in a business relationship after the dispute. This is obviously the clearest form of incentive to resolve a dispute. Alternative dispute resolution will definitely not be appropriate in certain other circumstances. Where one party urgently requires an injunction to prevent something from happening or from continuing to happen this method is unlikely to be useful: it is the continuation or imminence of damage that is of greatest importance at that point not a final resolution of any substantive issue. Alternative dispute resolution is also unlikely to be appropriate where a stance taken by one of the parties is purely tactics and lacking in any legal merit.

Unlike a court's judgment or the finding of an arbitrator the successful conclusion in agreement of an alternative dispute resolution is not of itself enforceable. Only when the parties draw up an agreement

Legal and Political Issues

between themselves reflecting the terms of that conclusion will this new contract be enforceable.

3.2.4 Litigation: the protection of general corporate knowhow

Intellectual property is a company asset which is being defended with increasing vigour. But if an executive can memorize important experience and information which his company has spent millions to obtain, then he also has in his mind knowledge which is worth millions to his company's competitors. He could then proceed to leave his company and work for one of their rivals, and expect a generous reward from his new company in return for divulging some of this priceless information.

This, perhaps, is where copyright law is inadequate. It is impossible to declare a person's memory, their chains of thought, as belonging to somebody else, or as bound to a company by law. It is well-known that under employment law clauses may be put in contracts binding people to secrecy, as is only proper when large sums of money are at stake, but the freedom of every individual to earn his keep often militates against such restrictive practices.

In a recent battle of the giants, Volkswagen in Germany has been under attack from General Motors of the United States, which wished to protect knowhow in the possession of a former employee.

In March 1993 Mr Lopez de Arriortua Jose Ignacio left General Motors to work for Volkswagen. He is a production and supply director, which means that his job is to ensure that the new series of Volkswagen cars are successful, both in terms of economy of production and popularity with the buying public. General Motors became extremely suspicious of Mr Lopez and six other former General Motors' employees, believing that some of General Motors' valuable research may have gone with them to their main rivals, Volkswagen. As is their prerogative under copyright law, General Motors ordered on 26 August 1993 a complete search of Volkswagen's headquarters and the homes of some executives, looking for anything, such as a floppy disk or a series of notes, which might prove this. The search was unsuccessful.

Anybody who has had their house or offices searched by a higher authority knows, from bitter experience, that it is a degrading affair. If you are innocent, as Mr Lopez assures us he is, then you are being falsely accused, which is enough to incite anger in anyone.

This is a train of thought which Mr Louis Hughes, president of General Motors Europe, has obviously not yet followed. He stated at the Frankfurt Motor Show that Volkswagen were only paying lip service to the probe which his company had instigated against them. A Volkswagen spokesperson replied that his remarks were unjust.

At the time of writing, the matter is still under review in the German courts, and General Motors are considering charges of industrial espionage, poaching of employees and theft of documents and data. We also hear that the accountancy firm KPMG have been unable to find evidence that the Volkswagen board could be accused of any malpractice over the Lopez case. This news appears to exonerate Mr Lopez but it is likely that the reverberations of the case will darken relations between the two companies for some years.

Irrespective of the guilt or innocence of Mr Lopez, this case is of general interest in that it shows how the courts are beginning to recognize the value of the intangible asset of **knowhow**, and the lengths to which the owner of knowhow may go to defend against its wrongful acquisition by a third party.

During the later stages of the preparation of this book, this high profile case was widely reported in the business press of many countries. The *Financial Times* reports featured the following headlines: 'Embattled VW chairman warns of enemies within' and 'Piëch speaks of enemies all around' (both 9 September 1993). The latter report mentioned a positive outcome of the dispute – the bringing together of management and workers at Volkswagen in a unified response. 'VW may agree

Legal and Political Issues

to suspend managers' (10 November 1993). This outlined a proposed settlement in which General Motors' managers who had defected to Volkswagen would be suspended.

3.3 Drafting an agreement

The agreement itself has to be negotiated by the legal advisors to the two companies and drafted in terms that will score in a court of law or arbitration tribunal. The exact terms are for legal experts and are not the subject of this book but this chapter reviews items that both parties are likely to put in front of their legal advisers before the negotiations begin.

An agreement is drafted to cement a business relationship between two parties. There are several schools of thought about the significance of the agreement itself.

One school of thought, popular among many businessmen, holds that the business relationship is all-important and that the legal document amounts to an expensive irrelevance to be kept, as they say, 'only to collect dust in a remote filing cabinet'. The only clause to matter, this school holds, is the one that enables you to extricate yourself if the relationship breaks down – an event that is usually not foreseen.

Another view is that the success of the relationship depends on the willingness of the parties to work through the terms detail by detail. In the eyes of this school, negotiating an agreement is vital to clarifying the aims, objectives and methods of operation before the project starts. Some take this view – the one that is closest to the authors of this book – to the length of recommending an extended period of planning to ensure that nothing is left to chance. This chapter aims to identify the issues that will occupy the planning and the negotiations, the raw material with which the lawyers will be asked to work.

3.3.1 THE TECHNICAL AND BUSINESS AGREEMENTS

Most of the issues under this heading have already been discussed and will be briefly summarized here.

The primary purpose of an agreement is a business one: the development

Legal and Political Issues

of the business interests of the partners in a particular market.

To this end, the most important contents are technical points of law, the specification of patents and knowhow to be sold by one partner and to be used by the other. The licensor will wish to list the uses to which the technology can be put and will attempt to limit the markets within which it can be sold, as far as it is legal to do so.

3.3.2 REMUNERATION

Most licences are paid for by a royalty based on a percentage of net sales or numbers of products. Sometimes the percentage will be reduced if very large sums are involved. The licensor usually prefers the royalty system as it provides an incentive to the licensee and because it ensures a share in the success of the project, but a lump sum payment is sometimes negotiated where a large royalty income is seen as less than certain. There is also a combined lump sum and percentage arrangement which effectively ensures a minimum payment. There may also be a minimum royalty per year which has the same effect. The size of the royalty varies greatly from around five per cent up to 25 per cent, but is usually towards the lower end.

A share in the success of a project can also be obtained by taking some equity in the licensee's business, perhaps in lieu of start up royalties.

3.3.3 MARKETING AND OTHER SERVICES

We have already explained that the aim of most licensors is to produce a relationship which gives the client maximum independence, and thus keeps to a minimum the demands the project makes on top management time in the licensor company, and that this aim seldom works in practice. The commercialization of technical knowledge usually implies more than its transfer from one company to another. There may be a package of expertise covering many company functions such as marketing, personnel, training and many aspects of production.

Sometimes the project will not work without the whole package. If this is foreseen, the necessary provisions have to be incorporated.

3.3.4 DURATION AND SCOPE

Decisions on the length of time for which an agreement will run will depend on the ambitions of both parties. A licensee will not be able to finance a substantial project without adequate security. Its bankers will be interested in the track record of the technology and its prospects. Similar considerations apply to the extent of the technology covered. Duration and scope are decisions whose resolution is particularly subject to negotiation. So is a clause on future technology. Both parties may aim to extend the duration with an option on future licences in the same technology. Such a clause would appear to offer special advantages to the licensee but is also favoured by licensors as enabling them to lock the licensee into future deals.

A licensee is likely to prefer an exclusive licence to handle the product within the agreed territory where it is legal to make this arrangement; the exclusive licence may give rise to problems if a third party imports the product from elsewhere. A non-exclusive licence leaves the licensor free to award licences to others in the same territory in competition with the licensee. A small company may prefer this as the only means of obtaining a licence.

3.3.5 REVIEW, RENEWAL AND TERMINATION

Those who enter a licensing agreement are naturally interested in a clause which provides an escape if the project fails. The licensor looks for a clause which denies the licensee any rights after termination, but in some developing countries such a clause is illegal. In particular the results of the licensee being liquidated vary with different national laws; this is an issue that has to be considered in drafting a contract.

Legal and Political Issues

3.3.6 Provisions for the settlement of disputes

Disputes between licensors and licensees are resolved by arbitration procedures usually stipulated in the agreements. These procedures are discussed in Chapter 3.2.

Disputes between the partners and third parties over issues like infringement of copyright can be pursued by either with the contract stipulating which. Normally the licensor is most interested in ensuring that the licensee protects its rights and properties but, if legal action is initiated by a third party, the contract is likely to stipulate that the licensee must protect the interests of the licensor provided it has furnished the relevant information. Product liability claims are usually directed at the licensee which needs a liability insurance policy.

3.3.7 Insurance and liability

The licensee will be contracted to undertake insurance on various risks that are expected to arise including the product liability just mentioned. A motive of the licensor in choosing a licensing option may well be to avoid product and personnel liabilities in the country of manufacture; to this end the licensee's insurance cover will be important.

3.3.8 Confidentiality and the right of inspection

A concern of the licensor is for the **confidentiality** of its business secrets including both the patented technology and the knowhow that goes with it. Confidentiality is detailed in different ways in licensing agreements.

There will usually also be a **right of inspection**, but the licensee will be able to insert a clause asserting its need for compensation in the event of a leak.

3.3.9 QUALITY

Both parties are concerned with quality issues. The licensor needs to ensure that the products are manufactured to acceptable standards that will not damage its reputation or the sale of the product and that there is adequate after-sales support and service; the licensee needs to know that it, in its turn, will receive sufficient support and that the technology will be regularly updated.

Trade mark protection is a key concern of licensors. Some countries have laws giving additional protection when the licensor adopts strong measures of quality control.

3.4 The political background

Licensing agreements do not appear to be activities designed to provoke controversy. On the face of it, they bring advantages to both parties – revenue from an expensive development process for the licensor and a major step towards a new business for the client. In keeping with this mutual advantage, many governments encourage licensing arrangements, but others legislate to restrain abuses they perceive. For instance, there are sometimes tax and regulatory controls on licensing arrangements to ensure that useful technology is transferred at a reasonable price.

There are two closely related pressures relevant to licensing in the counsels of world politics. One is for greater freedom of trade in all services and the other is for harmonization in patent regulation; the latter is a condition of the former. Progress is slow on both these counts partly because of conflicting interests among the industrialized nations and suspicions in the developing world. One move towards harmonization is the patent worksharing treaty which may well have moved closer to reality by the time this book is published.

One reason for the suspicion among some developing countries is that a large proportion of the licensing agreements within their borders are between two units of a multinational company; they do not provide local entrepreneurs with business opportunities but the restrictions that result do not distinguish between licensing within a company and that between two independent concerns. Licensing agreements which appear to enhance the power of foreign firms still cause suspicions although more countries have modified their constraints to encourage investment and the employment it brings. The general thrust of developing country regulations has been aimed to make more technology available and to limit restrictive clauses in agreements.

In industrialized countries, constraints on licensing are even more indirect, mainly deriving from laws of contract and competition to prevent licensing agreements which used to contain restrictive clauses limiting, for instance, the areas within which the licensee could

Legal and Political Issues

sell the products. In a sense all licensing contracts (like patents) are restraints on competition since they give the partners a monopoly, if only a temporary one. In recognition of this, the European Commission has granted the so-called 'block exemptions' to prevent legitimate agreements from being attacked under the competition legislation. The block exemptions are considered elsewhere, meanwhile agreements are held to be 'legitimate' on the grounds that the technology transferred would not be made available without the safeguards provided.

The conflict between a need to promote trade and to foster competition at the same time is a fundamental political dilemma that cannot be separated from licensing. The measures just noted may well turn out to be indications of how regulators in the future will cope with this dilemma.

Most international agreements that affect licensing concern the subject matter not the licences themselves. The protection of intellectual property and the registration of patents, both subjects of Chapter 3.1, are essential to licensing projects.

There are other **characteristics** of licensing that have political implications and the following quotation is taken from Dr Piero Telesio and reprinted with his permission.

> If governments restrict the outflow of foreign direct investment, the outflow of licensing will increase unless also restricted. Licensing can partially substitute for foreign direct investment in the transfer of technology abroad. However, the technology owner is likely to realize lower returns from licensing undertaken because of restrictions on foreign direct investment than from a controlled foreign direct investment.
> If, on the other hand, licensing is restricted and foreign direct investment is not, it is not likely that foreign direct investment will increase significantly, because it typically is not a substitute for licensing. For example, if a company chooses to license because an

investment would not be profitable, it would be unlikely to undertake the unprofitable investment if licensing were restricted.

Licensing restrictions would hurt firms by reducing royalty income. In addition, technology from competitors would most likely replace restricted U.S. technology in third-country markets. For example, a relatively small U.S. multinational enterprise, if not permitted to license, might have to forego establishing a manufacturing presence in foreign markets; direct investment would probably be too costly. Similarly, a U.S.-based multinational enterprise with high product diversification that licenses older technology would most likely abandon some markets to non-U.S. competitors and thus lose royalty income. In both of these examples, the chances are that technology would still be transferred, but from a source other than the United States, with the U.S.-based multinational enterprise losing both market presence and income and the United States losing taxes on royalties. In addition, licensing restrictions would produce indirect effects for both the firm and the nation involving a long-term loss of competitive strength vis-à-vis foreign competitors. This analysis is consistent with the finding that U.S. firms generally invest abroad for defensive reasons, as they would otherwise lose the foreign markets to non-U.S. competitors. And restrictions on U.S. foreign direct investment would be damaging to the United States in terms of the balance of payments and the skill levels of employment.

Restrictions on reciprocal licensing would succeed in keeping certain innovations at home but could prevent firms from acquiring important foreign technology. Innovative firms might then fall behind the technology of firms in other countries that do allow licensing. If the United States were, for example, to impose such restrictions, U.S. firms in the pharmaceutical, chemical, and electrical industries would probably have access to fewer new technologies, as they would be deprived of the benefits of R&D carried out by other firms abroad. With a deteriorating competitive position, they might then return fewer benefits to the United States. Of course, foreign firms would fall behind the U.S. firms in certain fields, so they too would return fewer benefits to their home countries.

Countries that want to restrain the influx of foreign investment

Legal and Political Issues

will often find licensing an attractive alternative. Still, government policy makers should be realistic with regard to the technology they can obtain through licensing. Often, certain technologies are not available for licensing without control, especially if the licensor is a large single-product-line firm. For example, it would not be easy to convince an automobile producer seeking area-wide production integration to operate in one country through a licensee. Moreover, developing countries are likely to obtain only limited access to advanced technologies in the pharmaceutical, chemical, and electrical industries, since it is unlikely that they could offer valuable technology in exchange.

Finally, while Japan provides a striking example of how a country can make use of foreign licensed technology, not every nation will be able to match its performance. Developing countries, for example, sometimes do not have the capabilities to use manufacturing technology without the transfer of management skills associated with foreign investment. For these countries, a policy of denying foreign ownership of investments might result in denying the country access to needed technologies.

A case study can be found in a Canadian book on international management (see P.W. Beamish, et al. (1991), 'Evaluating a licensing agreement', *International Management: Text and Cases*, Irwin, pages 249-258).

3.4.1 CHARACTERISTICS

Governments are constrained to hold a balance between two opposing pressures in handling issues that concern patents and other forms of protection for intellectual property. On the one hand protection is a restraint of trade and may be held to violate competition policies, on the other hand lack of protection for patents discourages innovation by making it difficult to ensure repayment of the costs of research.

Most governments do not feel the need for a policy on licensing as such – although legislation on patents and other industrial property is more usual and may be considered as a form of protection for licensees, but when they do the issues will be considered under the following headings.

DECISION-MAKING

How can inward licensing projects be steered to match national capabilities, national needs and national objectives? The government may well be anxious to promote business activity and the opportunities for domestic investment offered by licensing; it may also be anxious to steer these investments to areas where facilities are already available or where work is scarce. In countries where the role of government is seen to be small, the steering will be by the use of incentives, others may use more directive methods. In either case, the success of the licensee will be assisted by the provision of facilities for leasing and of loans. Any government is interested in providing an environment in which new enterprises can prosper.

APPRAISAL AND MONITORING

Government departments need to monitor the consequences of licensing projects for the national economy. Are the projects bringing income through increased tax revenues? Do they provide employment and a stimulus to existing businesses through competition? There is a narrow dividing line between healthy competition and damaging conflict; only a sophisticated system of appraisal can judge where controls are needed to replace incentives. Policies will be formulated and reformulated as the projects work through the system.

REGULATION

Most government intervention is likely to be through incentives, controls and taxation (see Chapter 4.3); in selected industries there will also be a regulatory system in place especially when the licences are in

Legal and Political Issues

pharmaceuticals or other high profile products with the possibility of dangerous side effects.

3.4.2 INTERNATIONAL ORGANIZATIONS

International organizations such as the United Nations and its affiliates have interested themselves in licensing agreements or their contents like patents. The one most quoted is the **Paris Convention** (first signed in 1883) which was established to safeguard intellectual property including patents. One of the many revisions of the Convention (1967) established the **World Intellectual Property Organization** (WIPO, an offshoot of the United nations, see Chapter 3.1). Also important to licensing people is the **International Centre for the Settlement of Industrial Disputes (ICSID)**, see Chapter 3.1.

Many world organizations can offer advice, information and sometimes assistance for licensing projects. Indeed major initiatives will depend on financing from the **World Bank** or one of the regional banks and the proposals before these organizations provide valuable indications about where licensing opportunities are likely to be available. Other sources, like the World Bank affiliates of the **United Nations** are listed below. Addresses can be found in Chapter 7.2

UNITED NATIONS INDUSTRIAL DEVELOPMENT ORGANIZATION (UNIDO)

A comparatively recent offshoot of the United Nations, UNIDO provides business opportunities in its economic development initiatives including the promotion of industrial cooperation in developing countries and emerging markets. UNIDO also claims to reduce the costs of technology transfer by training programmes for practitioners and government officials.

3.4.3 REGIONAL TRADING ORGANIZATIONS

Countries wishing to regulate trade, in this case licensing and related activities, are apt to find that this is ineffective if not counter-productive when operated on the part of a single nation which may not be sufficiently attractive to foreign concerns to induce them to invest and accept the regulation. This is especially true of competition legislation as members of the European Union have discovered. The larger unit can impose regulations which the individual country cannot. This and other similar insights have stimulated a rapid increase in regional treaties in various parts of the world. The following are the ones most likely to be important to you.

> ECOWAS (Economic Community of West African States)
> ANCOM (Andean Community and Common Market)
> CEAO (Communauté économique de l'Afrique de l'Ouest)
> CARICOM (Caribbean Community)
> ALADI (Latin American Integration Association)
> ASEAN (Association of South East Asian Nations)
> NAFTA (North American Free Trade Area)

See also Chapter 5.2; for addresses see Chapter 7.3.

3.4.4 TRAINING

All countries need training for skills for those to be employed in licensing projects, but developing countries have special training needs to ensure that:

1 there are sufficient people with technical skills to staff the newly appointed licensees; and
2 there is a corps of people with negotiating skills to match up to the licensor company. The negotiations will be available for recruitment by licensees to promote their interests and by government departments to provide a service to local entrepreneurs.

3.5 A typical technology transfer agreement based on knowhow and a trademark

Many companies and licensing practitioners have standard agreements which they use as the basis for negotiations for patent, trademark and knowhow licences. In practice, every such text (with the exception of a few very simple patent or trademark licences) is altered during the negotiations, and compromises are made in the cut and thrust of the commercial power game.

Some international organizations, such as ORGALIME, sell standard texts for such agreements. ORGALIME have representatives in all European member countries, and are represented in the United Kingdom by BEAMA (Legal Department). Full details of addresses of ORGALIME and BEAMA can be found in the list of useful organizations (Chapter 7.3).

Other draft texts are reproduced in legal works such as the excellent book by Leslie William Melville, *Forms and Agreements on Intellectual Property and International Licensing*, published by Clark Boardman Co. in New York, and by Sweet and Maxwell in London under ISBN No. 0421053002 (revised third edition 1979, revised 1990).

Since average business people will not want to draft their own licence texts, such works are for reference purposes only, but anyone wishing to involve themselves to any depth in this field would be well advised to study a number of standard agreements in order to observe the points covered and the style of the documents. One of our legal advisors recommends the text of the software licences on the packaging of standard computer software packages for spreadsheets or word processing, as good examples of the way in which licence agreements are structured.

As we have stressed throughout this work, the legal matters should be dealt with by a solicitor or patent attorney experienced in such matters: not only is a little learning dangerous, but the field is changing almost daily from topic to topic and from country to country.

Legal and Political Issues

The following draft agreement is given to demonstrate how the particular problems of a knowhow agreement are dealt with in a practical working environment. In this case, the licence to use the (fictitious) trademark 'LOCOM' is included in the body of the agreement. Alternatively, relatively simple trademark or patent licences may also be appended to the agreement. This not only keeps the body of the main agreement simpler, but may permit the extension of the main agreement in spite of later expiry of patents, or changes in the trademark situation.

A number of additional clauses could be included in the ideal agreement: for example in relation to the parties helping one another to resist infringement of a patent or trademark, protection of goodwill and methods, or *force majeure* (that is events beyond the control of either party which may frustrate the outcome of the agreement).

The appendices showing the drawings of the licensed product are not included, but in a knowhow agreement, great attention should be paid to the unambiguous definition of the knowledge to be transferred. Otherwise, there can be endless disagreements on what trainees are and are not allowed to see, or whether the licensee is entitled to improved models later developed by the licensor. Hence, if the licensed product is defined in a sales manual, it is as well to define the issue date of the particular manual concerned.

The Specimen Agreement

This agreement is made the   day of   19.... between company 'a' whose registered office is in country L (hereinafter called 'A') of the one part and company 'b' whose registered office is in country M (hereinafter called 'B') of the other part

WHEREAS

(a) 'B' wishes to undertake through its Manufacturing Division (hereinafter called '*B*') the assembly manufacture and distribution of the range of power transmission units designed and manufactured by company *a* of country L (hereinafter called '*A*')

(b) '*A*' markets the said range of power transmission units (hereinafter more particularly defined and called the Units) under the trademark 'LOCOM' and wishes to establish manufacture and distribution of the same in the Territory as hereinafter defined

(c) Both 'A' and '*A*' are subsidiaries of XYZ (a public company incorporated in country L) and 'A' has been designated by XYZ as the subsidiary company responsible for entering into overseas distribution and manufacturing contracts on behalf of subsidiary companies of XYZ

(d) By separate contracts between 'A' and '*A*', '*A*' has undertaken to fulfil the obligations entered into by 'A' in this contract.

NOW IT IS HEREBY AGREED AS FOLLOWS:

1 As used in this Agreement the following expressions shall have the following meanings

Expression Meaning

Units   Sizes 1-10 (inclusive) gear boxes similar to or as shown in '*A*' product guide No. 6 reference 12345 appended hereto as appendix 2.

Assembly   The dis-assembly of Units supplied by 'A'/'*A*' and their subsequent re-assembly with the substitution or addition or modification of components manufactured by either '*A*' or '*B*' for the purpose of changing gear ratios or adapting the Units to suit market requirements in the Territory. Assembly shall additionally mean the original construction of the Units using components some of which will be manufactured/supplied by '*A*' and some of which will be manufactured/supplied by '*B*'.

Territory Country M

Trademark The name style and title 'LOCOM' or in the event that it should prove impossible to register in country M the name 'LOCOM' such other name style or title as 'A' or '*A*' may nominate.

Legal and Political Issues

2 This Agreement shall remain in force for ten years from the date hereof and unless terminated by either party giving to the other not less than twelve months notice in writing to expire on the tenth anniversary of the date hereof will continue in force after such tenth anniversary until either party terminates it by not less than twelve months notice in writing to the other.

3 'A' hereby grants to 'B' an exclusive right and licence to manufacture the Units in the Territory and a non-exclusive right for the distribution Assembly and sale of Units in the Territory. The manufacturing and Assembly rights herein contained shall not include the right to grant sub-licences.

4 (a) In consideration of the rights hereby granted 'B' shall pay to 'A' a royalty calculated at the rate of 5% on the Net Sales of all Units manufactured by 'B'/'*B*' or upon which 'B'/'*B*' has carried out an Assembly operation Net Sales shall mean 'B'/'*B*''s invoiced price to customers after deduction of all charges for packing freight insurance taxes rebates and sales commissions returns duties and brokerage as well as the FOB UK port value of Units or components of the Units purchased by 'B'/'*B*' from '*A*' during the royalty calculation period concerned. During the life of this Agreement the following minimum royalties shall be payable:

For the first year £
For the second year £
For each of the remaining years £

(b) The royalty provided for in Clause 4 (a) shall be paid as follows:

(i) The minimum royalties after pro-rating in the first year shall be paid on the 1st day of January in each year during the continuation in force of this Agreement the first payment to be made on

(ii) On the 30th day of April and the 31st day of July October and January in each year during the continuation in force of this Agreement 'B' shall remit to 'A' the royalty on net sales calculated in accordance with the rates in 4 (a)(i) above in respect of the immediately preceding three months periods ending 31st March 30 June 31 October and 31 December respectively.

In determining the amount of these quarterly royalty payments 'A' shall give and 'B' shall receive credit for the minimum royalty paid on 1st January. The computation of royalties shall be made in (currency of country M) Payments will be remitted in US dollars to the account of 'A' at a bank to be designated by it at the rate of exchange ruling on the date of remittance

(c) Coincident with the remittance of quarterly royalty payments 'B' shall provide to 'A' statements setting forth a list of all Units or components of the Units sold and if so requested by 'A' the names of the customers therefore during the relevant quarterly period. Interest shall be charged on all overdue royalty payments at the rate of 3% per annum above the Bank base rate at the time being calculated and payable monthly

(d) In the event that the current double taxation treaty between country L and country M which provides that country L Licensor shall receive royalties without deduction of any tax at source should be changed 'B' agrees that the royalty percentage stipulated in 4 (a) (i) above shall be adjusted to the end that 'A' shall continue to receive a net five percent on Net Sales and the royalty calculated in accordance with this Agreement shall be received by 'A' without deduction of any kind whatsoever

(e) 'B'/'*B*' agree to maintain books records and accounts in accordance with generally accepted accounting principles covering its operations and containing all information necessary for the accurate calculation of the net sales of Units or components of the Units and will deliver to 'A' with each remittance referred to in clause 4 (b)(ii) hereof a statement verified by its accountant or auditor confirming the amount of Net Sales of Units and components of Units for the preceding quarterly period

(f) In the event of any subsidiary or associated company of 'B'/'*B*' being concerned with the sale of the Units or components

Legal and Political Issues

thereof or carrying out an Assembly operation the provisions of this Clause 4 shall apply to that company and sales or an Assembly operation by that company shall be deemed to be a sale or an Assembly operation by 'B'/'*B*' for the purposes of this Agreement

5 'A' hereby agrees:
   (a) to procure the supply to '*B*' of the Units and components of the Units at the prices shown in '*A*'s standard pricelists minus the percentage discounts indicated against each individual size of Unit in Appendix I hereto. '*A*'s current standard pricelists (which are contained in Appendix I hereto) are established on an FOB UK port basis exclusive of packing. '*A*' shall inform '*B*' on each occasion that there is a requirement for an adjustment to '*A*'s standard pricelists and agrees to accept orders for shipment within the 90 days following the notification of such adjustments at pre-adjustment prices for quantities of the same Units or components of the Units up to the number ordered during the three months immediately preceding such notification but after the expiry of the said period of 90 days such revised prices shall forthwith be applicable to all Units supplied to '*B*' and shall be accepted without demur by '*B*'

   (b) to facilitate the shipment of purchases by '*B*' through the forwarding agents and to the destinations in the Territory and in such manner as '*B*' may from time to time request

   (c) to assist '*B*' in promoting sales of the Units in the Territory by making available on loan existing artwork and the like for the preparation by '*B*' of promotional material

   (d) to permit the use by 'B'/'*B*' of the Trademark in association with sales by '*B*' of the Units and components of the Units within the Territory for so long as during the currency of this Agreement 'B'/'*B*' maintain the standard of quality prescribed by '*A*'. 'A' further agrees to bear the responsibility and expense of maintaining the Trademark in force

(e) to procure the supply to '*B*' of information assistance and expertise available at '*A*' in connection with the Assembly manufacture and sale of Units and components of the Units. For this purpose 'A' shall procure that '*A*' shall make available personnel to visit the factories of '*B*' or distributors or customers in the Territory up to a commitment of not more than four man/weeks per year as may be mutually agreed. Additionally 'A' shall procure that '*A*' shall accept visits by '*B*' personnel to '*A*'s factory if required up to a total commitment of not more than four man/weeks per year or as may be mutually agreed

(f) to procure that '*A*' shall inform '*B*' of evolutionary improvements which '*A*' may make in connection with the design of the Units or their components or for the materials or techniques used in their manufacture and provided that the same are not subject of patents or patent applications permit 'B'/'*B*' to adopt and use the same without payment of any royalty additional to that hereinbefore set out. In the case of improvements the subject of patents or patent applications 'A' agrees not to grant to any party other than 'B' in the Territory the right to use the same without having first offered such right to 'B' nor subsequently to grant such rights to any third party on terms more favourable to such third party than those finally refused by 'B'

6 'B' agrees to procure that '*B*' will:

(a) use its best endeavour to promote sales of the Unit in the Territory on a scale consistent with early achievement of maximum market penetration

(b) give to '*A*' the right of first refusal to supply all the requirements of 'B'/'*B*' for the Units or components of the same

(c) pay for goods purchased from '*A*' within thirty days from dispatch of each shipment from '*A*'s factory in such a manner as '*A*' may from time to time stipulate it being clearly understood that notwithstanding '*A*'s Conditions of Sale the

Legal and Political Issues

property in such goods shall not pass to 'B'/'*B*' until payment in full therefor shall have been received by '*A*'

(d) pay the royalties reserved under Clause 4 hereof in accordance with the provisions contained therein

(e) maintain accurate accounts books and records of all transactions and activities relating to the sale and manufacture of Units and components of Units and make the same available for inspection by a member of '*A*''s auditors or accountants for the purpose of verification

(f) (i) prominently display the Trademark on each Unit sold by '*B*' and indicate that the Trademark is a Registered Trademark provided that registration in the Territory shall have taken place

(ii) use the Trademark in all promotional and packaging material associated with the Units and where practical the components of the Units and acknowledge in the case of each such use that the Trademark is the property of '*A*' of England

(iii) not use in association with the sale by '*B*' of products other than the Unit any trademark which is confusingly similar to the Trademark

(iv) maintain the standard of quality prescribed by '*A*' in respect of units or components of Units assembled or manufactured by '*B*' and make such products available for inspection by '*A*'. In the event that and for so long as '*B*' shall fail to achieve the prescribed standard of quality 'B'/'*B*' shall forfeit the right to use the Trademark

(g) inform '*A*' of evolutionary improvements which '*B*' may make in connection with the design of the Units or their components or for the materials or techniques used in their manufacture and that a royalty-free exclusive licence inclusive of the right to grant sub-licences will be granted to '*A*'/'A' covering all countries of the world except the Territory in respect of any such improvement whether or not the same shall be patentable

(h) take complete responsibility with regard to Units or components of Units sold by '*B*' which have neither been manufactured by '*B*' nor upon which '*B*' has carried out any Assembly operation for any warranty which '*B*' may give to '*B*'s customers which is more favourable to such customer than any warranty given by '*A*' to '*B*'

7 'B' agrees that '*A*'s liability in respect of products supplied by '*A*' to '*B*' shall be strictly limited to the extent provided for in '*A*'s Conditions of Sale a copy of which is attached as Appendix II hereto.

8 'B' hereby certifies that it carries liability insurance covering both 'B' and '*B*' against suits claiming product or public liability and 'B' agrees to furnish to 'A' and/or '*A*' a certificate of insurance showing that such coverage is adequate in amount and in full force and effect and further agrees to keep such insurance in force at all times during the term of this Agreement. In addition 'B' agrees fully to indemnify 'A' and/or '*A*' against claims or demands for damages and expenses including legal fees and expenses which may arise in association with or resulting from demands causes of action or suits claiming product liability or public liability during the existence of this Agreement.

9 'B' agrees that during the existence of this Agreement and for ten years thereafter it will not and will procure that '*B*' will not enter into a similar agreement with any other supplier or manufacturer of Units which are competitive with the Units. (Note: this type of clause should be reviewed in the light of the competition law and other laws relating to countries L and M.)

10 'A' and 'B' mutually agree that:

(a) each party will bear its own expenses in connection with visits made by its representatives or personnel to the other's country provided that in the case of visits made by '*A*' representatives at '*B*'/'B''s request under the provisions of Clause 5 (e) 'B' shall pay the business class return air fare from country L to country M and hotel expenses of such representatives while in the Territory

Legal and Political Issues

(b) each party will maintain and will procure that its respective employees (including employees of '*A*' and '*B*') will maintain in the strictest confidence all and any technical and commercial information which it receives from the other and at no time disclose the same to any third party except in so far as such disclosures may be necessary to enable the party properly to fulfil its obligations under this Agreement

(c) neither party shall be entitled to assign the benefit of this Agreement other than for the purpose of amalgamation or reconstruction without the prior written consent of the other which consent shall not unreasonably be withheld

(d) this Agreement shall be construed in accordance with and governed in all respects by the laws of country L

(e) any dispute arising out of or in connection with this Agreement which the parties are unable to settle between themselves within one month of the appearance of the dispute shall be submitted to arbitration on the application of either party.
Final settlement shall be made by a single arbitrator appointed in accordance with and operating under the rules of conciliation and arbitration of the International Chamber of Commerce. Any such arbitration shall take place in the capital city of country L. The parties accept that any arbitral award shall be binding upon them and executory against them

(f) Any notices which may be required to be sent by either party to the other shall be properly given by telex or by being sent by pre-paid registered airmail letter and shall be deemed to have been delivered seven days after posting

(g) Either party may prematurely terminate this Agreement by written notice having effect immediately on its receipt in the event that the other party shall have a receiving order made against it or shall have gone into liquidation or bankruptcy (under voluntary liquidation for the purpose of amalgamation or reconstruction) or shall have made a composition with its creditors or shall have made default in performing or observing any of the covenants or agreements herein contained and by it to be performed or observed and if curable shall not have cured such default within sixty days of being called upon so to do

(h) From the date of expiry of this Agreement or the date of its termination for any reason whatsoever 'B'/'*B*' shall forthwith cease to use the Trademark (other than in the disposal of Units in '*B*'s inventory at such date) and shall from such date onwards make no further use of drawings or designs associated with the Unit which '*A*' may have supplied to 'B'/'*B*' and which are hereby acknowledged by 'B'/'*B*' as the property and copyright of '*A*'

(j) If this Agreement shall be prematurely terminated by 'A' because of a default by 'B' 'B' shall pay to 'A' (in addition to royalties accrued due but not yet paid to 'A' at the date of such termination) a sum calculated as the minimum royalties which would have been payable by 'B' to 'A' in respect of the period between the date of such premature termination and the date upon which this Agreement would naturally have expired
OR
the highest annual royalty amount payable hereunder in any year preceding the date of premature termination multiplied by the number of years which but for the premature termination would have represented the remaining years of life of this Agreement whichever shall be the greater

(k) This Agreement shall be conditional on any necessary approvals hereto being received from country M authorities before ....

IN WITNESS WHEREOF the parties hereto have executed this Agreement in accordance with the requirements applying to their respective corporations the day and year first before written

The Common Seal of 'A'
was hereunto affixed
in the presence of:

Legal and Political Issues

Director

Secretary

The Common Seal of 'B'
was hereunto affixed
in the presence of:

Director

Secretary

Part 4

Managing the Licensing Agreement

The legal document will have been drafted by lawyers; once the agreement is activated the business executives of both parties need to design a management system to establish a profitable relationship between two independent organizations; neither of them can exercise authority over the other, but each has objectives that must be fulfilled by the other.

Some departments in the licensor's company may not consider the licensing arrangement to be ideal for its purposes and may have difficulty in giving the project the necessary priority. The licensor, too, may have in mind a direct investment if this becomes viable. The licensee is aiming at developing a profitable business in the shortest time that can be achieved. The objects of both must be made feasible as a result of the management system. This system is divided, in this Part, into six Chapters: organization (4.1), planning and control (4.2), finance and profits (4.3), marketing (4.4), personnel and other services (4.5) as well as a general review of the relationship in the last chapter (4.6).

4

4.1 Organization and communication

One company has divided its licensing activities under a number of headings such as 'line aspects' (including design, manufacture, marketing), 'specialist aspects' (personnel, programming, techniques) and 'financial aspects' which control all the rest. This list, although the words may change, provides a practical checklist for establishing a control and monitoring system. It has to be remembered, however, that at present the activity itself is unlikely to be departmentalized.

A licensing agreement may well be a first venture into international business on the part of either or both parties. As a result, a process will start which renders obsolete the existing organization. New posts will appear which have been designed to meet the demands of international communications and these demands will burst established links and produce a reorganization. Three typical organizational structures are shown in Figure 4.1.1 (see page 163).

None of these organization structures is satisfactory under all circumstances; each provides a priority for the control of licensing without the need for extra specialist staff. If a company's main business is licensing, a different structure would be viable; but this is unusual, a licensor draws its strength from deriving saleable knowledge from its main business. The most probable course is to allocate licensing to the marketing department. The danger of this is that the department may have other priorities and a conflict of opinion can arise about the best way of servicing a particular market. As a result the three-way split (Figure 4.1.1(C)) appears the most logical, but like all logical solutions it is not necessarily the easiest to operate; it may also lead to demands for extra staff who may not find themselves fully loaded.

4.1.1 AUTHORITY AND RESPONSIBILITY

A licensing department is a centre of expertise. Its customer is a user of the expertise, not a purchaser of products (although it is likely to be this as well). The authority of the department is, therefore, external

Managing the Licensing Agreement

and not towards other units within its own company. It looks outward towards an independent concern, the licensee. The authority derives from developing and displaying the expertise so that the customer continues to need it which means close liaison with the research and development department and other sources of information within the licensor company.

The licensing department has parallel responsibility to develop relationships with existing customers and to expand into markets which can be most economically serviced by licensing.

One company has adopted its characteristic scheme for allocating responsibilities between the various departments involved in its licensing agreements for formulating policies and negotiating with their opposite numbers in the licensee. The responsibilities are allocated under three headings.

Resource

Senior managers in all the departments are responsible for obtaining information, establishing and modifying policies on the knowhow to be sold and ensuring that the knowhow is maintained and updated. At the middle manager level, these policies are executed by:

1. setting up the knowhow within the licensee organization;
2. supplying training, documentation and updated information;
3. ensuring that the licensee uses resources effectively through quality control, marketing and other activities;
4. providing assistance when needed; and
5. arranging visits by licensor staff of the correct personnel and at the right level.

Risk

Senior managers outline the types of agreement required, the safeguards needed and the policies on such matters as patents and trade marks.

Middle managers are held responsible for ensuring that employees of the licensor play the parts stipulated in the agreement. They also handle disputes and ensure that the interests of the two parties are safeguarded against one another as well as against third parties.

RETURN

For senior managers, this means determining policies on costs to the licensor and the minimum returns required. For middle managers, the task is to ensure that costs are kept to budget and that the licensee pays within terms set by the agreement. The implication is to ensure that unrealistic cost concessions or profit expectations do not threaten the success of the project.

An allocation of work between the licensor and the licensee is illustrated in the options set out in Table 4.1.1.

Table 4.1.1 Degree of delegation of work in various company resource-utilization strategies

Department	Marketing of goods		Marketing of knowhow etc.			Investment			
	Direct Selling	Overseas Agent	Limited Scope	Medium Scope	Broad Scope	Joint Venture		Wholly-owned Subsidiary
						Limited	Broad	
Design	1	1	1	1	2	1	1	1
Manufacture	1	1	2	2	2	2	2	1
Marketing	1	2	2	2	2	2	2	1
Techniques	1	1	1	2	2	2	2	1
Programming	1	1	2	2	2	2	2	1
Personnel	1	1	2	2	2	2	2	1
Finance	1	1	2	2	2	2	1	1

Key: 1 = Licensor activity   2 = Licensee activity

Managing the Licensing Agreement

The allocations will obviously change if a project develops towards a direct investment or joint venture arrangement, but the table demonstrates the maximum use of the foreign partner in a licensing agreement under the heading 'Marketing of knowhow'.

4.1.2 ORGANIZATION

To achieve its position of authority and responsibility a licensing department has to be slotted into the structure of a company. In most large companies, it is not regarded as a top level responsibility – a reason, no doubt, for its slow growth. In smaller companies, with greater dependence on income derived from the sale of technology, licensing is more likely to rate a higher level of supervision.

The commitment of a company to licensing, and indeed its assessment of the department's usefulness, can be understood by examining the level at which licensing decisions are taken. A look at the organization chart will also show the skills expected of the licensing staff. Figure 4.1.1 illustrates three options available to the licensor.

The figure shows the three departments which relate to the licensee as design (or research), manufacturing and marketing. In 4.1.1(A), the licensing department reports to none of the three, but to the company secretary; in this case, the department is mainly concerned with legal issues; it provides a service to the departments more directly involved – a service that may or may not be cost effective. This arrangement is not usually to be recommended.

Figure 4.1.1(B) places the patents' department within design and licensing services in marketing, while the licensing department itself reports to marketing. This more complex organization, splitting those involved in licensing between three departments, is intended to ensure that licensing arrangements are sensitive to the needs of all three departments. Finally 4.1.1(C) shows another arrangement in which licensing responsibilities are split; this time between a small service department that reports to the chief executive (the international policy department) and design within whose authority licences are negotiated.

Figure 4.1.1 Organization structures

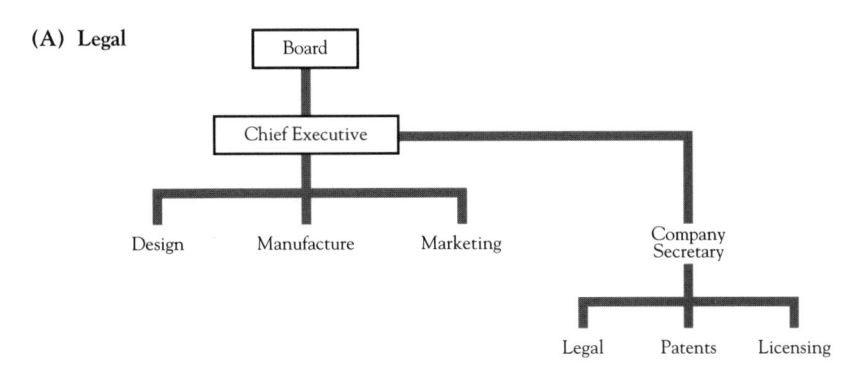

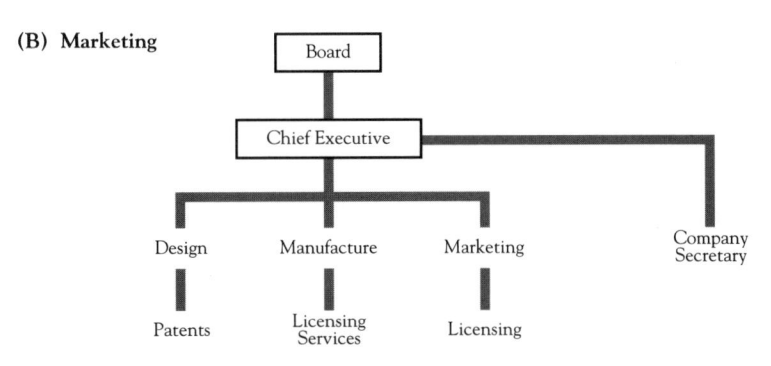

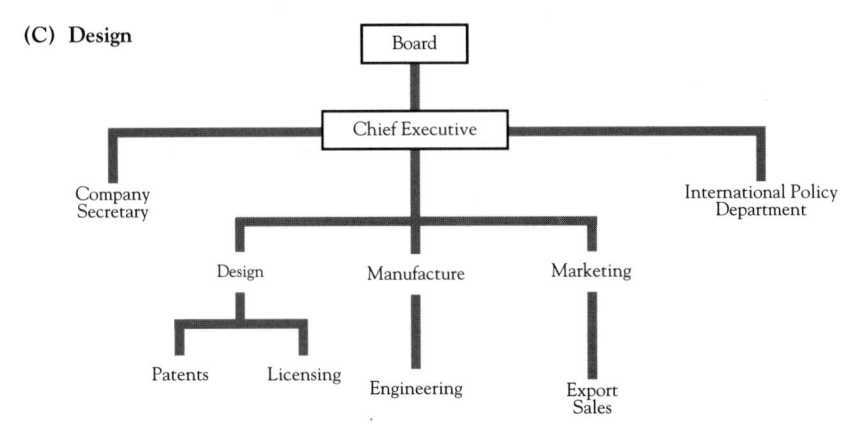

(A) Legal

(B) Marketing

(C) Design

Acknowledgement: Diagrams (A), (B) and (C) are reproduced from a training manual used by the Glacier Metal Company (now incorporated in Turner and Newall plc).

163

Managing the Licensing Agreement

CONFLICT

The containment of conflict is a normal function of organization and a number of conflicts occur during the operation of licensing agreements. The following are included.

1   Conflicts within the company affect the sales department which sometimes resists the loss of a territory to a licensee. Production is another department affected if engineers have to be sent abroad to train a licensee when they are needed at home. Both these possible conflicts make it desirable to bring the departments into the decision-making process. The organization structure needs to be framed to ensure the commitments of sales and engineering.
    An example has been recorded in which a factory manager would not allow the licensing staff onto his premises for fear they would sell his latest invention.

2   Conflicts between the licensor and the licensee arise when the latter perceives that inadequate information and services are being provided or that the licensor is moving too fast. Competition in export markets is another possible cause of complaint.

3   Conflicts between the parties to the agreement and their other trading partners. These can be more difficult to provide for when the structure is worked out; they can be eased if a close relationship is established; otherwise they can only be handled by the agreement itself. For instance, a problem can arise when a good customer of either party transfers its purchasing office to the country of the other and one party loses its business. Another problem, to be found in the business environment, arises when the government of the licensee's country stops remittances because of balance of payment problems.

Licensing agreements are often designed to last for many years and the departments involved need to keep adequate records to ensure that the arrangements survive staff changes. Licensing and other technical staff are inclined to promote their specialization with the claim that knowledge is the company's 'most valuable asset'. The organization will usually demonstrate the extent to which that view is accepted within a firm. A board or executive committee which regards knowledge in this light will arrange a direct line to a director or senior vice-president for the licensing department. Even the establishment of a specialist department demonstrates some commitment.

MOHPAM COMPONENTS: A CASE EXAMPLE OF A COMPANY ORGANIZING FOR LICENSING

Mohpam Components is an example of how a small company (less than ten employees) was organized to fulfil the requirements of a licensing contract for the production of a new design of passive electronic components. The licence agreement was with a much larger international component producer, which had advanced facilities for large scale production and access to mass markets throughout the world but which lacked the specific design and production technology covered by the Mohpam licence and patents.

Since the managing director only had a small team at his disposal, the work associated with negotiating and operating the agreement was split between four people – shown in Figure 4.1.2.

Figure 4.1.2 Organization of senior management of Mohpam Components

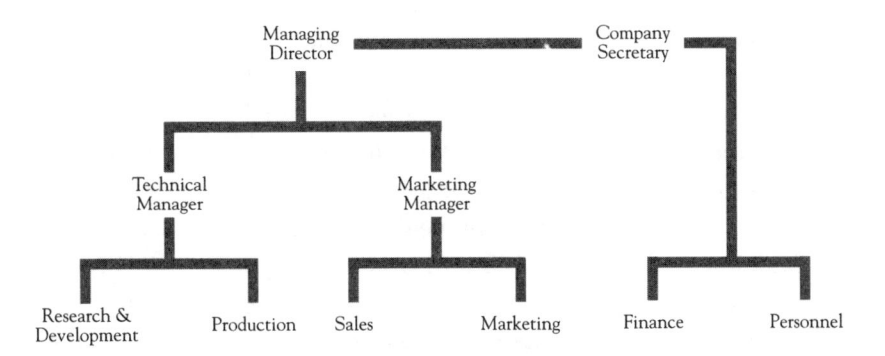

Managing the Licensing Agreement

The managing director, who took responsibility for the company's long term planning, was involved with the choice of licensee and the negotiation of the agreement.

The technical manager, who was in charge of both research and development and production, was responsible for obtaining patent cover for any new technology developed by the company and for maintaining suitable cover. Unfortunately, at the beginning of the company's history when financial resources were limited, some patents had only been obtained within the United Kingdom with the result that the main technology was not protected outside the country. Subsequently a number of patents of addition had been obtained and registered in the main European Union countries and the United States, but not in Japan and the Far East. One of the reasons for choosing a large and powerful company as licensee was to ensure worldwide exploitation of the technology without the need for negotiating separate agreements in individual countries.

In addition to patent matters, the technical manager was also responsible for producing and updating process and training manuals. Originally, these manuals had only been designed for internal use, and their rewriting was a substantial additional cost. The technical manager employed a freelance technical writer to rework the manuals over a period of six months while the licensing negotiations were being completed.

Once the deal was signed, the technical manager was also responsible for training the licensee's personnel in his own factory and for supplying technicians and operators to visit the main plant of the licensee where the principal training was to take place. The agreement was that the licensee would then train other personnel for other factories as an internal process, but that Mohpam would provide two weeks' supervision by a plant supervisor and a lab technician at the commencement of production at any new site. The licensor also provided an on-going quality supervision service, whereby a statistical sample of products from the licensee's plants was checked at Mohpam's laboratory once a quarter during the first two years of production at any plant of the licensee. The licensee paid for the cost of these quality checks.

Mohpam's marketing manager was responsible in the early stages of the choice of licensee for assessing the market penetration of each of three candidates in various markets and assessing the quality of their selling and advertising. In addition, he checked on the number of major world customers served by each of the three possible licensees. He also advised his managing director on possible negative consequences of the licensee selling to foreign associates of Mohpam's British customers. He confessed some concern as to the licensee's future pricing policy since it was quite likely that the licensee would eventually achieve prices considerably lower than those of Mohpam. As part of the agreement, the managing director included in the licence a right for Mohpam to purchase from the factories of the licensee.

Once the agreement was negotiated, the marketing manager arranged sales training for a core group of the licensee's sales personnel, and made a number of joint visits to key customers with the licensee's sales staff. These visits also had the effect of reassuring certain large customers about why components which had been hitherto supplied only by Mohpam were suddenly being offered by a different company. Finally, the marketing manager was also responsible for the supply of certain raw materials to the licensee's factories until such time as it became possible for the licensee to arrange more suitable sources of supply. From licence years two to five, Mohpam was buying substantially larger quantities of certain expensive raw materials than would have otherwise been the case, and this had a positive effect on Mohpam's own cost structure for a period of three years.

The company secretary of Mohpam was the senior manager most familiar with legal matters and, once the managing director had come to a general agreement on terms with the representatives of the licensee, it was the company secretary who worked with Mohpam's own legal representatives to produce the final agreement. In view of his line responsibility for the company's accounting and financial

Managing the Licensing Agreement

arrangements, he worked with the managing director during the negotiations in order to ensure that the likely costs and benefits of the agreement were budgeted for and that the return on the agreement, after offsetting costs, would be adequate.

Once the agreement was in force, the accounts department supervised the regular receipt of royalty statements and payments from the licensee, and kept control over the internal costs and budgets associated with operating the agreement.

Apart from the day-to-day operation of the licence agreement, the managing director made sure that it was raised on the agenda of monthly management meetings, and ensured that the company secretary entered into the diary well in advance any key dates in the agreement, such as review dates for re-negotiating certain agreed costs, and option dates for the sale of Mohpam improvements, or the purchase of improvements from the licensee.

4.1.3 Decision-making and Communication

Two purposes of an organization are to facilitate decision-making, by providing lines of authority and feedback, and communication. Other purposes are also served, like the provision of a career structure. This is essential to use the staff most effectively. A structure that makes licensing a dead end is likely to create problems; it will not meet the needs of a technical transfer, to be generated by a highly motivated staff, in the future.

The decision-making process is a difficult one when it has to be operated between two independent organizations; places for executives from both need to be fitted into the scheme.

The organization structure, for its part, will need to provide lines of authority and feedback; it will also need to facilitate communications, especially contacts between the two independent companies (licensor and licensee) over a period that may last thirty years or more. Most organization arrangements are complicated like those in the figure; they have to match up to complex situations and decision-making processes in order to improve communications.

For the licensor, the requirement is that departments dealing with design, production, marketing, financial and legal affairs may have to be brought in on the act. Channels to update the expertise must be maintained as must a system for sending trouble-shooting teams to licensees with a problem. One aspect of the communication is to provide opportunities for the different departments to work out how the licensing department's activities will affect their plans. The licensee company, for its part, is likely to be smaller, but may still need to mirror the expertise available to the licensor as far as possible. This 'mirroring' means that the licensee will set up departments and make appointments capable of communicating with their opposite numbers in the licensor company. Such an arrangement will be essential if cross-licensing and the reverse sale of technology or only the cross-fertilization of ideas is expected. The involvement of numerous departments ensures that a range of expertise is available to the licensee.

4.1.4 Data transfer: machinery and process manuals

The transfer of information is a key issue in licensing. Clearly this is not carried out only by the circulation of technical papers and blueprints. These have been found inadequate within a company, between a parent organization and its subsidiaries, and must be additionally inadequate between separate companies. The passage of technical information includes a programme of exchanges of engineers and of training schemes but still manuals will remain an essential part of the transfer process and will have to be translated in the light of the client company's customs and traditions as well as its language. In drafting the manuals, it need not be assumed that they can instruct the uninitiated in every technical or commercial detail, but a backup hotline will be required to allow discussion between the executives responsible within the organizations of the licensor and the licensee.

Managing the Licensing Agreement

The provision of manuals can represent identifiable quantities of knowhow for which payment can be obtained.

One company's briefing to its licensing department contains the following policy directions.

1. We work to ensure that the licence is renewed or replaced by an alternative form of co-operation.
2. If it is not renewed, we part on friendly terms with the licensee — there is a great difference between friendly competition and cut-throat competition.
3. At the same time, optimum return is sought from the agreement by supervising the licensee's marketing and manufacturing progress and offering assistance where necessary.
4. Measures are also taken to ensure that the licensee does not break the agreement, but wherever there is conflict between the agreement and our own or the licensee's requirements, we try to discuss the matter constructively, before either party insists on its rights to the literal interpretation of the clauses.

4.1.5 Updating the licence

The agreement should provide a method for revising the licence either when it is due for renewal or when both parties agree that renegotiation is sensible. Their organizations need to provide a process for carrying out the revisions. The process will be activated by either party on realizing that the objectives of the agreement are not being fulfilled. This usually means that the licensee is not being informed of new developments in the technology being licensed. The situation may come to light as the result of a complaint from the licensee, but will usually be stimulated by the licensor's research department anxious not to acquire a reputation for falling behind the competition. Both parties have much at stake and regular revisions may be stipulated in the contract; if they are not, they are still necessary. The licensee needs to feel it is being kept on the leading edge, at least of the technology that it can handle — and being pushed beyond. The licensor's business is not promoted by a slow-moving unwillingness to feed in changes.

4.2 Planning and controlling the licensing process

This chapter is contributed by Dr Carl C. Thunman of the University of Uppsala in Sweden. Carl wrote a thesis on licensing in 1988 (ref: Acta Universitatis Upsaliensis, Studia Oeconomiae Negotiorum, 1988). References in this chapter show Thunman 1988 in brackets. Other references show full details in brackets while a list of sources is to be found at the end of the chapter.

The selling of technology is not just a matter of providing patents and blueprints for a fee. It comprises a process involving two or more parties, various resources and extends over a number of years. It is therefore useful to participants in the licensing process to develop a pattern against which to assess the progress of a licensing relationship through its various stages. The licensee and licensor have to interact to develop an enduring collaboration that can cope with emerging problems in the development process. The relationship is built, maintained, and sometimes temporarily discontinued. During this process the parties must be able to overcome various difficulties, to solve different types of problem, and to execute exchanges in a number of dimensions. Our knowledge of what happens during a licensing development process is far from complete. Only a few writers have focused on this issue (Thunman, 1988). Even less have taken into account the cultural aspects in international operations. The development of the international licensing process consists of interaction between business people and their companies with more or less different cultural backgrounds. The cultural aspect is a substantial part of international marketing and includes people who form associations and situations in which long-term reciprocity enhances trust between various parties (this was affirmed by J.C. Unusier (1993), *International Marketing - A Cultural Approach*, Prentice-Hall).

When planning a licensing agreement the implementation can be viewed as a development process with distinct stages regarding the activities carried through to reach the goals of each stage. Corresponding to these stages are distinct characteristics and problems which may be more or less common to a great number of licensing deals. By realizing

Managing the Licensing Agreement

the potential problems and features of a particular stage the licensing firms can increase the control over the development by, for example, planning resources better, taking appropriate measures, foreseeing costs or changing various aspects of strategy. In this chapter such a stage by stage licensing approach is outlined as a basis for the planning and control of the licensing process.

4.2.1 THE LICENSING DEVELOPMENT IN FIVE STAGES

The licensing development process entails the five distinctive stages. The stages occur sequentially but may in some situations overlap. The stages involve different kinds of problem which the licensing manager must be able to cope with in an adequate manner (various authorities have identified this feature, see the publications by Ford, Teece and Thunman at the end of the chapter). The process described is based on a production licence, but the principle extends to other licensed activities.

PRE-NEGOTIATION STAGE

The development into a relationship begins with activities designed to open communication between the parties. The initial stage may also start from an existing relationship which is developed into a licensing one.

NEGOTIATION STAGE

The development process will pass into the negotiation stage when each party views the other as a possible licensing partner. This stage ends with the signing of the contract.

KNOWLEDGE TRANSFER STAGE

When the contract is signed the bulk of technology transfer can start in the form of training programmes, instruction, supervision, plant installation services, marketing assistance and others.

Manufacturing start-up stage

When the transfer of knowledge is concentrated on the specific problem of bringing the production on stream. This becomes less significant when the operations reach the planned level of output.

Long-term development stage

After the primary implementation of the technology transfer the development of the relationship between the parties can fade-out or take other directions.

Licensing development processes can have different features conditioned by different background factors such as industry characteristics, the licensing parties' capabilities and experience or the culture of their countries. The possibility of building a successful licensing relationship depends strongly on the successful management of progress through the stages.Needless to say, the process may be interrupted at any stage, temporarily or finally, as a result of the parties' assessment of features in the development process or changes in the environment. The stages will now be analysed in detail.

Pre-negotiation stage

This stage is characterized by actions taken to establish contacts between the parties when each aims to obtain information about the other to continue the dialogue. A number of activities and decisions precede the development into, or the formation of, a licensing agreement. Most texts on licensing stress the strategic aspect in the decision-making process of the licensor (see the works by Brooke, Caves, Rugman and others): when to use licensing and which licensee to select. Similarly

Managing the Licensing Agreement

the licensee has options, to licence-in or to execute its own research and development activities and to seek out an appropriate licensor. The choice of (the right) partner is a crucial decision in the licensing process. From the licensor's point of view it is incumbent on the licensee to apply the transferred technology in the market and, from the licensee's perspective, the licensor should facilitate this transfer. The correct partner means that there is not only a potential for good social and other exchanges but also an appropriate fit between the companies. The licensing relationship is also determined by a larger national or international framework of business relationships which may reduce the parties' discretion. A particular relationship can serve as a link or bridge to the other party's industrial network and needs to be evaluated in this context.

There are a great many aspects to evaluate at this stage which should at least encompass a 'rigorous analysis of potential markets, distribution costs and benefits, commercial practices in the prospective partner's locality, the legal situation (particularly with regard to patents), and the general technological climate which may well affect the successful marketing of the licensed product'. (This quotation as well as the one below is from the publication by McCall and Warrington.)

These evaluations cannot readily be made on flying visits but demand detailed information. It is also important to go further and to see how the potential partner relates to others by contacting its suppliers, customers, other licensing partners.

The evaluation of the other partner's competence is a process involving personal judgments, as well as objective facts. As the interaction between the parties continues with increased mutual information, these judgments are refined. The complex evaluations which have to be made are more or less rational but the approach of most companies can be characterized by comments like the following. 'We use the back of an envelope to compute profitability'; or 'I just try to get a rough feel for the attractiveness of the deal'; or 'My approach is intuitive'. Such an approach is undoubtedly indicative of most organizations' approach to licensing, which is essentially passive, with many licensors granting a licence simply because they have been approached.

This approach is in contrast to the view in which technology is seen as a product which has been developed for sale and sent to market. There is however, evidence that technology is seldom produced to be sold – rather to improve the competitive position on product markets. Sometimes licensing parties are more interested in the side-effects of licensing, such as the sale of goods, or to secure a market position. This means that costs related to licensing and payments made are often inadequate indicators of the relative importance of a licensing agreement.

The background of the licensing relationship is therefore different in different cases, and the parties may or may not have previous experience of each other or the potential (licensee's) market (country, industry or technical application). An Australian study revealed that for those firms with five or less foreign licensing agreements two out of five were preceded by exports. In a Swedish study 22 per cent of 72 foreign licensing agreements had been preceded by export. In these circumstances established patterns of contacts exist so that the incorporation of a licensing agreement may be a fairly smooth process and the evaluations directed towards special issues related to the transfer itself instead of general information about the other party.

In these cases the search for a suitable licensing partner involves a gradual involvement between the parties by means of agency or distributor agreements, for example. In other cases the selection of a licensing partner starts more from scratch or the parties are well aware of the international market situation and approach one of the prospective partners for discussion regarding a licensing deal.

In all industrial commercial deals it is necessary to enter into personal relationships with individuals in the other organization (if the relationships do not already exist due to the prior contacts) before more regular interaction can take place. Face-to-face meetings in the early licensing stages are important. The whole process may be started by licensor, licensee or third parties all of whom may be more or less active. Since

Managing the Licensing Agreement

the majority of companies are not in the market for selling technology instead of products they are likely to adopt a passive role and respond only if necessary. Other, research-intensive firms may adopt a strategy of selling technology to meet their development costs. The adopted strategy has consequences for the whole process and the success of the technology transfer.

A particular problem is to recognize and plan for the differences between the companies' capabilities in different respects. If the acquired information shows that there is a large misfit in technical development or other capabilities a new assessment of the costs of transfer must be made. A great effort must be directed to understanding the production capability of the licensee, with such connected aspects as equipment and imports of components. When dealing with developing countries the lack of implicit technical knowledge can present substantial impediments. The market capability in terms of established networks to customers must also be assessed. As the whole process is lengthy, with unforeseen problems and resource consumption, the parties must have sufficient financial resources to sustain long periods of contacts before results emerge.

When a completely new relationship is created the initial exchanges are of a personal and information nature to generate knowledge on each other and to execute joint planning for forthcoming activities. If this first stage in the licensing process reaches a common acceptable level the process can continue to a stage where the parties opt for the formal licensing agreement.

NEGOTIATION STAGE

This is characterized by actions taken to reach a formal licence contract. When the parties view each other as suitable licensing partners the development process assumes the form of negotiations to reach an agreement which can provide terms and conditions for the future behaviour of the parties involved. The result of the negotiations is a contract which superficially is a document signed by both parties. But a main value of a licensing agreement lies in the long-term relationship including future expectations. Inter-organizational agreements are rules, and like other rules (such as laws, rules of etiquette and bureaucratic red tape) they are not always followed nor are the rule breakers always punished. They are often the finishing touch in the process of negotiating future behaviour. All licensing agreements are compromises and the difficulties in their negotiation consist in the selection of terms that fall within the acceptable range of the parties. Otherwise a party will have an incentive to circumvent the agreement.

There are a number of factors which affect the course of the negotiations. The time spent on negotiations is conditioned by the interference of governments and the experience of the negotiators. It has been estimated that the time taken to conclude a licence contract was: in Europe 2 to 2.5 years; in North America 1.5 to 2 years; and in Japan 1 to 1.5 years. Some of the issues discussed in the negotiations are more divisive than others; for instance commercial issues are more likely to cause conflict than technical issues. The degree of conflict is also affected by the experience and negotiations between parties which have been doing business for a long time, know each other well and come from the same environment may involve fewer conflicting issues than those between two unfamiliar parties. If there is an atmosphere of trust (generated either by earlier exchange or by the negotiations) 'the parties begin to feel increasingly comfortable about the fact that the negotiations could proceed further, then further disclosures enable the parties to present their evaluations of the technical and legal worth of the proposed licence'. (Quoted from McCall and Warrington.) The conduct of the negotiations is rather complex because the issue of compensation (in such forms as royalties, down-payments and fees) is discussed simultaneously with, and as a function of, what should be included in the transfer (for evidence of this see the publication by Farouk Contractor).

When the parties opt for licensing it is important to have realistic expectations regarding the conditions for an agreement. Standard licence contracts used in western markets are not always a proper basis for agreements in regulated countries where certain conditions are

Managing the Licensing Agreement

improper; these include tied inputs, prohibitions of sub-licensing and exporting and certain duration limits. Also in western countries the legal situations differ, for instance with lengthy elaborated contracts in the United States. The more realistic the expectations in this respect the less time-consuming the negotiation stage will be in avoiding repeated renegotiations.

The better the licensor's knowledge of the conditions the less the licensee can utilize them to increase its bargaining power.

At this stage the parties regard each other as prospective contracting partners. The evaluations made earlier must now be refined. When the process is a response to a licensee proposal there is a risk that the licensor will not devote enough resources for evaluating the project. The problems inherent in the cultural distance between the parties can also make evaluations more difficult.

During the negotiation stage the activities of the parties become more intense, particularly over the exchange of various types of information, personal contacts, knowhow and some exchange of documents. There may also be early shipments of products from the licensor when customers are in immediate need of the goods. When the contract is finalized and signed between the parties the transfer of technology can commence.

Knowledge Transfer Stage

This stage is characterized by the actions taken to transfer knowledge between the parties. Once the agreement has been signed, the implementation of the transfer process can start. The content of the transfer is conditioned by the scope of the total agreement, for example to the extent that equipment and training are included. A detailed contract may itemize all major forms of exchanges such as the number of persons to be trained in the licensor's facilities, number of months of supervision in the licensee's plant, drawings and other specifications to be sent. The contract may also state that supplementary consultation is to be provided by the licensor upon request and at an agreed tariff. In some extreme cases, the licensing contract may only permit the use of a proprietary right, such as a patent which is already known to the licensee, or to enable the transfer of a particular chemical formula. In such cases the knowledge transfer process is limited.

If the earlier activities have been efficiently pursued the transfer of knowledge may run smoothly: the pre-negotiations have opened up channels of communication between the appropriate individuals or departments in the two firms, the information exchange has covered all crucial aspects of the implementation of the licence and the negotiations have resulted in a suitable contract. However technology transfer, even when commercial negotiations have been successfully completed, is sometimes an expensive and difficult process. Minor items of knowledge are transferred immediately after the parties have begun discussions of what technical and organizational issues a licence agreement should encompass. But after the signing of the contract the bulk of knowledge transfer normally starts.

The technical fit between the two parties with their implicit technological knowledge will be important in determining the development of the knowledge transfer stage. It is also at this stage that the purchase and delivery of machinery and equipment of the right quality will take place. Equipment and components for production call for planning activities related to installation services and production schemes. As the process unfolds the involvement of top management in the early stages is now supplemented by lower levels of staff with production and process technicians who sometimes lack an understanding of local cultural and technical conditions. Cultural strain seems therefore to be more frequent the closer the transfer comes to on-the-job training and direct supervision on the shopfloor.

When training programmes in the country of either party are implemented some aspects become manifest. The differences in technical and cultural attitudes can obstruct the transfer of technology. For example, when transferring technology from Europe to India theoretical aspects do not seem to offer any problem, but the learning of knowhow by

Managing the Licensing Agreement

practical operations is difficult for the licensee's engineers who are not accustomed to dirtying their hands. When lower level personnel, who do not understand English, are trained or supervised, the language can be a problem when instructions must be interpreted (Thunman, 1988).

As drawings are an important means of transferring technology the problems related thereto must be appropriately solved. Drawings are often constructed for particular situations in particular countries. In other countries where conditions are different, in terms of activities ancillary to the process for instance, the necessary size of storage space, and the availability of standard and other industrial goods, the use of the original drawings without modifications can involve unnecessary expense and friction in the process.

The mutual engagement has now reached a high point with involvement by a number of departments in the two organizations with individual specialists and with hopefully rapid and smooth problem-solving.

Manufacturing start-up stage

This is characterized by actions taken to bring production to the planned level of output. When the transfer of knowledge has been executed the process will reach a stage when the activities will be directed to starting up the production. Manufacturing knowhow from the licensor is needed to tune up the plant, to true up the composition of inputs and components and to make other necessary adjustments. If the total transfer of knowledge has been successful the manufacturing will start without delay, but if the transfer and absorption of the knowledge have been poor this will now be apparent. When equipment has been installed the activities take the form of production assistance. New technology may demand cleanliness in the workshop or other requirements which are more or less implicit. The differences in the latter may be seen as a manifestation of the different technical levels of the two countries.

If the agreement does not specify additional terms of continuous technology upgrading or marketing support the implementation of the technology will be concluded at this stage.

LONG-TERM DEVELOPMENT STAGE

This stage is characterized by actions taken to implement the long-term strategy when the original licensing agreement has been implemented. This is the final stage in the lifespan of the licensing development process. The licensor's product or process is now in the licensee's market with production and existing or emergent relationships to customers. In the internationalization process of the licensor the licensing relationship may be seen as an increased commitment to this particular market and the development can take various directions; for instance the licensing contract may be supplemented with another agreement for other products or processes. How the original contract is renewed on expiry, how the parties increase their range of transactions or how, in the worst case, non-compliance with the contract leads to legal proceedings. But licensing relationships long sustained may become standard organizational procedures, their origins eventually being forgotten. Over time the circumstances once prevailing when a contract was signed may change: laws may be more vigorously enforced, new businesses may enter a market as buyers, sellers or middlemen, new pools of resources may be discovered or other resources become scarce. The intra-company circumstances may also change, new owners or managers may pursue different international strategies. All such changes can render agreements less useful or favourable than they once were.

There are also favourable aspects of licensing in the internationalization process, creating other marketing possibilities, and 'in the long run, it can become a springboard or bridge to these other openings. Within this context licensing can be approached as a long-run international penetration strategy, even though the firm may have been forced back into using it, in the short run, because of for example,

Managing the Licensing Agreement

foreign restrictions on exporting.' (See entry under Carstairs and Welsh (1981) in the booklist and page 24 of that publication.)

In the best case the licensing interaction process has resulted in mutual benefits. The licensee has, at a relatively low cost, acquired and absorbed a profitable technology with future prospects as well as a relationship with a useful partner. The licensor, although the compensation for the technology is sometimes modest, has added supplementary deliveries of goods or equipment, increased its ability to handle licensing deals in foreign markets, built a valuable relationship with foreign parties with prospects for additional licensing or other agreements, or deliveries; it has also forestalled foreign competition by having its own product established on the market.

In the worst case, the licensor has wasted resources on a futile project, acquired bad experience of foreign cooperation or even gone bankrupt. The sampling procedures in most research should exclude a great number of failures at the different stages which is presumably the reason why most reported licensing cases have a positive evaluation of the agreements.

It is possible to discern three different directions for the development of the agreements.

1. The agreement runs for the stipulated time and includes technology transfer programmes and deliveries of hardware along with other items; it is not renewed. The licensee might then become a competitor unless there are strong relationships between the parties or other factors limiting potential competition.
2. The agreement is renewed after the stipulated time or is supplemented with additional clauses concerning other products with an intensified involvement between the parties.
3. The foreign production unit may serve as a bridgehead in regional markets making use of local conditions and expertise (eventually with ownership).

4.2.2 THE CONTROL AND MONITORING OF THE LICENSING STAGES

The relationship which evolves is not a featureless link between the parties. It has distinct features each contributing to the available options in different stages of the developing of the process. It is not so much a matter of the decision-maker evaluating the risk of losing the firm-specific advantage when licensed, but adjusting to the conditions of a relationship which at times may not offer any real alternative. The development of licensing agreements seems not to be a calculated decision in the traditional sense by the licensor but rather a complex process involving economic and social elements. Aspects, often neglected in earlier writings, are the importance of the parties' mutual knowledge, personal relationships, mutual planning requirements as well as the mutual interdependence of the partners. The personal relationships incorporate the trust which facilitates the disclosure of technical information and knowhow. In this way the relationship can develop in loops, where one aspect affects the development of another which in turn has an impact on others.

According to the narrowest definition, licensing consists only of a contract with provisions for payments. This occurs, however, only in rare cases (such as cross-licensing of the licensing of formulae in the pharmaceutical industry) when licensing relationships are not complex. So the decision to enter into a licensing agreement is not so much a legal formality as a commitment of the organization to a long-term relationship with subsequent co-operation and problem-solving together with another organization.

The strategy can be more or less conscious in adaptations to the other party; in due course, the experience of the parties involved in the process increases not only in terms of the capabilities and knowledge of the other organization and its environment but also in the licensing development processes themselves.

The networks of the parties are important for defining the capabilities and experience related to licensing, but also the position of licensing in a global marketing plan. Well developed international operations

Managing the Licensing Agreement

on the licensor side may ease evaluations of, and exchanges with, licensees in different markets. For the licensee a well developed network bringing in customers is an advantage in securing the demand for the licensed products. If the licence involves a diversification in terms of market orientation a network of new customers is built by the licensee. The licensing relationship may also alter other parties' perceptions of the licensee. The licensor, on the other hand, acquires an additional production unit in its global network.

A broad division of countries with respect to licensing within different business environments means that a licensor situated in an industrialized country can work to three scales. The first scale considers the level of industrialization (industrialized or developing countries), the second involves the differences in culture (similar or dissimilar mental programming) and the third scale is the level of central planning in the economy with reference to licensing (unregulated or regulated). This last results in different environmental situations, some of which are common in licensing.

Licensing interaction processes between firms in industrialized markets with similar cultures seem to involve the least friction. This type is the base for most theorizing on licensing and is also the most frequently used in global licensing. As the technical and other conditions are similar, differences in the companies' capabilities can easily be recognized if the parties are reasonably experienced in licensing and emergent problems can quickly be recognized. It is, however, not always certain that the licensee fully understands the markets for the product. A good mix between the parties may contribute to the quality of the relationship, to more mutual problem-solving at a high technical level. The similarity in technical level also enables much of the information to be transferred via impersonal means. The most decisive factors influencing the licensing interaction process are the resources of the parties and also the type of industry. From here the licensing process must pass through the various stages and overcome different problems. Such aspects of the relationship as social and information exchanges are important in the pre-licensing processes. These are also important from the point of view of evaluation –

whether to withdraw early from an unsuitable deal.

The largest differences in the background of the parties are to be found in licensing between firms in industrialized and developing countries. The difference in technical level appears to be the most common determining factor of the licensing development process to a developing country. Differences in technical procedures and training, and supportive infrastructures, imply differences from the same licensing process to an industrialized country. It is, therefore, necessary to understand and plan for such impediments when licensing to developing countries.

Some general problems that will occur during licensing negotiations prompt a few notes of advice for licensing partners:

1. the greater the difference in culture, the greater the friction in face-to-face interaction at lower levels;
2. the greater the difference in industrial development levels, the more numerous the problems originating from the lack of implicit knowledge of technology; and
3. the more regulated the licensing within a particular market, the more time-consuming and difficult the whole process.

The progress of licensing developments through the various stages has implications for managers who discover that licensing to foreign partners is a far more complex matter than they had been led to expect, particularly the development of a long-term engagement with another party by a process which imposes demands for adaptation at different stages. To succeed both parties must be able to create a relationship within the cultural frameworks.

The control and monitoring of the licensing process is by no means an easy task. By applying the approach suggested here on each licensing deal the manager can increase the possibilities of anticipating the problems and costs that will unfold in the development process. When passing through the stages the following checklist of questions is useful.

1. What do we want to achieve at this stage?

Managing the Licensing Agreement

2   What problems do we anticipate at this stage?
3   What information can we reveal at this stage?
4   What are the prospects of building a long-term trusting relationship with the other party?
5   What extra-contractual means of dependence are involved?
6   What will the consecutively acquired information imply on a short-term and long-term basis regarding resources and costs?
7   Shall we continue or discontinue the process?
8   Do we need to reconsider our original strategy as a consequence of new information?

PUBLICATIONS

The author consulted the following publications in preparing this chapter (some of which have already been referenced).

Ardisson, J.M., and Bidault, F. (1985), *Technology Transfer Strategies as a Means to Building International Networks*, 2nd Open I.M.P. Seminar on International Marketing, Uppsala 4-6 September 1985

Beamish, P.W., Killing, J.P., Lecraw, D.J. and Crookell, H. (1991), *International Management. Text and Cases*, Irwin

Brooke, M.Z. (1986), *International Management*, Hutchinson (now Stanley Thornes)

Carstairs, R. and Welch, L. (1981), *A Study of Outward Foreign Licensing of Technology by Australian Companies*, report prepared by the Licensing Executives Society and Industrial Advisory Committee of Australia, (rev. edn, December 1981)

Caves, R.E. (1982), *Multinational Enterprise and Economic Analysis*, Cambridge University Press

Contractor, F.J. (1981), *International Technology Licensing*, Lexington Books, D.C. Heath and Company

Ford, D. (1982), 'The Development of Buyer-Seller Relationships in Industrial Marketing' in Håkansson, H. (ed), *International Marketing and Purchasing of Industrial Goods*, John Wiley and Sons, pp. 288-304

Ghauri, P.N. (1983), *Negotiating International Package Deals*, Acta Universitatis Upsaliensis, Studia Oeconomiae Negotiorum 17 Uppsala

Killing, P. (1975), *Manufacturing Under Licence in Canada*, unpublished Ph.D thesis, University of Western Ontario

Lowe, J. and Crawford, N. (1982), *Technology Licensing and the Small/Medium Sized Firm*, Interim Report, September, University of Bath

McCall, J.B. and Warrington, M.B. (1984), *Marketing by Agreement. A Cross-cultural Approach to Business Negotiations*, Wiley & Sons

Roberts, E.G. (1981), 'Licensing: An Effective Alternative', *Les Nouvelles*, 16, September, pp. 220-225

Rugman, A.M., Lecraw, D.J. and Booth, L.D. (1985), *International Business. Firm and Environment*, McGraw-Hill

Teece, D.J. (1976), *The Multinational Corporation and the Resource Cost of International Technology Transfer*, Ballinger Publishing

Thunman, C. (1988), *Technology Licensing to Distant Markets*, Acta Universitatis Upsaliensis, Studia Oeconomiae Negotiorum 28, Uppsala

Thunman, C. (1992), 'Managing International Licensing Relationships', in Forsgren, M. and Johanson, J. (1992), *Managing Networks in International Business*, Gordon and Breach

Tutle, E.G. (1982), 'Evaluating Licensee Candidates', *Les Nouvelles*, 17, June, pp. 127-128

Unusier, J.C. (1993), *International Marketing - A Cultural Approach*, Prentice-Hall

Welch, L.S. (1983), 'Licensing Strategy and Policy for Internationalization and Technology Transfer' in Czinkota, M.R. (ed), *Export Promotion*, Praeger, pp. 5-23

Managing the Licensing Agreement

Welch, L.S. (1985), 'The International Marketing of Technology: An Interaction Approach', *International Marketing Review*, 2, Spring, pp. 41-53

4.3 Finance, prices and costs

The licensor expects to receive an adequate return for investment of knowhow and trained personnel, and can also expect certain strategic benefits in relation to home, host and third-country markets. The level of remuneration is determined by a number of factors, not least relative bargaining power in the initial negotiations. The range of financial and strategic benefits differs greatly from company to company, from contract to contract and from country to country.

Among the general influences on prices are the protection offered for patents and trademarks in the licensee's country. The licensor is able to claim a higher fee where these are strong because protective legislation ensures that the project is of more value to the licensee.

4.3.1 Revenues and costs: the licensor's profit

'Knowhow and patents have no value in themselves; they have value to the user when their use brings new profit opportunities or reduces risk. Their value is increased if the knowhow can be absorbed easily and bring rapid start-up for the licensee. The significance of this was illustrated in the case of a chemical plant when design costs were reduced by 50 per cent and building costs by 30 per cent and the efficiency of the process increased by the purchase of outside knowhow.

A problem for both parties to an agreement is how to assess the value of the knowhow. An answer frequently given is: 'by experience and knowledge'. As in other activities, experience can be a misleading guide. For instance a licensor company that considers itself to have lost out on a highly profitable project may well hold out for a fee that the market will not bear on a later agreement which turns out to be a disastrous loss. This chapter aims to improve the 'knowledge'.

Fixing a price on the strength of experience could be described as an **art dealer** theory: an inspired guess based on similar deals. In the case of patent licenses, the art dealer method would suggest a price on the

Managing the Licensing Agreement

basis of what patents for similar products or processes have been fetching in similar fields, or what percentage royalty might be expected on the basis of similar deals. Who has access to such information in any case? This global approach may be better than nothing but begs the question about what is a similar product or process, when the potential of the patent is relatively untried.

Where analogy fails, some more scientific assessment needs to be made, although as in any pricing decision, there is a large element which depends on the politics of power between the negotiating parties.

A difficulty for a licensing executive is to find some criteria by which to dictate prices when experience of a similar deal is limited or non-existent and when the market is not working efficiently. This consideration suggests that some method of payment by results is likely to be preferred. The pricing options are: a lump sum, a payment per product produced under the terms of the licence, a percentage of sales or a percentage of the licensee's profits. None of these options are satisfactory under all circumstances and the licensee is likely to try to vary the method or to press for a combination of methods. If the payment is to be per product, then a minimum royalty sum is needed to fix a minimum income for the licensor in case the licensee's production does not reach the target volume. Further, the licensor feels impelled to study the market opportunities of the licensee to determine that expansion is likely to take place; the need for this study may itself prove an advantage of per product pricing.

In negotiating a payment system, a licensor will be influenced by problems that are likely to occur in the future such as political and economic changes in the licensee's country that may disrupt the market there (see Chapter 6.2). If there is serious danger of political changes disrupting the licensee's market, the licensor will seek a maximum lump sum down payment. Revenue or profits based pricing systems are of questionable value in an unstable country unless the instability is a prelude to an economic turnround.

Whichever method the licensor succeeds in negotiating, some criteria will be needed to determine the lump sums or percentages that result. Clearly the method most readily accepted by both sides is to follow the amounts stipulated in other similar licences. Even this would only be a basis for negotiation because differences in industry sector, nationality and market would make the similarity inexact. Other factors which the licensor will consider include:

1 the **opportunity costs** – the amount of revenue that the licensor could expect by selling the product rather than the knowhow (bearing in mind that the market might be limited by various barriers to access);
2 the **real costs** of selling and negotiating the agreement and of servicing the project; these may well be balanced by other revenues such as sales of components or consultancy fees;
3 **other value to the licensor** – if the project plays an important role in the licensor's global strategy, this will affect its bargaining position. This will apply especially if the licensor also supplies the licensee, for instance increased volume production of raw materials or components to provide for the licensee may reduce the licensor's own cost base;
4 **anticipated value to the licensee** – if the licensee is understood to have an excellent market a higher (probably percentage) charge is likely to be the aim; a higher charge will also be demanded if the licence is exclusive (in countries where exclusivity is still permitted).

Table 4.3.1 sets out the considerations in the form of a questionnaire addressed to the licensor.

Table 4.3.1 Pricing a licensing agreement: questions for the would-be licensor

1 (i) What were your **costs** in obtaining (a) knowhow (b) patent?
  (ii) Over what period were these costs incurred – should you include an interest factor?
2 (i) What will be the running costs of:
  (a) a knowhow agreement?

Managing the Licensing Agreement

      (b) a patent agreement?
  (ii) How do you intend to share the running costs with the licensee? If fixed rates are agreed, e.g. for payment per man-hour, should these include an inflation factor?
  (iii) Is it better to include these costs as part of the down-payment? annual fee? or invoice them as they are incurred?

3 (i) What is the market for the product? Over what period?
  (ii) What will be the licensee's competition?
  (iii) What will be the licensee's market share during agreement period?
  (iv) Will the licensee's market share be enhanced by:
      (a) patents, or
      (b) knowhow
         influencing the licensee's exclusivity or prices?
  (v) Are there any localizing factors which allow the licensee to enjoy a bigger market or better prices than would be otherwise expected. Can you assess the value of this benefit in terms of: increased sales, increased prices or saving, in customs duties, transport and other distribution charges? How do you want to share these benefits?
  (vi) Is the licence to be exclusive or non-exclusive?

4 (i) What would be a fair estimate of the licensee's profitability throughout an agreement period?
  (ii) Will knowhow give it any appreciable savings over a former process or competitor processes?
  (iii) What will be profit income for the licensee over the life of:
      (a) the agreement, or
      (b) the useful life of patent or knowhow.
  (iv) If the licensee can get income from your knowhow for a period longer than that of the agreement, the licensor might want to claim a greater price.

5 (i) How much is it worth to the licensee today to buy its way into this market by purchasing the licensor's knowhow or patents:
      (a) as a lump sum? or
      (b) as an annual fee (either fixed or by a percentage)? or

(c) as a combination of (a) and (b)?

(ii) Are there any factors which influence the **utility** of the know-how; is the product or process fully developed, for instance, or will the licensee have to carry out development work of its own?

6 (i) What profit opportunity will the licensor be **losing** by setting up the licensee? The former will normally want a licence opportunity unless there are overriding strategic reasons.

(ii) For **licensees**, consider other uses to which they could put their money – would other investments bring a better yield, or are there overriding strategic reasons for entering the agreement?

7 (i) What total price such as downpayment and instalments (including interest factors if necessary) will satisfy these requirements?

(ii) Is the licensor prepared to accept more, or less, for policy reasons? (e.g. to establish its trademark in licensee's country it might accept less from the patent agreement). Or do other considerations such as global strategies influence its pricing policies?

(iii) Should the licensee be expected to pay more for policy reasons?

8 (i) Does the figure produced by the last question (no. 7) correspond to a 'felt fair price' such as the rate other people are charging the same industry?

(ii) Are there any other factors, such as sales goodwill resulting from the prestige of the licensor's firm, which justify a higher price?

(iii) Are there factors such as income from sales of raw materials which would justify a lower price?

(iv) How is the future of the licensee's trade likely to be affected by political and economic conditions in its country? How is the answer to this question likely to change the prices?

9 (i) How will these amounts be affected by foreign taxation and other legislation (such as the setting of a maximum royalty rate) for:
(a) knowhow? or
(b) patents?

(ii) Is it therefore better to have high patent and low knowhow fee

Managing the Licensing Agreement

or vice versa?

(iii) Is it better to have low downpayment and high annual fees, or vice versa? A low downpayment makes it easier for the licensee to set up, but represents a bigger risk for the licensor, unless guaranteed minimum annual fees fall due if the licensee defaults.

10 Is it now time to 'dress the package for negotiation'?

General considerations

If the licensee's country is one that has strong protection for intellectual property, this may increase the value of the licence while reducing the price to the licensee.

Whatever method is used, one fact stands out clearly in most reports – the need to aim for maximum market share. Where the licensee does not achieve a high market share, the project lapses into low profitability and perhaps disuse. This consideration often persuades the licensor to become involved in marketing, an involvement which may increase costs and ultimately reduce profitability unless the market share objective is achieved.

In practice, licensors adopt one of three policies for the determination of prices: a policy based on cost, market or income criteria. The cost policy is acceptable to the licensee, in that it stems from the costs involved in developing the technology from scratch rather than buying it from outside. The income approach, often preferred by licensors, is similar to the cost criteria in that it is based on financial rather than market considerations. While costs and income will always enter into the bargaining process, the market-based policy – adopt prices indicated by similar products in the same market – will usually be accepted where it is possible; this policy is assumed in this chapter. A problem of market criteria is that there may be no established market price for the most valuable (unique) technology. This is overcome when the parties have a mutual understanding about the commercial value of the licence and are able to justify this value in the light of other criteria.

Parties will be entering the agreement in order to obtain the maximum income from the technology being licensed and will have considered other options for the same investment. For the licensor the income has to fit a global strategy and to ensure that other options will have higher costs.

An additional consideration in the pricing policy is how to share any benefits that a particular licensee may expect in addition to those anticipated under normal circumstances. There may, for instance, be a number of local considerations such as a monopoly or restricted market, customs concessions, transport facilities which could produce windfall profits in which the licensor needs to participate. Another additional benefit occurs if the licensee is able to obtain income from the know-how beyond the period of the agreement.

Whether or not the licence is exclusive is another factor in pricing policies. In those countries where exclusive licences do not fall foul of competition regulations, exclusivity brings to the licensee a valuable asset, possibly a monopoly position.

An analysis of costs to the licensor has used the following classification (see note 1 at the end of this chapter).

1 **Development costs**. These include the costs of obtaining the know-how and the patents. A question for the licensor is the period over which the costs have been incurred and whether interest or inflation factors should be taken into account.
2 **Direct transfer costs**. These are usually known as the running costs and include design, ongoing training, manufacturing, marketing and post contract servicing.
3 **Indirect transfer costs** include legal payments costs and general management overheads as well as supervision and audit costs.

Among the costs – both direct and indirect – will be the senior management time focused on stimulating and controlling the project.

4 **Opportunity costs**. This covers the loss of revenue that **might** have

Managing the Licensing Agreement

been generated by another method of conducting business, either export or direct investment. The idea of opportunity costs may be treated as hypothetical, but it is often a determining factor in the decision for or against licensing.

The contractor with an adequate appraisal system will be balancing overall costs against all sources of income.

5 **Dissipation costs**. One authority (see the book by Rugman and others in Appendix 7.2) refers to 'dissipation' costs incurred by the licensor. This means the effects on the use or misuse of the company's name, image and technology by a licensee. These will eventually become straightforward accounting costs if the need for correction filters through the system.

4.3.2 REVENUES AND COSTS: THE LICENSEE'S INTERESTS

A licensee can find two benefits from an agreement – a quick route into a business, or an expansion of an existing business. In paying for a licence it is buying a technology and, as a rule, updates when necessary without the costs of research and development. The licensee company can make a relatively straightforward calculation to balance the costs of conducting the necessary development itself against the payments to the licensor. For both it is easy to underestimate the management costs incurred in running a project. Otherwise the licensee firm's costs and revenues are easier to forecast than those of the partner company, although it will need to take into account the size and growth of the market which is being entered or retained by the knowhow.

In the end the market, represented in the bargaining positions of the two parties, will determine the price which the licensor will then have to consider in the light of income expected over the lifetime of the patent; another consideration is the utility of the knowhow, whether it can be applied to other projects or is capable of profitable development in other spheres. Some unique and clever ideas are less difficult or expensive to apply than others and will have greater value to the user. The position of the licensee as well as that of the licensor is identified in Table 4.3.1.

Some licensees manage to save money by negotiating profit-sharing agreements.

4.3.3 Sources of funds

The search for sources of funds is a problem for the licensee which frequently becomes a worry for the licensor. Normally a licensee is a growing company and will be heavily geared (leveraged) with a high ratio of loan finance from banks. Obtaining more of this for a new project depends on the track record and prospects of the licensee, although the principal's reputation is a help in obtaining loans – this is one of the advantages of a licensing agreement. A project with a good track record and strong possibilities for expansion can justify more equity finance and this improves the licensee's debt:equity ratio.

The injection of equity into the licensee by the licensor is one way of ensuring that the licensor shares in the prosperity of the project, although this may not be the original purpose of the equity which is likely to be the need for a less expensive form of capital (one that does not require immediate annual repayments as does loan finance). The equity may also be regarded as a first step in a takeover of the licensee and, if that happens, the project changes from a licensing (in the sense used in this book) to a direct investment business.

4.3.4 Fees

A number of fee bases are possible for most knowledge agreements. The chosen base will depend on the relative bargaining positions of the two parties. A licensor desperate to enter a market and finding other routes blocked will be more willing to agree a fee base favourable to the licensee; under normal circumstances, the licensee will find itself in a weaker position but a project which is an optional extra for one party may still be a major part of the business of the other; the bargaining power of the licensee is likely to be weakened by competition

Managing the Licensing Agreement

with other would-be licensees as well as by the significance of the deal to its business.

A major choice is between fixed fees and percentages. The fixed fee, which can be paid in instalments, releases the licensor from risks of failure by the licensee but it also deprives the licensor of the benefits of success unless a specific clause stipulates extra payments or renegotiation if a certain level of business is attained. Such clauses are too speculative and, be it said, difficult to enforce, to be popular with either party, and some form of percentage fee is common. In this case there is another pair of options – between a percentage of gross income (usually up to ten per cent) and a percentage of profits (around 30 per cent). Some countries place an upper limit on the percentage in either case. A lump sum may be negotiated either as an advance on royalties or in their place. The licensor may seek additional benefits by supplying materials or components to the licensee. Equally there may be a reverse sale of goods from the licensee to the licensor. Both parties will be looking at the total sums involved; total revenues will be the ultimate test of success or failure.

Fees and down-payments should also be examined in the light of tax efficiency. Some one-off knowhow costs associated with plant sales may be regarded as costs by the licensee's government and not subjected to tax at source.

A problem for the licensor is how to verify the correctness of the licensee's payments. An agreement to accept the verdict of the licensee's auditor is likely to overcome this but a right to inspect the licensee's books may be written into the agreement. The licensee then takes over two problems – the threat of disruption when the inspectors come and a worry about a possible breach of confidentiality after their visit.

COUNTERTRADE

Fees may be paid in kind by a countertrade agreement. This is sometimes compulsory, especially for enterprises in countries with a non-convertible currency or balance of payments problems.

Countertrade has been increasing in spite of premature forecasts of its demise and there are a number of methods by which it is conducted. One is a buy-back agreement when the licensor agrees to accept products resulting from the licence in payment of royalties, another is a barter arrangement whereby the licensee pays in other goods. Neither of these arrangements is wholly satisfactory to the licensor as the resale of the goods may be difficult and costly, but many do accept countertrade as a means of entering a market likely to be important in the future. A number of companies have grown up to provide a sales service for products acquired through countertrade.

One arrangement, especially useful in a country where the remittance of royalties and fees may cause difficulties, is the translation of the initial sums into equity. This method was used when Pilkington (the British glass manufacturer) established a plant in India in 1987.

The arrangement for the licensor to accept part payment in products of the licence agreement is common in China. It was also used by Wilkinson Sword in part payment for razor blades manufactured in Poland from machinery installed under a licensing agreement there.

In some instances, governments may insist that part of the purchase price for machinery or of the fees for training or technology transfer is paid for by means of the licensor purchasing back certain volumes of licensed products from the licensee.

If there are compelling reasons why buy-back is difficult or impossible for the licensor, the countertrade may be possible in other more saleable products of the licensee's industrial sector, or even in products of other industrial sectors.

The problem for the licensor is that it cannot receive payment for the deal unless it agrees to market considerable volumes of products from the licensee's country. If these products are saleable by the licensor's marketing resources the problem is manageable. However, if the

Managing the Licensing Agreement

countertrade is in products from a completely different sector, the licensor will then have to contact specialists in countertrade who, for a fee, will turn the products into cash.

The difficulty then arises that increasing volumes of countertrade products have to be marketed in order to generate a given amount of convertible currency. Another difficulty is that the appearance of large numbers of products on world markets may ruin the markets as the glut lowers the price.

For instance, if a manufacturer of FHP electric motors was paid in motors which he could sell easily, he might be able to generate $100 000 net income by purchasing motors worth $200 000 at the production price of the licensee and selling them on at a mark-up of 60 to 100 per cent.

If the same income had to be generated from purchases of aluminium saucepans the licensor's countertrade dealers might have to buy $400 000 worth from the licensee's country. In a jam for machinery countertrade deal with an Eastern European country, the countertrade dealers had to purchase $600 000 worth of assorted fruit jams so that the licensor could obtain $100 000 net income.

Not surprisingly, a considerable number of potential licensing agreements are frustrated by the inability of the licensor to arrange a satisfactory outlet for the countertrade.

The economics of countertrade are heavily influenced by the immediate saleability of the countertrade product where countertrade is offered in perishable foodstuffs or fashion goods which may become obsolete; additional safety margins must be allowed to insure against part of the countertrade articles becoming unsaleable. In such cases it is usual to persuade the licensor's government to discount the cost of the countertrade product to safeguard the licensor against its possible deterioration.

Companies confronted with the need to accept countertrade find themselves faced with considerable problems about how to sell the unwanted goods. If these are products which the licensor itself sells, it will not wish to disturb its existing markets and the goods will be skilfully and carefully inserted into an existing marketing programme. If unrelated goods are accepted, the most cost effective means of disposing of them is likely to be through one of the organizations that have sprung up for the purpose of selling the fruits of countertrade agreements.

4.3.5 Taxation

An advantage of licensing is that money paid for this type of business is usually taxed more lightly than for other types. Some countries, giving top priority to acquiring knowhow, allow royalty payments free of tax. A similar advantage is that royalty payments may still be allowed when a country clamps down on remittances abroad to conserve currency.

One advantage of a lump sum royalty payment can arise if it is accepted as a capital transfer for tax purposes.

The same taxation benefits apply to management fees but, in this case, it may prove hard to justify the payment. A taxation officer can see the results of a licensing agreement; management services may not prove so acceptable. For this reason, some companies charge a composite fee for licensing deals which includes management costs. This makes it possible to defend the payment on the grounds that it is charged for a tangible benefit. Table 4.3.2 lists withholding taxes levied by some countries on royalty payments.

In some countries, the tax benefits for royalty payments only apply to royalties paid by independent local companies, not subsidiaries of foreign groups.

Managing the Licensing Agreement

Table 4.3.2: Withholding tax on royalty income (%)

Destination Country of origin	Non-treaty countries	Treaty countries	Notes
Argentina	21.6 or 28.8	15-28.8	
France	33.33	5-33.33	
Germany	25	5-25	Special provisions for lower rates
India	30	10-30	Special provisions for variable rates
Italy	30	15-28.8	Some reduced rates non-treaty on 70% of royalty
Japan	20	10-20	0 in some treaties, rates vary
Malaysia	15	0-15	
Netherlands	0	0	
Russian Federation	15	0-20	Most treaty countries 0
Singapore	31	10-25	
Spain	25	5-15	
Switzerland	0	0	No withholding taxes on royalties at present
United Kingdom	25	0-25	No withholding taxes to other European countries nor to United States and many countries outside Europe
United States	30	0-30	No withholding taxes to European and many other countries

Source: figures compiled from *Corporate Taxes: A Worldwide Survey*, Price Waterhouse 1992

The tax position may well be the determining factor in the choice of licensing (for the licensor). Most countries are keen to import technology and fix low rates of withholding tax which is normally the only tax that affects licensing agreements. There is no profits tax, as with dividends, although a sales or value added tax may be levied as well.

NOTES

1 See Contractor, Farouk J., 'The cost of technology transfers in overseas licensing', *Working Paper*, 8 November, 1978. In this study, indirect costs were shown to be 22.7 per cent of all transfer costs.

4.4 Marketing

It has been claimed that 30 per cent of overseas licensing ventures from the United States fail, chiefly because of an unsatisfactory marketing approach and the lack of a wider understanding of their implications. The vetting of the market and the licensee (or partner) are the only ways of reducing the risk that arises from outside a company. Within a firm, the whole of the expertise of its management must be brought into the planning and promotion of the venture (see Chapter 4.2 and 4.4.2).

The target market in a licensing strategy will be companies in relevant industry sectors in a limited number of countries. The country will largely be determined by the type of technology and the potential for its sale in that country.

The approach to marketing will be determined by an over-riding strategic decision, whether the company: (1) sees licensing as a business method to be developed in its own right; or (2) as a fallback when other methods are unlikely to work; or (3) as a method to be undertaken when an opportunity occurs; or (4) as a protection for a company's knowledge. The implications of each for marketing will be considered in turn.

1 The promoter of licensing as a revenue earner in its own right needs to:
   (a) identify clearly the opportunities for application;
   (b) describe accurately the technologies to be licensed;
   (c) involve technical staff at an early stage to ensure that the project is a company effort; and
   (d) build up a reputation as a successful licensor. Some evidence has been assembled that the reputation of the licensor is all-important in the search for a partner.
2 The promoter of licensing as a fallback when other methods are unlikely to work needs to:
   (a) develop criteria for determining which markets cannot be serviced by other methods (for example: too protected for export or too risky for direct investment); and

Managing the Licensing Agreement

    (b) ensure that the expertise and the facilities are available when a need for licensing arises.
3. As a method to be undertaken when an opportunity occurs. The considerations in this approach are similar to 2 above, except that more detailed planning is usually undertaken. Marketing this option will mean retaining contact with known entrepreneurs who might be expected to be looking for new products.
4. As a method of protecting a company's knowledge. Facts exposed in Chapter 1.6 have shown that defence of the business, especially of existing trade, is the most common, and most lucrative, use of licensing.

The marketing of technology in its own right has been identified (by R. Adoutte, Director of Contracts, Battelle-Europe, in a speech to the Les Pan-European Conference, reprinted in *Les Nouvelles*, December 1988) in the following stages:

1. identification of need,
2. internal research – creation of intellectual property,
3. validation,
4. development,
5. technical evaluation,
5. market evaluation,
6. financial evaluation,
7. protection,
8. definition of commercial strategy,
9. sale.

The same speaker also listed a number of 'other avenues' made available for exploiting the knowledge including technological feed-back to the company and a gearing effect produced by the technology.

The desire or, indeed, willingness to sell licences varies with circumstances. According to one authority (see Mark Casson (1986), *Multinationals and World Trade*, Allen and Unwin), the benefits of large-scale production in the motor car industry are enormous but American manufacturers have in the past been unwilling to grant licences which might dilute the technological lead they believed they had. The same authority demonstrates that most of the major producers of synthetic fibres originally entered through licensing agreements.

4.4.1 THE FOUR STAGES

The marketing breaks down into four stages which form the sections of this chapter: innovation (at which stage the product idea is adapted commercially, a stage critical to all later development); market research and assessment; the marketing thrust itself including promotion; and selling.

INNOVATION

It is often said that innovation is the ability to bring a deal to the stage of becoming a product or process which someone can succeed in marketing profitably.

Innovation is a broad topic on which many books have been written but its success is largely a success in market research (often involving **future** research), marketing and financing. The chances of a given idea becoming a successful innovation are minute. In the case of undeveloped technology only around one in five of ideas submitted to the now-defunct British National Research and Development Corporation (NRDC) each year were even accepted and these ideas must have been already on the way towards becoming developed before anyone would think of submitting them; a still smaller proportion come to fruition. In the United States, UPI – a company of knowhow brokers – found that only five to ten per cent of technological ideas adopted led to any satisfactory results, whilst Research Corporation, a company which took up ideas early on in their life, found that only four per thousand (that is, 0.4 per cent) produced any royalties and less than one per thousand (that is, less than 0.1%) produced over $50 000 per year in royalties.

Figure 4.4.1 illustrates the decision process for an innovation and

Managing the Licensing Agreement

explains the percentage chances of success at each stage.

Figure 4.4.1 Operation sequence for early innovation decisions (year 1) (showing "go" paths only)

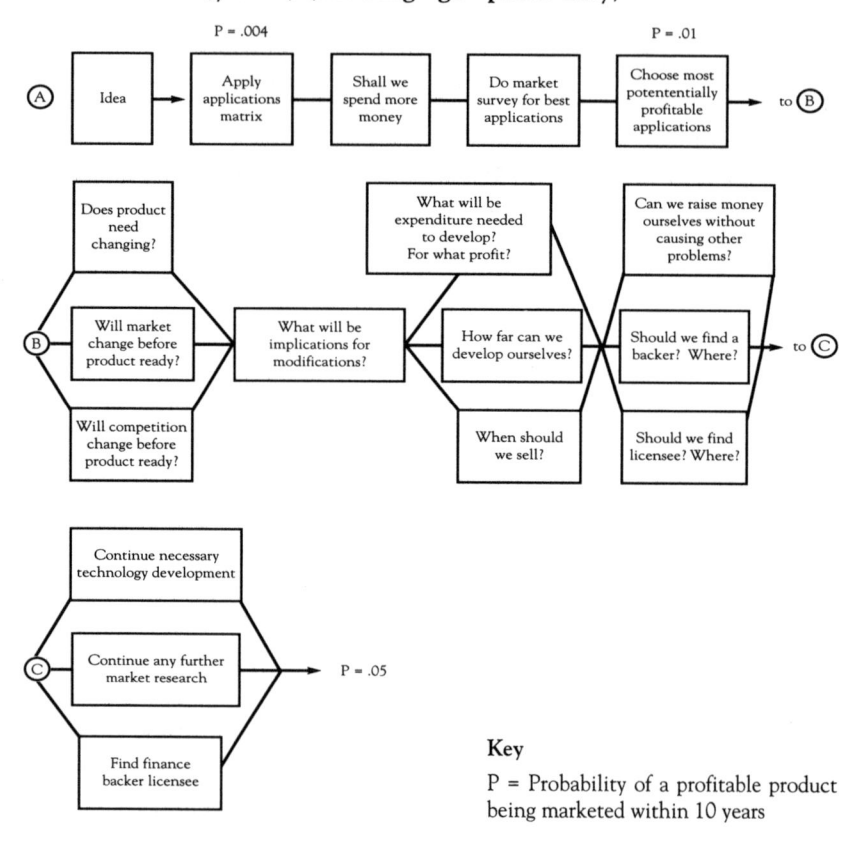

```
(A) Idea → Apply applications matrix → Shall we spend more money → Do market survey for best applications → Choose most potententially profitable applications → to (B)
         P = .004                                                                              P = .01

(B) Does product need changing?
    Will market change before product ready? → What will be implications for modifications? → What will be expenditure needed to develop? For what profit?
    Will competition change before product ready?
                                                                    How far can we develop ourselves?   Can we raise money ourselves without causing other problems?
                                                                    When should we sell?                 Should we find a backer? Where? → to (C)
                                                                                                         Should we find licensee? Where?

(C) Continue necessary technology development
    Continue any further market research  → P = .05
    Find finance backer licensee
```

Key
P = Probability of a profitable product being marketed within 10 years

NEED FOR MARKET RESEARCH

The reason for market research is that customers are not impressed by elegant concepts, they are impressed by something that fills a need. An engineer in Switzerland spent many leisure hours perfecting a self-winding watch movement which turned out to be so expensive that it would never cater for the mass-production market; it was also a little insensitive so that it could not capture the Rolex type market. If he had thought about this earlier on, he could have saved himself a lot of time and expense.

A typical idea goes through four stages: conception; goal oriented experimentation; pilot production; and full scale production.

The conception stage may come in the form of finding a market for some aspect of theoretical research. For example switches are now being produced from special types of glass which are electrically conducting at one voltage, and insulating at another – an effect discovered by a Russian called Ovshinsky. Alternatively, conception may result from deliberate experimentation stimulated by a market need – pollution control devices for transportation equipment are an obvious example. However, at each successive stage, market research and financial analysis **must** be carried out to see whether:

1. the next stage in the process is correctly oriented and aimed towards achieving the right goals;
2. the pay-off from developing the idea one stage further will balance and give a profit on the new expense to be incurred;
3. the results may also give rise to a problem about how to raise finance for the next stage without adversely affecting the liquidity of the research company – this is an especially acute problem for small research companies; and whether
4. there is a right moment to launch the product; as an example, interest in the Sterling cycle engine has been renewed by interest in pollution. Also **timing** is important since by the time the product is ready, the market or one's competitors may have changed radically.

In the case of **developed technology**, which is usually the case in international licensing, innovation merely means introducing a concept which has been tried in one market into another. The market research involved is usually based on **facts**, since the market characteristics are well-known for the country of origin and have to be evaluated, compared and contrasted for the recipient country.

In the case of **non-developed technology**, elements of conjecture, insight and hunch are stronger, reflecting greater uncertainty about the outcome. However, improved techniques in **forecasting** and **futurology** can help.

Managing the Licensing Agreement

FINANCIAL IMPLICATIONS

In the early years, the foreseeable probability of success is low. However, the research manager has to look ten years or more into the future (for the early Xerox it was more like twenty years, with the early Wankel engine some forty years and for Leonardo da Vinci's helicopter design some 400 years!).

In the early stages, the development costs are usually low, and it is therefore feasible to spend a limited amount of money on a wait and see basis.

As the idea becomes increasingly developed, and the outcome increasingly clear, the double or quit problem becomes increasingly acute, and many small research companies have to start looking for a licensee before the prototype stage, since developing a prototype places great strain on their financial resources.

At this stage, the value of the knowhow will be low compared with its possible value at a later stage. In year one, knowhow may not be clearly **identifiable**; although it is theoretically **useful**, it has **low utility** and is not easily **transferable**. In such a case the potential licensor, if short of money, will stand a much better chance by persuading someone to buy the idea or finance its further development. However, at this stage, the likelihood of success is so low that the buyer will hardly be likely to sign a licence agreement on a royalty basis. Hence a lump sum payment may be more appropriate.

Clearly, if inventors can finance the idea to a fully licensable product, they might be able to obtain a disclosure fee, to offset their development expenses, as well as an ongoing royalty.

The licensor's situation will be better if it can sell its idea three or four times (in Japan, the United States, the United Kingdom and Germany for instance). In order to make these sales, the licensor will have to persuade foreign buyers of the likely market for its ideas.

4.4.2 Market research and assessment

The assessment of the market for knowhow and the search for potential knowhow partners is a second order function imposed upon the market for the primary product. In an assessment of the market for beer brewing processes in the former state of Yugoslavia, the market research first had to assess the market for different types of beer, both among the local population and the considerable tourist industry. The tourist industry meant that there was a seven month period of high demand for lager type beers, and some foreign specialty beers such as English ale which could be produced by related processes. Since Yugoslavia at the time of the survey had only a semi-developed agricultural economy and low reserves of foreign currency, difficulties were anticipated in finding reliable supplies of the feedstock for the beer. A process had to be developed whereby a variety of grains and even other forms of carbohydrate could be used to supplement the basic feedstock in case of problems of supply.

The design of plant eventually chosen was also capable of producing local beers for the autumn and winter season in order to ensure at least a basic level of plant utilization. Some lager type beers were produced in winter for winter sports areas.

Whereas a normal market research project would have concentrated on a particular type of beer or group of beer types, the knowhow marketing project had to consider the overall beer-brewing opportunities in the Yugoslav market of the time. Indeed, in order to balance capacity in the bottling plant, additional surveys were carried out to assess the potential for bottled mineral water and soft drinks.

Market assessment

The above example shows that market research for a licensing venture is a much more entrepreneurial process than the simple assessment of the market for the primary product.

Managing the Licensing Agreement

Clearly the market for the primary product is a satisfactory point of departure although, in the case of United States companies seeking licensing partners in Europe, investment criteria such as the prices of land and buildings, labour costs, local taxation and many others may be more important than the presence of an immediate market in the country concerned. The Caterpillar plant at Gossilies in Belgium is a particular case in point; it was designed to service the total European market and not simply the market in Belgium.

It can be difficult to gain any figures about the existing market for a product, especially in the case of developing countries. Government statistics are often non-existent or misleading and it may be difficult to draw parallels between the market for a product in a developed country and a developing country. There is an enormous market for outboard motors in Malaysia and Indonesia, although sophisticated European and American types have had a relatively small share for many years. The reason is that local ingenuity has enabled small two-stroke engines from a variety of agricultural machinery, and even second-hand motor car engines, to be adapted to drive a propeller.

Other traditional methods of market research, such as postal or telephone surveys, are also rendered more difficult when working in foreign markets. Apart from questions of language and translation, the attitudes of the public to giving such information may vary enormously. A postal survey to a number of large food stores in Nigeria regarding the acceptance of a new brand led to very misleading results because the respondents felt obliged to say good things about the product so as to qualify for the free gift which was given to respondents.

Since many developing countries have excellent civil services, import and export statistics are often a good indicator of market characteristics especially if a licensed product could replace imports.

Although the **sum of competitors** method of assessing market size is useful in developed countries where the turnover figures for individual companies are obtainable, this method also has limitations if some producers are manufacturing large volumes for export, or if local production is supplemented by substantial imports.

Whatever the quality of statistical information available, it is always good to speak to knowledgeable personnel in the embassy or consulate in the country concerned. In desk research, one should not forget to check what information may have been compiled by world organizations such as the OECD, the World Bank, various United Nations organizations, and even government authorities from other countries: for example, valuable statistics and market assessments of foreign markets can be obtained from sources in the embassies and consulates of the United States and Germany, as well as the United Kingdom and France.

Government studies, reports on anti-trust proceedings and the annual reports of large companies are also useful on occasion.

Some trade associations produce reports on world trends, and the market research departments of large multinational companies can also be helpful in providing information to non-competitors.

Linear Power Ltd: A case example on market research and the location of a licensee

A small electrical engineering company, which developed a number of product ideas for cheap linear motors, had to decide what to do with the invention.

Market assessment using national statistics and published information

The first step was to do some desk research on the possible applications of linear motors. The aim was to launch prototypes on the United Kingdom market and then to look for licensees in other countries.

A number of countries have input-output tables showing the inputs from each industrial sector into the outputs of every other sector.

Managing the Licensing Agreement

Table 4.4.1 Linear Power Ltd: Technology application matrix using input-output tables

INDUSTRY	VALUE OF OUTPUT	APPLICATIONS (a) = moving coil (b) = moving core [5] = years development time
Agriculture, forestry & fishing	£1339m	Harpoon (a); Sack hoist (a); [5] Conveyors (a) (b) [5]
Coal mining & other mining	£819m	Conveyor (a) [6] Propelling magnetic slurries along plastic tubes (b) [8]
Coke & coal tar	£151m	Conveyor (a) [6]
Chemicals, dyes drugs & perfume	£681m	Actuators (b) [5]
Soap, polishes etc.	£121m	Actuators (b) [5]
Oil refinery & greases	£476m	Actuators (b) [5]
Paints & plastics	£194m	Actuators (b) [5]
Iron & steel smelting & casting	£810m	Conveyor (b) [5]
Iron & steel plate & tubes	£158m	Conveyor (b) [5] Guillotine (a) (b) [3]
Non ferrous metals	£404m	Conveyor (b) [5]
Automobiles & cycles	£875m	Conveyor (a) [5]
Aircraft & aerospace	£305m	Rivet gun (b) [5]
Railway rolling stock etc.	£213m	Conveyor (a) (b) [5]
Shipbuilding & marine	£313m	Rivet gun (b) [5]
Mechanical engineering	£1300m	Conveyor (a) (b) [5] Guillotine (a) (b) [3]
Electrical engineering	£916m	
Precision instrument	£206m	
Miscellaneous metal goods	£633m	Rivet gun (b) [5]
Spinning & weaving	£1011m	Throwing a shuttle (b) [7]
Clothing & shoe manufacture	£1180m	
Foodstuffs	£1916m	

4

Table 4.4.1 continued

Drink & tobacco	£1442m	
Timber & furniture	£423m	Gun for shooting nails [3] (b) Guillotine (a) (b) [3]
Paper & board	£366m	Guillotine [3] (a) (b)
Printing & publishing	£435m	Guillotine [3] (a) (b)
Rubber	£210m	
Building	£283m	Hoists (a) [5] Passenger lifts (a) [5] Door openers (a) (b) [3]

Table 4.4.1 shows an excerpt from a census of production showing the value of equipment supplied to various industrial sectors, and possible uses for the embryo device. In each case the assessment team separated the potential applications between devices having a moving coil, and those having a moving core, and gave an estimate of the likely development time to bring each development to a practical product.

The product designed by Linear Power was particularly suited for sealed units to supply motive power in corrosive or polluted environments. It also had only one moving part, which eliminated many complications of using conventional rotating electric motors with rack and pinion drives.

It was therefore decided to narrow the search down to actuators for various types of valves used in a wide variety of industries. It looked as though this offered a large market for a product with a development time of about five years.

Further research on national statistics gave the value of construction projects in hand over a period of time (say two years), and investment in new plant in a particular year (see Tables 4.4.1 and 4.4.2 A and B).

From a search of literature on chemical and allied plant and after discussions with two contractors Q and R, an assessment was made of the breakdown of plant cost. This gave a figure of about ten per cent of plant value in piping and valves, of which actuator systems came to

Managing the Licensing Agreement

about two per cent (see Table 4.4.2C). The total market value for the type of actuator used was therefore about £5.5m.

Table 4.4.2 Chemical and other plant construction

(A) Value of projects in hand

SECTOR	VALUE (£m)
Petroleum	181
Town Gas	69
Heavy organics	108
Synthetic fibres	73
Inorganics	34
Plastics & resins	26
Fertilisers	24
Dyestuffs	19
Industrial gases	10
Pharmaceuticals	11
Synthetic rubber	4
Coal chemicals	–
Other	17
TOTAL	576

(B) Investment in plant

Gas manufacture	£87M
Petroleum refineries	£93M
Chemicals	£95M
	£275M

(C) Breakdown of plant hardware cost

Hardware type	Chemical plant %	Gas plant %	Contractors Q R
Heat exchangers	15	5	– –
Piping, valves etc.	10	10.6	12% 15%
(of which actuators)	(2)	(1.8)	(3) (1)

Table 4.4.2 continued

Pumps & compressors	7	2.8	–	–
Filters, centrifuges, mixers	8	0.8	–	–
Other	10	38.8	–	–
TOTAL	50%	48.0%		

MARKET ASSESSMENT USING THE 'SUM OF COMPETITORS' METHOD

The method of assessment used in this case is rather theoretical and is based on many assumptions; on the other hand, it is fast and cheap.

The next step was to look at the total market already served by competitors (Table 4.4.3A). For this purpose, the definition of 'competition' was kept fairly wide, covering the function performed rather than particular product designs. Import-export statistics were also consulted to make sure that the production of the manufacturers was absorbed by the local market, and also whether the market might offer opportunities for import replacement.

Table 4.4.3 Linear Power Ltd: Other survey results

(A)

Competitor Times mentioned in Survey(B)		Actuator for valve with bore size inches	Share capital £K	No of employees	Actuator turnover £K
A	2	0.25 – 36	2,900	3,000	250
B	4	0.50 – 12	1,000	4,000	1,000
C	4	0.50 – 6	120	200	700
D	1	0.50 – 4	10	195	400
E	5	0.50 – 6	1	800	1,500
Others	–	0.25 – 36	–	400	1,200
TOTAL				–	5,100

Managing the Licensing Agreement

Table 4.4.3 continued

(B) Telephone (postal) survey

Contractor	Size range used inches	Competitor mentioned	Size inches	Price £	Actuator usage	Need for LP type %	
M	4 - 8	D C	5 7	25 75	£100K	10	£10K
N	0.50 - 6	B E	2 0.50	10 7	£50K	7	£3.5K
O	0.50 – 14	A B	1 10	8 150	£250K	6	£15K
P	3 - 6	E A	3 5	15 35	£75K	4	£3K
Q	0.50 – 2	C E	2 1	13 6	£25K	12	£3K
R	0.50 – 6	E B	5 0.50	30 5	£100K	11	£11K
S	1 – 6	C B	3 1	13 7	£50K	14	£7K
T	1 – 12	E C	1 3	7 19	£25K	6	£1.5K
TOTAL	0.50 – 14				£675K	8%	£54K

There are about 50 contractors in the United Kingdom

The sources of information were the annual reports of companies to their shareholders and publications of associations of plant producers, supplemented by buyers' guides such as Kompass and company information sources such as Dun & Bradstreet. In some cases, and especially with the residual group 'others', it was necessary to estimate production from numbers of employees or other circumstantial information.

It was also necessary to recall that not all the production facilities or the employees of each company were engaged in the manufacture of actuators. For this reason, the most useful information came from middle-sized, specialist producers, rather than from the larger and more diversified companies.

This method gave a market size of £5.1m.

TELEPHONE SURVEY

On the strength of the above prospects, it was decided to invest in a telephone survey of users, which in some cases was supplemented by a postal questionnaire. The survey covered:

1. size range used,
2. makes used,
3. price information,
4. total value purchased per year, and
5. opinion of the users on the percentage which could be converted to the Linear Power design.

Out of 50 users contacted, only eight provided useful information, giving a usage of £657 000 per year. This method gave rather lower market assessment of £675K x 50/8 = £4 220K, of which eight per cent could be converted. The results are shown in Table 4.4.3B.

When evaluating the market from the purchases of users, factors such as stock changes, imports and exports by users should also be borne in mind.

The information was further developed to give a picture of the relative importance of the competitors, the sizes required, and the demand frequency of each size. With the aid of competitor sales literature and price lists, similar techniques may be used to reconstruct the price and discount structures of competitors.

Managing the Licensing Agreement

In this case, it was felt that the Linear Power device could replace about 40 per cent of the products on the market, particularly in the larger size ranges.

SEARCH FOR A LICENSEE

Two years later, when a viable product was well on the way to acceptance, similar desk surveys were carried out to obtain a general comparison of the size of markets in continental Europe, the United States and Japan. It was decided to concentrate on the European market, and to try to find two potential licensees, one for Germany, Benelux, Austria and Switzerland, and one for France and Italy.

The company already had some experience in exporting its existing product range, and felt that the achievable turnover would be too low in view of its limited sales network and, more importantly, that the speed of penetration would be too low to benefit from the market advantage offered by the patent.

The sales manager contacted British embassies in France, Germany and Italy, and obtained the names of 50 competitors, along with basic details of creditworthiness, business reputation, turnover, and product range. In addition, discussions continued with a German competitor which had contacted them independently when it heard about Linear Power's new product.

Five companies were chosen from each country and, after contact by post and telephone, a short list of seven was drawn up. These companies were compared by drawing up tables showing their location, share capital, number of employees, size of sales force, turnover, export percentage, markets covered, chief products, market share and market reputation. A credit rating was also obtained through their banks.

After further correspondence and a number of visits to the most promising candidates, four were chosen of which two were in Germany, one in France and one in Italy. In evaluating these four, meetings were held between the directors of Linear Power and their prospective licensees. Attention was paid not only to the present management team but to questions of succession and the future prospects of each company. Production facilities were assessed by Linear Power staff rather late in the proceedings, as there was some suspicion from the potential licensees until more confidence was established.

As a result of these efforts, licence agreements were made with one German and one Italian company.

Tables 4.4.1 to 4.4.3 contain the results of the survey.

Even though the problem of presenting a product to the public in a particular market may seem quite straightforward to both knowhow partners, it is as well that both partners call into question their existing strategies, asking: should the licensee profit from advertising developed by the licensor for other markets or will the slogans and graphic material prove unsuitable for the local market?

In this section the word marketing is used to describe a wide interface between the company and its customers, including the presentation of the company and its products to the market place – public relations, advertising and sales.

Licensing represents an extension of the way a company views itself, and is the result of a more entrepreneurial view of its activities. The licensing approach does not require any new vision with regard to the primary products or processes of the company, but involves taking a new look at how a better return may be obtained on its total resources.

This means that the marketing function of a particular company or profit centre is transformed into a primary and a secondary level. The primary level involves the market for the principal products and services supplied by the company; the secondary level involves the market for the company's expertise. It should be recognized that there is an inherent conflict between the two levels: the market for a company's knowhow will probably involve working with existing or

Managing the Licensing Agreement

potential competitors. The sale of knowhow is always a compromise in the interests of speed or depth of market penetration. A large and financially powerful company with good worldwide market coverage would be unlikely to licence out its knowhow, unless it was thereby able to increase its opportunities in certain markets (for example where there were substantial import barriers) or reduce threats (by gaining income from a potentially unstable market without the need for direct foreign investment).

In markets with a high cost of entry licensing may in fact represent the most cost effective method of gaining a modest income. This is seen frequently in the automotive industry where the cost of building an engine plant in a particular market may prove excessive if its capacity would not be fully utilized until (say) ten years after start-up due to slow market penetration. In such cases, it has proved more economical for the engine manufacturer to licence a well established competitor in that market for a particular range of engine models, and thereby to benefit from a modest income per engine on a large portion of the market. In such cases, the opportunity cost is zero or perhaps even negative, since any other profitable method of market penetration might be impossible.

Advertising

In the case of developed technology, the products of the licensor are often sufficient of an advert to attract technology buyers: in the case of The Glacier Metal Co Ltd, a United Kingdom bearings manufacturer, licensees first approached Glacier in 60 per cent of the cases. In a further 20 per cent, the would-be licensee advertised, asking for a technology supplier, and elicited a response from the eventual licensor.

With non-developed technology there are two distinct requirements which may, in fact, conflict. Up to the **pilot plant** stage, all the inventor needs is a backer with finance available. Although it would be useful to have marketing expertise working on the project earlier, it only becomes crucial when the inventor has a product to sell and clearly the best financiers are not always the best marketing experts.

Moreover if, at the early stages of development, the inventor contacts a company which will eventually manufacture and market it, such a company may want to change the invention, file its own patents – and indeed may emerge as a competitor before the idea has reached a marketable stage.

Hence it may be that advertising in respect of projects in the very early stages would be better directed at investors, who would then share in the proceeds at a later date when manufacturing licensees would be contacted.

To do this, one may advertise in *International Licensing, Technology Mart* or one of the other knowhow exchange journals, but these journals are not necessarily read by those whom one would like to contact. It may be the patents manager who receives the copy and not the production manager, the executive who has the problem.

In some cases, this grape-shot technique may be appropriate but more often a carefully aimed direct mailshot launched towards a carefully selected target is more effective. A typical response rate is 10-20 per cent.

These ideas all tie in with the complementary skills and resources of the potential partner; in the early stages the emphasis is on finding a partner with financial and development expertise. Later the partner must have manufacturing and marketing skills. In either case, it will help to find a suitable partner if an appropriate knowhow profile can be drawn up before starting to contact people indiscriminately.

4.4.3 The Marketing of Technology and Advertising

Profitable innovation does not merely depend on developing an interesting scientific principle to a point where it is of practical benefit, but on successfully integrating into and balancing in the new product a

Managing the Licensing Agreement

wide variety of data and decisions concerning the present and future market environment while assessing the financial and technical requirements of each step.

A shower accessory which was marketed as a relatively expensive upper-market product in the United Kingdom only achieved significant penetration in Germany when its packaging and presentation were changed to give it a much more utility image – in other words, its image had to be down-graded to achieve any significant market penetration. In the United States, the attitude to many domestic accessories is utilitarian and it proved impossible to market this particular shower accessory in that country at all since the market was well supplied with lower quality but perfectly acceptable alternative products. In the licensing of components, consideration must be given to possible interactions between the licensee and associate companies of key customers of the licensor. A common problem is that the licensor or the licensee can come under price pressure from the customer group which notes significant differences between prices for apparently similar products. Problems of interchangeable quality can also arise when spares from the factories of both the licensor and the licensee are eventually found side by side in the warehouse of a multinational customer.

4.4.4 Selling

Normally, the methods of selling an end product are similar from country to country, although the licensee should decide at an early stage with the licensor whether to emphasize or play down the foreign origin of the licensed product. Depending on the attitudes of the public, the foreign origin can give a cachet of quality and exclusivity, or it may be seen as a threat to local producers and distributors or even to the local way of life.

At all levels of development, the establishment of a local producer frequently means that importers, agents and distributors who have enjoyed a good living from selling the imported product at a high premium may be displaced. Bearing in mind the experience of these companies and individuals, it is well to make a deliberate decision about whether to incorporate some of them in the future sales and distribution network of the new licensee. Sometimes this is impossible, since the importers have built up their reputations on the virtues of a particular imported product, and lose their credibility when changing to a cheaper local product. Sales agents who work on a commission basis may suddenly see their incomes reduced by 50 or 70 per cent when selling a locally manufactured product which is substantially cheaper.

A lower priced locally manufactured article does not necessarily win the support of the local public. When a particular kind of medical suture was produced in an Asian country in which many doctors had been trained in Europe, the licensor had to arrange a campaign of visits and advertising to the local hospitals to persuade surgeons that the licensee's product was equal in quality and performance to the traditionally imported version. In Turkey in the 1960s and early 1970s, imported spare parts for cars and trucks would sell at a premium of 100 to 200 per cent over the locally produced product which was technically equivalent in every way.

4.4.5 OTHER MARKETING ISSUES

We will not repeat here the warnings about the different symbolism of colours in different countries that stress the potential blunders which can occur in the transfer of trademarks from one language to another or the errors which can occur in the translation of technical documentation, product operating instructions and other necessities. These matters are routinely dealt with in exporting circles. However, one important matter which can seriously affect the success of a licensing deal is the question of presentation and packaging. Years of successful advertising have meant that the Coca-Cola bottle with its distinctive shape is almost as essential a part of the 'Coca-Cola experience' as its contents. Licensing partners should therefore give serious consideration before setting up production as to the form in which the product

Managing the Licensing Agreement

should be presented to the public, answering the questions: does the packaging knowhow then become part of the licence agreement? Is the royalty payable on the contents of the pack, or on the total price of the pack including packaging materials? Who pays for the research and re-design of the packaging to suit a new market?

Such issues were recently raised in the United Kingdom when a European yogurt manufacturer set up a local licensee, and it was found that the packaging and presentation of the product required radical change.

It must also be said that for less sophisticated economies, the packaging of certain products may need to be down-graded: under a licence for electrical spares for an Eastern European market, it was decided to eliminate the elaborate blister packaging which is used to supply small quantities of spares to retail outlets in favour of loose packing the products in boxes of 50 and 100 pieces.

Although it is illegal (almost everywhere) to use a licence agreement for the purpose of price fixing, it may be advantageous for the licensor and licensee to understand the principles on which a product is priced. Where a cost plus price system is used, pricing policy is relatively uncomplicated. In other cases, the price of a product may be determined not by the cost of its constituent parts or ingredients, but as a reflection of the function it fulfils.

The licensor of a medical product to a Third World country could take the view that its particular product was very expensive to develop and that its price should be based on the fact that the recovery rate of patients is shortened by several days. The licensee, as well as the health minister of its country, on the other hand, might take the view that the research costs would already have been covered by sales to other markets, and that the medicine should be sold at a price based on production cost alone. This in turn might mean that the licensor's foreseeable royalty income is reduced by over 50 per cent. Since in most cases it is illegal to use a licence agreement for the purposes of the restraint of trade, the problems can be compounded if exporters in the licensee's country then start distributing the cheaper product in third markets in competition with the more expensive version produced by the licensor. In order to forestall this possibility, some licence agreements include the right of the licensor to purchase the surplus capacity of the licensee, at an agreed price basis, so that the licensor can control the distribution of the licensee's products in third markets.

The pricing of raw materials and semi-finished products supplied between the licensor and the licensee is also a frequent bone of contention. The licensor may expect to make a good profit margin on raw materials and semi-finished products supplied to the licensee. On the other hand after transport costs, import duties and other charges, the raw materials may become so expensive as to endanger the profitability of the venture to the licensee. The licensor may expect to buy semi-finished or finished products from the licensee at favourable rates reflecting the lower cost base of the licensee's country. However, the results of such comparisons can be surprising: in the 1980s when the cost of labour in West Germany was over 60 per cent higher than in the United Kingdom, the higher efficiencies and longer production runs in the factory of a German manufacturer of components for domestic electrical equipment meant that its costs were still ten per cent lower than those of its United Kingdom licensee manufacturing on identical machines.

Similar conflicts of interest may arise in quality matters: a licensor may agree that the licensee produces a lower quality version of a product for a particular market, only to find some years later that the lower quality product competes against its own products in third markets, or in the case of components, that a multinational customer complains at the non-interchangeability of products from different sources. Apart from questions concerning the sale of the end product, the existence of a licensing agreement may affect other aspects of the life of the sales department. For example, should the sales personnel of the licensee be invited to the licensor's annual sales conference? On the one hand, this can prove an excellent way of keeping the licensee informed about the licensor's progress on world markets; on the other hand (especially where the licence agreement only covers part of the licensor's product

Managing the Licensing Agreement

range) the licensee may thereby obtain access to valuable information outside the scope of the licence.

There is a difference between the sales organization used for selling the end product and that used to sell the knowhow. This is usual in marketing policies as a whole. In finding purchasers for knowhow, contacts are more likely to arise between chief executives, research departments or production departments than between sales and purchasing departments. This means that executives who normally have little exposure to legal and commercial problems may be confronted with very complex issues affecting many aspects of a company's sales and marketing strategy. This is why a team approach is to be recommended in the search for and assessment of licensing partners. The chief executive or team leader should be aware of the particular biases to which different team members may be subject: it is, for instance, difficult for the sales manager of a company who has regarded a particular competitor as an enemy to regard the same individuals as friends merely because a licence agreement has been made between the two companies. Production personnel from either partner, on visiting the factories of the others, may be unnecessarily critical about the quality or cost of production in the other factory.

The selling of knowhow requires a much more strategic and long-term approach than the sale of an end product: a product is sold to fulfil an immediate demand; knowhow is sold in order to benefit from a strategic opportunity.

Blood transfusion equipment: A case example in licence marketing

As a fall-out product from a theoretical research project, the physics department of a university designed and applied for patents for a device used in blood transfusion and dialysis. Discussions with doctors indicated that it might have commercial potential, but the department did not know how to go about assessing the market or setting up production and marketing facilities. The department did not have a budget for the commercial exploitation of this idea and stipulated that, apart from a limited amount of office support and a limited expense budget (for travelling and other expenses), the project would have to be self-financing.

After the initial filing of a United Kingdom patent application, progress had to be made as fast as possible because the university was not prepared to pursue registrations in other countries without firm commercial prospects.

Through personal contacts, one of the professors located a licensing consultant who agreed to carry out the initial assessment on an expenses only basis, followed by a payment by results remuneration package.

By questioning a number of hospitals on their use of similar equipment, and from information in the press and discussions with sales personnel in medical supplies companies, the consultant came to the conclusion that the European market for the product was about 130 million units per year, with about 26 million in the United Kingdom. Discussion with United Kingdom suppliers showed considerable resistance to change, since the purchasing specifications of the national health system stipulated low prices and rigid technical requirements. Considerable supplies came from Italy, but these were at the cheaper end of the price range so it was decided to contact two of the larger German manufacturers who were interested in a high quality product.

Contacts by telephone, followed up by descriptive literature, led to a meeting with the market leader who felt that the idea was worth following up. A disclosure agreement was signed to ensure that the company would not abuse any information disclosed during the negotiations. The university then produced a small number of prototype units, which were tested in simulated clinical conditions by the prospective licensee.

After successful completion of the trials, the parties met to negotiate an option agreement to cover further development. Under this agreement,

Managing the Licensing Agreement

the licensee agreed to pay a disclosure fee to allow the university to finance further tests and modifications to suit the device for large-scale manufacture and further undertook to fund the production of a test batch of 10 000 units.

The option lasted for nine months, and successful completion of manufacturing and market tests would lead to the licensee obtaining worldwide rights to the invention. The period of the option was chosen so that the university would be able to proceed with patent registration in a number of markets if things seemed to be going well.

The university usually started royalty negotiations at a rate of about five per cent of sales but, in view of the price pressure on the product, this was later reduced to a sliding scale below two per cent. Since the prospective licensee was funding the development of the final product, the disclosure fee would be offset against future royalties.

There was considerable discussion on the status of inventions made during the collaboration. It was agreed that the university would give the licensee first refusal on all improvements made by the university during the option period, while any registerable improvements made jointly would be jointly registered and owned by both parties.

During the option period, the terms of the licence agreement were to be negotiated. This would include a period of exclusivity for the licensee, in which it would have the chance to develop a market for the products. Minimum royalty rates were agreed as a guarantee of performance. If these were not achieved in the year concerned, the agreement would become non-exclusive. Agreement was reached in principle on all these matters, but the production tests took longer than anticipated, so that the parties had to meet again to agree an extension of the option period, subject to an addition to the disclosure fee payment on a monthly basis.

During the development period, new information came to light on the medical requirements for the use of the equipment, and the emphasis of the development was changed towards use in mobile systems, such as emergency ambulances and field hospitals. At this stage the option expired, and the parties agreed to reassess their positions.

Although the collaboration has not yet led to a final agreement, it served to finance the full-scale production and market assessment of the invention by the university. At the same time, the prospective licensee was able to gain rapid access to a new technology which may well have future potential in its core market.

4

4.5 Personnel and other services for licensor and licensee

To match the organization called for in an earlier chapter (4.1), both licensor and licensee need to recruit and train specialist staff who will develop the skills for negotiating and operating an agreement effectively. This chapter looks at recruitment, conditions of employment, training and other management services.

4.5.1 RECRUITMENT, STAFFING AND CONDITIONS OF EMPLOYMENT

The adoption of the licensing strategy brings with it a change in the culture of the licensor and the licensee companies. In particular, the fulfilment of the obligations under the licence agreement may mean that production or research staff who were recruited for one specialist activity within the company may have to spend long periods away from home, and carry out training and management functions for which they were not originally employed. At the same time these foreign assignments are not permanent and one advantage of licensing is that it does not tie up qualified personnel indefinitely.

The personnel department needs to ensure that suitable provisions are made for staff who are away from home for long periods, including arrangements for travel and health insurance. In some countries, staff from foreign companies carrying out training functions still have to get temporary work or residence permits. The trade unions in the companies of either partner may object to members of other companies working on their premises, even when performing a training function. There was one case in which a production expert from a European licensor was prevented from operating machines in the factories of an American licensee. Local union officials took the view that he could instruct on the process, but not do the work of a local employee.

Attention should also be given to the training of company members visiting foreign countries to fulfil the terms of a licence agreement. In particular, they should be given guidelines on how to handle exceptional circumstances which may arise. For example, a junior lab technician

Managing the Licensing Agreement

from the licensor company may be suddenly confronted with a serious breakdown at the licensee's plant. Without suitable discipline, he might well be drawn into trying to solve problems which are outside his authority and expertise. Similarly, a visiting sales manager might be expected to make judgments on the quality of the licensee's products, which he or she is unqualified to do.

The personnel department may also become involved in the health and welfare of foreign visitors. Considerable strains were placed upon the senior management of a European licensor when the president of their largest Far Eastern licensee fell seriously ill during a routine visit. Since the patient was too ill to return to his country, nursing staff and medicines had to be flown out to ensure a suitable standard of care.

On a less dramatic note, it can be quite difficult to ensure suitable recreation opportunities during weekends and holidays for visiting trainees who may have limited financial resources and who do not speak the local language. Questions of standard of accommodation and the type of food to be provided should also be discussed between the partners well in advance. Various groups of trainees from Eastern European countries visiting factories in Western Europe preferred to be accommodated in simple furnished rooms with cooking facilities rather than to stay in expensive hotels. In this way they were able to gain greater benefit from their limited supplies of Western currency. On the other hand, it is difficult for many European and United States nationals to entertain Japanese guests on the lavish scale which is usual in many Japanese companies.

Apart from the normal laws of hospitality, each licensing partner has a general duty of care towards visiting executives or trainees and some attention should be paid to the needs and problems of foreign visitors who are away from their homes and families for substantial periods of time.

Once a licensing strategy becomes part of the company culture, recruitment policies should be changed to include wherever possible a provision that employees may be asked to spend periods of (say) six months per year abroad, or to ensure that linguistic and communication skills are included in key job specifications.

4.5.2 Training

The training requirements for setting up and operating a licensing operation vary according to the size of the company. The same functions need to be fulfilled but, as we have seen in Chapter 4.1, the degree of resources committed to each function depends on the overall scope of the activity. A large company with a small licensing activity may have a smaller training requirement than a small company suddenly catapulted into agreements with several licensees.

Although we will concentrate primarily on the licensor, the training needs of the licensee are similar.

STARTING FROM SCRATCH

If an individual inventor or a small company were to start from zero, the most important thing would be to find a good patent agent with experience in the field of activity, and a lawyer with a proven track record in preparing and defending licence agreements. Sources of information might be the Licensing Executives Society, the Institute of Licensing Practitioners, larger chambers of commerce, specialist legal advisers and patent agents.

The patent offices of most countries produce information on how to prepare and register patents and trademarks, and there are a number of courses from one day introductions to detailed seminars lasting one week or more to familiarize the newcomer with various aspects of protecting and exploiting intellectual property. The number and quality of such training activities will depend on the other priorities (in time and money) of the individual or company concerned but, in general, small companies tend to underestimate the importance of proper protection of their knowhow and proper agreements for its

Managing the Licensing Agreement

exploitation. More than in any other field, loose arrangements based on a handshake and an exchange of letters written by non-experts can cause enormous problems if the invention later becomes a success.

It is relatively cheap and easy to file a patent application, and even an amateur should do this before showing his invention to anyone. Potential backers, subcontractors, competitors, business partners have all been known to misappropriate ideas with good earning potential aided by the goodwill, relative inexperience and limited finances of the inventor.

One off-putting factor for the smaller company is the sheer cost of good advice: an inventor in London who wished to warn off a potential infringer was quoted a fee of £300 per hour by a firm of solicitors solely for examining the papers.

However, it is possible to find firms who will adjust their rates to the pocket of the plaintiff and at least advise on whether it is worth taking the matter further. In this respect, firms in larger provincial towns with lower overheads and a less affluent clientele often charge more reasonable rates than their counterparts in national or regional capitals.

Training for a complete beginner is therefore more a question of familiarization with the issues and problems involved, and finding the right advisors, than of trying to acquire instant expertise. Contracts for the sale of goods, and even basic property conveyancing are relatively straightforward, and can be undertaken by a careful amateur, but contracts for the exploitation of intellectual property are much more varied and complex.

Training in a smaller company

In a small German engineering company the technical director was its most capable representative in almost all activities. He had added considerably to the company's patent coverage, was its best designer and technical salesman, and carried out licensing negotiations together with the company's owner.

When he prepared for retirement, his understudy had to be trained. The successor was a metallurgist, and had been involved in production and design. He was put in charge of the design departments to gain technical expertise in the application of the company's knowhow to practical problems, including technical discussions with customers and their commercial implications in terms of pricing. He then began to take over the correspondence with the company's patent agent on existing patents and trademarks, and later concerning new patent applications.

Over a period of eighteen months, he attended a structured set of one and two day courses on the law of contract, the protection of intellectual property, legal aspects of the licensing agreement and negotiation. Through his technical contacts with customers and licensees, he improved his command of English.

The aim of this training was not to make him an expert on the intricacies of exploiting intellectual property, but to teach him enough to hold informed conversations with the patent agent and to provide the patent agent with the best information to further the company's objectives.

He was then given various projects of liaison with and visits to the company's overseas licensees. These involved technical sales support, arranging training programmes, with particular emphasis on reaching practical conclusions with the licensees, agreeing a programme, reporting to his company and supervising the implementation.

The next stage was to involve him in the renegotiation of part of a licence, where he worked together with his manager, but was responsible for reporting and implementing the changes in the agreement. The reporting element included the preparing of the brief for the company's intellectual property solicitor and vetting the agreement text to ensure that the technical and commercial aims of the company had been fulfilled. He was also introduced to the company's auditors

Managing the Licensing Agreement

and bankers who, as the company's financial advisors, vetted the agreements for problems arising from taxation and exchange control.

Through supervising and re-negotiating existing agreements, he familiarized himself with the issues involved and built up a good working relationship with the company's advisors, so that on the retirement of the technical director, he was able to take up responsibility for the whole of the licensing activity.

It is unlikely that it would be worth a small company employing its own full-time patents officer or intellectual property solicitor unless the daily volume of work over the years makes it economically defensible.

The method of hiring an in-house technical expert who takes on most of the control and liaison functions connected with the exploitation of intellectual property may be varied according to the needs and history of the particular organization.

An alternative to the technical expert taking responsibility for the licensing activity would be to choose a member of the commercial or legal department. The training programme would be similar as far as attendance at courses on patents, trademarks and licensing and collaboration with in-house or external financial and taxation advisors are concerned, but in the case of a non-technician, attention should be paid to familiarization with the technical and research activities of the company. In some cases, the commercial specialist is provided with a partner from the technical side in order to ensure that he or she is properly briefed on technical matters. The commercial specialist may also be a regular participant at meetings on monthly research and development progress or on factory technical planning. It is important that the individual concerned is understood to be a useful member of the technical team and not felt to be a spy from another section of the company.

Due to the breadth of exposure to the whole of the company's activities, such roles require individuals of unusual mental flexibility; they are excellent stepping stones to a general management function.

Other training requirements are likely to arise in the departments responsible for providing the training under the agreement. There is a considerable difference between training one's own employees, who have a familiar educational background and a minimum of communication difficulties, and training individuals from other companies or countries, who start from a different factory or national culture.

Hence, engineers, scientists and commercial specialists who have to become trainers of licensee staff need to be made aware of the problems of the staff of the other company, with especial emphasis on the need to check regularly that the teaching has been fully understood, both factually and in its wider implications.

TRAINING IN A LARGER COMPANY

Once the volume and frequency of licensing activities justifies it, a company is likely to appoint an in-house patents officer or an in-house solicitor to deal with the protection of intellectual property and licensing matters.

In the first instance, it is probably better to recruit suitable staff ready trained, perhaps from another business enterprise in a similar field, or from a professional practice.

The training for these newcomers will be in the form of familiarization with the company's activities and culture. Again, the provision of liaison partners from research and factory departments and the attendance at routine progress and planning meetings, will enable them to remain fully informed about the technical resources of the company. It is frequently necessary not only to know the status quo, but also the direction of development of a company if one is to avoid giving away access to future possibilities.

An even larger volume of work may make it necessary to employ or develop sales personnel to specialize in selling licences and associated plant and equipment, skilled negotiators, project managers and even

Managing the Licensing Agreement

translators able to cope with the technical jargon of the particular industrial or service sector.

One very important individual is the licensing engineer. In many different companies, we have encountered this skilled technician, with years of experience in the licensor's factories and a love of travel and other cultures. He (and, in particular cases in a shoe factory and a transport company, she) typically has a background in one of the armed services, the merchant navy or an airline. He or she is a reliable and methodical worker, who can be depended upon to dispatch daily faxes reporting the progress and problems of the previous day, and who is typically a Mr or Ms Fix-it – they can solve many practical problems on their own initiative. On the other hand, they know when they are reaching the limits of their own capability or authority and will check with their managers before exceeding them. They are also well respected in many departments in their own company and can often solve problems by means of a well-targeted telephone call rather than involving kilometres of red tape. Any company planning a substantial commitment to licensing should endeavour to develop or recruit such individuals (Mr or Ms Fix-it) at an early stage.

The greater the involvement of the company in licensing, the greater the requirement for a full-time licensing or business development manager or director. At this level the activity covers a considerable element of strategic planning, investment analysis and interaction with many other company functions at a corporate level. Product design, sales policy, international pricing, the organization of international sales or licensees' conferences all require the formulation and agreement of policy with other departments. The whole business policy of the licensor company becomes affected: does one continue certain minor but expensive research projects in-house or farm them out to licensees in lower cost economies? Does one continue the local production of older product versions or, much as VW relinquished production of the Beetle to its Brazilian subsidiary, extend its life by having it produced by a licensee?

The recruitment profile and training for the licensing manager become increasingly those for an able general manager, responsible for steering a team of specialists and obtaining information and services from other departments of the company. In many larger companies, such an individual, given a staff of 50 or 100 specialists, can be responsible for as much of the company's profit as the manager of a large factory or division.

Training for the licensee

Training for the licensee is very much the mirror image of the situation with the licensor. A licensee reading the above descriptions can readily imagine an opposite number to each of the roles described.

At the one person level, the licensee will need to consult experts to check that the knowhow he or she is buying is properly protected and that the agreement is fair from the company's point of view. As far as the absorption and application of the knowhow are concerned, the licensee is in a good position; it should understand its own business and can presumably learn quickly the key aspects of the business of any licensing partners. The most serious danger is the difference of scale between the two operations: if a one person licensee has to absorb information from a large licensor with many departments and individuals, the relationship may suffer from the sheer complexity of communication. Also the small operator is unlikely to have learned some of the discipline in recording and documenting information which are necessary for an efficient transfer of technology.

In larger licensee companies, problems may arise in the inward transfer and dissemination of knowhow. In a manufacturing project in Nigeria, the Nigerian licensee sent seven young graduate engineers and technicians to the French licensor for training. According to the local system, these were fairly privileged individuals from the leading families of their district.

They were probably a reasonable choice – they were familiar with the technology, had some practical manufacturing experience and succeeded

Managing the Licensing Agreement

in learning enough French to communicate.

However some of them had had no experience of operating machinery on the shop floor and there was a status problem when they had to be trained by manual workers in the French factory. It was difficult for them to accept that they (university trained specialists) had to learn from individuals whom they felt to be their social and educational inferiors.

The difficulties were further compounded when the male graduates returned to Nigeria and had to teach some of the process steps to unskilled female operators. Although the graduate trainees had by then mastered the mechanics of the process, they explained it in theoretical terms, and were not good at demonstrating the manual skills and quality checks; as someone aptly put it, 'they understood the theory but not the choreography'. In social terms, it was not acceptable to the Nigerian factory to send their women to France so, after much debate, it was decided that a female supervisor should be sent from France to train the Nigerian women operatives and the process was introduced successfully.

The licensee equivalent of the licensing engineer is an individual with a good knowledge of his company, an ability to communicate with the licensor's personnel, and who can be relied upon to get things done in his or her own organization. He or she will make sure that all the plant is set up and raw materials are available before the licensor's trainers arrive, that notes are written by the trainees to supplement training manuals, or that any subsequent operating difficulties are recorded and communicated to the licensor for resolution. This individual convinces by the quality of his or her actions and not by excuses.

Finally, in the licensee's company it is equally important to a certain stage that the licensing operation is run by competent generalists who can get the necessary support at the strategic level. They need to look at whether the company should start developing its own knowhow, and licence it back to the partner and other licensees. They should also look at other options to the purchase of captive plant and machinery from the licensor once the process is proven and operating well.

As the licensee's company develops, there will be many areas of potential conflict with the licensor: should the licensee export? To what countries and customers, at what prices? How should it advertise? – emphasizing its relationship with the licensee, or under its own identity?

When dealing with individuals working at corporate level, it is more a question of developing the understanding and scope of activity of an available or specially recruited manager than of training a person in a narrow sense. In such a role, a general understanding of the business and the market and an ability in project management are more important than the acquisition of particular skills.

If there is a training manager in the company, then the training audit should include the needs of the inward or outward licensing activity. Economies may be achieved by realizing when a particular training course being arranged for other functions or departments may be applicable to the licensing staff or even to personnel from the licence partner.

The training department can also use its expertise in organizing and documenting the training activities necessary for the fulfilment of the licensing contract.

In some companies with extensive licensing activities, it is necessary to separate licensing training from the internal company training function, so that a specialized department deals exclusively with the inward and outward training, concentrating on the special needs of trainees from other industrial sectors and other countries and cultures.

Where the provision of training is stipulated in the licence agreement, it is rare that the qualifications and status of the trainees and the precise methods and standards of training are satisfactorily defined. Before training commences, the partners should agree on where the training is to be carried out (in whose factory, in the training workshop, in the laboratory or on the production line), who should be trained (managers

Managing the Licensing Agreement

and supervisors who often have better language and communication skills, or actual operators who will have to carry out the process later), and the quality of training (the standard of comprehension and skill that should be achieved by each of the trainees).

The problem most frequently encountered in training is the choice of level of the trainers and trainees. The licensee may be tempted to send managerial and supervisory staff for training in hands-on production processes, although they may not have operated machinery for a number of years, and may not actually be the people best qualified to train operatives. The choice of trainer and trainee may also lead to status conflicts, such as when a 45 year old department manager is being instructed by a 21 year old machinist. Once again, wherever the budget permits, a team approach should be adopted in training. It should be ensured that as far as possible direct operators, supervisory and managerial staff receive training from trainers of equivalent status.

The duration and standard to be achieved by training should also be defined between the partners before training commences. Paradoxically, training is often seen as a burdensome overhead and a licensee who spends a million dollars on licensing a new process may quibble about an extra week's training for an operator at a cost of a few hundred dollars above budget. This amount of money could be lost in minutes if the operator later produces a batch of faulty products.

One training related aspect which also needs careful consideration is the scope of the information to be provided to trainees. This is particularly important in the case of licences covering restricted aspects of the production of one of the partners. It may be important to avoid the situation where trainees of the other party gain access to research information or production details concerning products not covered by the licence. This may not be a problem where training can take place in a specific laboratory or training workshop, but may lead to unavoidable tensions and conflicts of interest when training takes place in an area where work is being carried out on significant areas of secret technology, although in certain cases a partner has gone so far as to curtain off certain parts of the production area.

Finally, some form of certification of achievement of a training standard should be agreed and signed by both parties. This is very important for avoiding recriminations at a later stage when quality or process difficulties may occur. As one sees in the repair workshops of Volkswagen or Ford dealers, certificates of achievement of a required training standard can also play a significant role in spreading confidence among the ultimate users of the product or service supplied under the agreement.

4.5.3 Management services

The training and recruitment policies should be framed to provide the management services that the licensee requires but further strengthening is often required. However carefully a licensee is vetted before a contract is signed, it is taking on a large addition to its business and management problems do arise especially if it is unwilling to incorporate new services which increase overheads.

As well as developing the personnel department itself, the project will require production skills in planning and control. It may also need new facilities in distribution and scheduling.

A vital facility will be the ability to incorporate new techniques like just-in-time management.

4.6 The relationship between the licensor and the licensee

Companies bring together people internationally with large differences in values but small differences in practices.

These days when international deals are commonplace and are negotiated by executives who fly in the same aircraft to similar airports to stay in identical hotels and to do most of their business in the same language, it is hard to believe that other people's countries are not just an extension of one's own. The similarities are a trap for all negotiating internationally, they are an especial trap for those who have to negotiate and organize the delicate relationship required by a licensing project. No effort to get to grips with cultural differences is wasted including the reading of the excellent and practical book by Hofstede who is quoted at the head of this chapter. Many countries have courses aimed at helping executives to understand other ways of life (an example in Britain is Farnham Castle in Surrey, see the Centre for International Briefing in Appendix 7.3) and embassies and other national organizations can usually help. The need for this help is underlined by the stereotypes by which we have all been conditioned. Along with this necessary, if often-repeated, reminder of the need to equip oneself for negotiating across invisible but barely penetrable cultural boundaries must go a warning against exaggeration. Oversensitivity to local feelings may appear patronizing and sensitivities may be upset by too close a regard to out-dated susceptibilities. 'We are not as primitive as you seem to think' may be a more damaging comment than 'we don't do that here'.

The school of thought (outlined in Chapter 3.3) that suggests that the licence agreement should be taken as the blueprint for organizing the relationship will form the basis of this chapter. Depending on the size and scope of the arrangement, this view is prudent. Because a knowhow or licensing agreement may extend for a considerable length of time (30 or even 50 years is not unusual for the length of a successful licensing relationship) both parties must ensure that their policies are properly formulated, communicated, enacted and supervized for a

Managing the Licensing Agreement

business that may have to pass through many hands during its lifespan. This in turn means that some appropriate form of recording the licensing activities must be set up. When conflicts arise, it is often important to find a particular product specification sent from A to B five years earlier and the contract may have to be consulted many times. Files should be kept on correspondence, reports on meetings between the parties and documentary evidence on the fulfilment of particular provisions of the licence – if a process manual is sent to the licensee, the licensor should record somewhere that the licensee did indeed receive the document in good order. Where communication must take place in a foreign language, fast and dependable translation services are essential. In general, it is easiest for the parties to communicate in their native languages and leave the recipients to translate it for their own use. This is frequently a safer option than trying to find someone in the sender's country who can translate highly complex commercial and technical information into the language of the recipient.

If it is necessary to communicate both ways in a single language, it is as well for both parties to be aware that translation errors can occur.

The contact between the technical departments is all the more important where there is cross-licensing. A danger is that the 'contact' takes the form of a mass of technical documentation despatched at irregular intervals and which the licensee staff have little time to read. Even if there is time, the literature may well be framed in a language and a thought form which is not understood by the licensee. The language of the natural sciences, with its recognizable formulae, may be universal but most documents are written in a way that is considered **culture-bound** and makes assumptions about the beliefs and customs of the readers.

To say that there is no substitute for face to face meetings is not necessarily to say that an immense amount of travel is required – although it is at present. As the technology develops, a greater use of video-conferences and video-telephones may replace some of the endless programme of time-consuming meetings demanded by the conscientious licensor. The following paragraphs set out who makes contact with whom in the two enterprises.

In terms of the organization options for the licensor set out in an earlier chapter (Figure 4.1.1), the contacts will vary in the following ways. (The numbers correspond with those in the diagram.)

1 **Legal**. Where the chain of command to the licensing department runs through the company secretary's department, there is occasional contact between the chief executive or the company secretary and the licensee's chief executive. More regular contact will be made by the managers of the legal, patents and licensing sub-departments; with whom they normally communicate depends on the setup in the licensee company. Each will develop a relationship with an appropriate manager if not an exact opposite number.
2 **Marketing**, where the chain of command passes through the head of marketing. In this case, again, there is occasional contact between the chief executive or the head of marketing of the licensor and the licensee's chief executive. More regular meetings will be between a head of the licensing sub-department and the chief executive of the licensee along with the head of marketing, while subordinates in both marketing and sales departments will also establish contact. There will also be meetings between the technical officers in the licensee and executives responsible for patents and licensing services in the design and manufacturing departments of the licensor.
3 **Design**, where the chain of command passes through the head of design. In this case, parallel to the others, there will be occasional meetings between the chief executive or the head of design in the licensor and the chief executive of the licensee.

All these organization options imply a continuous dialogue between the named departments in the two organizations; in each of these departments, several staff are likely to be involved.

The purpose of the dialogue is to solve a major problem of licensing deals – the need for staff with different skills and disciplines to work together with conflicting business cultures and rival commercial

Managing the Licensing Agreement

interests in each partner as well as between the two. The commercial interests of licensor and licensee are likely to conflict but the technical interests of the scientists and engineers which are often divisive within each partner are likely to bridge the gap between the two. A related problem is caused by unrealistic forecasts on the part of those same engineers who anticipate market share and income in foreign markets which has never been achieved at home; one of the authors of this book records the following experience when:

> companies, which themselves have less than ten per cent market share and make less than ten per cent profit before tax at home, set up business plans for unknown foreign markets involving 25 per cent market share after five years and demanding a 7.5 per cent royalty on sales.

With new inventions it is difficult to distinguish between promise and profit.

In the case of **cross-licensing,** the dialogue is expected to be even more intense with ideas flowing backwards and forwards for new products and more methods of implementing plans. Companies that undertake cross-licensing usually have large research and development expenditures and a high degree of product diversification (according to Mario Telesio; see the reading list at the end of this book, Appendix 7.2).

The secret of a successful licensing arrangement lies in negotiating a workmanlike agreement, maintaining good personal relationships, and ensuring proper documentation. It is recommended that the relationship between the partners is actively managed with the same care as all other aspects of the agreement. Frequently communication costs are seen as undesirable overheads and insufficient time and money is invested by the senior managers of licensing partners in ensuring good communication.

The nature of a successful licensing arrangement – as is emphasized elsewhere – is the exploitation of a strategic opportunity rather than the sale of a specific end product. Bearing in mind that the partners are independent companies with different strategic objectives, separated by distance, language and culture, it is not surprising that conflicts occur within the partner companies as already indicated (in 4.1.2), at the interface between licensor and licensee, and at the interface between either partner and its trading environment.

However good the agreement and the organization of the partners, it is their desires and intentions which will decide the success or failure of the agreement in the long term.

One of the main reasons for the failure of agreements is the non-achievement of sales targets by the licensee. It may be that, in the initial market research, these targets were falsely assessed in the first place. It could also be that the licensee has taken on the product with a hidden agenda of blocking the market to the licensor and promoting its own products in the meantime. If the sales targets were indeed mistaken from the outset, it might be better for the parties to agree new targets and to continue their relationship, since the time and effort involved in finding new partners would be wasted. On the other hand, if the licensor has good reason for believing that the licensee is incompetent or is frustrating the agreement, the sooner it takes measures to remedy the situation the better.

It is extremely difficult to judge the rights and wrongs of some of these issues if the partners never meet after the initial training period. It is therefore prudent to legislate in the agreement for at least an annual meeting between senior managers of the two parties in order to review the progress of the agreement. Providing that the financial scope of the agreement merits the cost, such meetings are a good investment of time and money to ensure that operational conflicts are resolved at a strategic level.

A well-organized licensing executive or licensing department within a company will ensure that a monthly report is presented to senior management, outlining key data on the progress of the relationship and giving early warning of any impending conflicts.

Managing the Licensing Agreement

It is also prudent to recognize that not every licence agreement should be regarded as a precursor to a long-term relationship: in the case of licences between competitors, a licence may represent a realistic solution to a relatively short-term problem, and it may be in the interests of both parties to allow the agreement to expire when it has run its course. On the other hand, there are many cases when a licensing relationship has led to further agreements with wider scope or where one party takes up a minority shareholding in the other, or when such an agreement has provided the preliminary to a later takeover. Indeed, many agreements contain option clauses whereby the partners outline the terms for mutual investment or takeover in certain eventualities.

The licensing strategy and expectations of each partner may change in different phases of its development as a company. A small production company with good marketing skills may choose to buy in knowhow to provide a fast track entry into a new product range. Once it is established in the market, it may decide to carry out its own research and development activities in preference to buying in knowhow. At a later stage it may revert to licensing in ideas as part of its marketing strategy in order to protect and develop whole portfolios of products. This is often the aim in cross-licensing agreements between some of the large pharmaceutical, chemical and petro-chemical companies working in mature markets where innovations only affect minor aspects of production technology or product performance. Indeed, once it has developed its own resources for producing new technology, the original licensee company may wish to become a licensor in its own right. For this reason some long term licensing contracts legislate for the buyback of technological improvements by the licensor from the licensee.

In managing the relationship between licensing partners, it is useful that each side forms its own opinion on the position of its own company and its partner company in the make or buy cycle in licensing technology.

4

Problems

The progress of a project frequently leads to problems and these can be the result of success just as easily as the fruits of failure. Fortunately the former are easier to cope with than the latter. Success, for instance, raises the sights of both partners. The licensee may be looking to even more product adaptations to suit changes in its growing market while adaptations to a product that is successful at home cause heart searching on the part of the licensor. This problem is solved by close attention to changes in each market.

Problems to be anticipated and that commonly arise are listed in Chapter 6.2.

The transfer of technology

The main aim of a licensing agreement is to transfer technology from a possessor to a purchaser. The difficulty of ensuring that the knowledge and its accompanying skills do actually come into the possession of the licensee is one of the main problems.

One author (Helen Hughes in *Achieving Industrialization in East Asia*) distinguishes between the **formal** and the **informal** means of transferring technology. Most readers of this book will be glad to know that a reduction in the price of the formal means that the informal (we might call it piracy) becomes less attractive. Licensors would do well to remember that the imposition of costly restrictions and – it might be added – an unwillingness to reduce the licensee's costs by not providing adequate support and training, may bring back informal methods of transfer. The author goes on to say that the costs of formal licensing (for both parties) have been much reduced in a country like South Korea where access to markets and marketing skills already exist for the licensee.

Part 5

Licensing in Specific Countries and Regions

The issues for industrialized countries whose enterprises seek licensing (and more frequently cross-licensing) agreements to broaden their already extensive technological bases are different from those in developing countries where the main object is to import foreign technology to build up new businesses. In the developing and former communist countries the agreements are also vital to national development and government intervention is to be expected.

The field of registering, protecting and licensing intellectual property – throughout over a hundred countries which are actively involved in international trade – presents a complex and constantly changing scene. There are over 500 specialist journals, newsletters and reports which are regularly published on patents alone. A similar volume of international publications is devoted to trademarks and new areas of activity, such as computer software and biotechnology, are also generating their share of literature.

Although it is fashionable to talk about global trends, it must be borne in mind that the needs of particular countries at different stages of economic development are vastly different; although the general effect of the liberalization of trade, particularly under the influence of the United States, has been a growing trend towards free trade and a removal of obstacles to the free exchange of goods and money across international boundaries, protectionist lobbies exist in most countries, reflecting the interests of parts of the labour force and of particular industry groupings.

The reaction between the forces of free trade and protectionism can be seen in the prolonged negotiations in the current round of GATT

Licensing in Specific Countries and Regions

talks, or the fact that Canada is currently delaying the finalization of the North American Free Trade Area (NAFTA) agreements between the United States, Canada and Mexico in order to prevent the export of jobs to Mexico from further north.

The end of the cold war between the former USSR and the West has shifted not only the balance of political power, but the economic equilibrium of the former COMECON economies. This brings with it a trend in the western states bordering the European Union to turn to the richer western markets, rather than the markets to the east, which (although rich in natural resources) are currently much less developed economically. New groupings are also emerging based on linguistic affinity, as a number of former members of the USSR now look for associations with Turkey on the one hand or Iran on the other.

The economic development of the Chinese speaking block of the People's Republic of China, Taiwan and Hong Kong will have far-reaching consequences in the next century, while young and eager labour forces in Korea, Thailand, Indonesia, Malaysia and other countries of south-east Asia are pulling the balance of economic activity to the east. Those of us who have been involved in international trade since the sixties have seen enormous changes in the economic development of individual countries and their role in world trade. India, for example, has made enormous progress in developing from a largely agricultural subsistence economy towards a technology based economy anticipating and meeting the needs of its population. India – and other countries such as Taiwan and Korea which formerly depended heavily on the imports of technology, knowhow and equipment – are now beginning to licence out and export technologies in their own right.

Another tug-of-war is occurring between the opposing forces of regulation and de-regulation. Formerly, with the so-called planned economy countries (mainly COMECON) and protected economies such as Brazil and India, the licensing process had two or even three distinct stages: the first was to assess the business opportunity, find a partner and agree terms. The second was to obtain approvals from the various ministries responsible for economic planning and development and exchange control. If the import of plant, machinery and semi-finished products was involved, a third round of discussions had to be held with the authorities responsible for import controls and the transfer of foreign currency. Negotiations were often very complex because of the interactions between the various bodies involved, especially since the government authorities often saw themselves as watchdogs defending a line of government policy rather than facilitators aiding a necessary economic process.

The recent changes in Eastern Europe have been bewildering for international traders and knowhow practitioners at a time when every taxi driver seems to be an entrepreneur in his own right and the profit motive has oiled the wheels of bureaucracy.

Against this background, it is almost impossible to provide definitive listings of matters such as the period of duration of patents and trade marks, the precise details of exchange controls or taxation of royalties. The laws and regulations governing such matters both nationally and internationally are changing almost daily and the business executive involved in international licensing deals should consult the appropriate bulletins and journals which are updated on a monthly or quarterly basis or consult expert advisers.

What we are trying to achieve in this section is to sensitize the reader to the differences in dealing with various countries, or groups of countries, and the interplay of the different aspects of the licensing deal. From a practical viewpoint, these fall into five categories:

1   the registration and protection of intellectual property;
2   the notification and regulation of agreements concerning intellectual property;
3   exchange control;
4   taxation of royalties, knowhow fees and management fees; and
5   regulations on the import and export of goods and equipment, including regulations on transfer prices.

The information given is based on the most recent data and experience

Licensing in Specific Countries and Regions

available to the authors, but for the reasons given above the reader is advised to seek the latest update on any specific piece of information.

5

5.1 The industrialized countries (including the European Union)

The transfer of technology – inward, outward and within national boundaries – is a target for government action in most individual countries. Relevant policies exist in most countries as well as in the European Union and other groupings of economic interests.

5.1.1 THE EUROPEAN UNION AND THE EUROPEAN ECONOMIC AREA

The European Union, like its individual member states, has policies on transfer carried out by the SPRINT (Strategic Programme for Innovation and Technology Transfer) programme mainly designed for promoting the transfer of technology within the Union; schemes include: finance for technical innovation; technological cooperation between companies; innovation support services (establishing networks among specialists including licensing agents); and promotion of management techniques for innovation. Nine banks (two from Greece, two from Spain and one each from Ireland, Belgium, Italy, Britain and Denmark) joined a Technology Performance Financing Scheme and others are following.

Most of the reports arising from the SPRINT programme are not specifically concerned with licensing which yet remains a main method of buying and selling technology.

Most member countries also have incentives for the development of technical innovation. Spain has both regional and national as well as private sector schemes. Some years ago (in 1987) the European Commission published a report entitled *Supporting Structure for Innovation, Technology Transfer and Enterprise Creation in Spain and Portugal*.

Licensing agreements with outside countries and between member states are subject to a number of regulations, both of the Union as a whole and of individual governments. There may be differences between rules that apply to the licensing of patents and to **knowhow**

Licensing in Specific Countries and Regions

licences providing expertise. Union regulation stems mainly from the competition policy. A body of cases is being built up – and expert advice is required for individual agreements – but the principle is to disallow clauses which restrain trade by firms (licensees) registered within the Union. Relevant laws in member countries, like those on patenting, have tended to grow more alike although there are still notable differences.

Industrial countries restrict licensing agreements only indirectly by regulations about competition and about the transfer of technology. The latter mainly applied to the United States during the cold war period when the government prohibited the export of products and knowhow to socialist countries. The effect of competition (anti-trust) legislation on licensing agreements has already been mentioned in Chapter 3.1. This has been to exclude clauses which limit the areas in which the licensee can sell the products. The Treaty of Rome prohibits 'the limiting or controlling of production, markets, technical development or capital investment' and 'the sharing of markets or sources of supply'. The quotations are from Article 85 and prevent restrictions on the licensee's trade. There are some exceptions to this rule. For instance, within the Union (or with countries with which the Union has a free trade agreement) **active** selling (where a licensee seeks a customer) can be prohibited by an agreement, while **passive** selling (where a licensee responds to an order that comes out of the blue) cannot. Agreements for joint research are not prohibited.

COMPETITION LAW

Regulation 556/89 of the European Union Competition Law sets out the provisions allowed in a knowhow licence. It allows, for example, the granting of an exclusive territory to a knowhow licensee for certain fixed periods.

Under Article 85, the European Commission deems a no-challenge clause in a technology licensing agreement as anti-competitive because, as a result, there is a restriction on competition which deprives the licensee of possibilities which are available to everyone else. Any clause which restricts the exercise of the licence as opposed to the availability of the patent may be questioned under the competition regulations and this has been held to include the existence of a no challenge clause. Some restrictions are exempted under the Union's rules. For instance the uses of the product may be limited, perhaps as components in the licensee's own products.

It has been suggested that European regulations make a distinction between patents which of themselves provide a monopoly right in which case competition rules are likely to be more strictly interpreted, and other forms of protection for intellectual property rights such as copyright. (See Singleton, E. Susan, 'Intellectual property disputes: settlement agreements and ancillary licences under EC and UK competition law'. Readers seeking more information on settlement agreements should read this article and its cross references.)

All licences, whether negotiated in the usual way of business or whether agreed as a result of litigation, have to be examined in the light of European competition regulations. The scrutiny is designed to ensure that the licensee is only prevented from infringing the exact rights granted with the patent and that trade mark agreements avoid geographical limits where possible.

THE ROLE OF LICENSING

Licensing agreements play a less important role in the calculations of enterprises based in industrial countries than those in developing economies. They form an optional extra to be used when an asset cannot be viably exploited or protected in any other way. Thinking is biased towards direct investment, operating through foreign subsidiaries, rather than licensing. American writings usually emphasize two reasons for licensing. One is as a means of testing the market to check the viability of direct investment; the other is as a use for technology that is not central to the licensor's core business. The dangers of licensing, including that of promoting a competitor, are also emphasized.

Licensing in Specific Countries and Regions

Industrialized countries, by definition, have companies possessing research and development facilities and shortages of these facilities are considered problems to be corrected either by measures to foster them or by education and training for engineers.

EUROPEAN UNION REGULATION

Article 85 (on competition) is the main means by which agreements are regulated in European law to prevent the agreements reducing competition. The apparent rigour of the article has been modified by a number of 'Block Exemption Regulations'. That for licensing came into existence back in 1984. Various clues about how the regulations will be interpreted have been proposed but they must remain clues until more agreements have been tested. On principle, it appears, competition legislation is aimed at the effect of an agreement on the national or community economies rather than on the companies. The criterion is expected to be economic rather than legal. The regulations increasingly bar territorial restrictions in licensing agreements.

Council directive 89/104 sets out a structure and a timetable for the approximation of national trademark law. It was to have been implemented by 31 December 1992 in all the member states; some, including the United Kingdom, have not implemented the directive. The long awaited Trademarks Bill which was expected to implement the directive in the country had only just, at the time of going to press (December 1993), come before Parliament. Both content and timing of the United Kingdom implementing statute for the directives are thus unknown, although it is almost inevitable that significant changes to the administration of trademarks will be included, including the amalgamation of parts A and B of the register.

In the meantime, under the European Community Law Doctrine of Direct Effect, an individual (including a company) may rely on the provisions of the directive (or at least those provisions which are clear and unconditional and leave no discretion to the member state) in an action against the state (including an organ of it such as the British Trademarks Registry).

Under the European Law, Doctrine of Indirect Effect, even where the provision of the directive is not clear and unconditional or where it is to be enforced against an individual, relevant national law may be interpreted in accordance with the directive.

Finally, if an individual suffers loss as a result of a British failure to implement the directive a domestic action may lie against the United Kingdom under the so-called **Francovitch doctrine**.

A European applicant for a patent has a choice of three routes.

1   Under the Patents legislation of its country.
2   Under the European Patents Convention (EPC).
3   The Patent Co-operation Treaty (PCT).

A national patent alone will provide a fairly limited protection for a business which is likely to operate in markets including those outside the country, but it does provide certain advantages of priority for other applications made abroad, and represents an opportunity to test the water before making a series of expensive foreign patent applications. Also, if exploitation of an invention in Europe through licensing is envisaged, patent protection is likely to be important as a means of preventing unlicensed copying.

There is no such thing as a world patent. Separate national applications can be made in each foreign country likely to be significant in the exploitation of an invention. This will also involve instructing patent agents in each country. Once it is decided that patent applications are to be made in a couple of countries separate applications are likely to be expensive.

Licensing in Specific Countries and Regions

THE EUROPEAN PATENT CONVENTION (EPC)

A second route to patent protection abroad is to make an application under the European Patent Convention. Most Western European countries, the convention contracting states, are parties and an application filed under the convention will be effective in each of the states designated in the application. If granted, the effect of a convention patent is as one of a collection of separate national patents in the designated countries.

THE PATENT CO-OPERATION TREATY (PCT)

Where exploitation is to take place internationally the Patent Co-operation Treaty, to which the United Kingdom is a party together with 39 other states, is likely to be more appropriate. The application should designate the countries chosen. The Patent Co-operation Treaty is therefore a third route to a valid patent.

The European Patent Convention is not a European Union patent in the sense that it does not derive from the institutional structure of the European Union. It should be distinguished therefore from attempts to agree on the format for a community patent. Negotiations between member states led to the signing in 1975 of the Community Patent Convention (an agreement on the form of a community patent). The convention has not yet come into force because it has not been signed and ratified by all member states. Spain still has to sign. The convention (which is viewed as achieving the harmonization of patent laws and under which a single patent would be granted effective throughout the community) will come into force three months after it has been ratified by all member states.

There is no equivalent to the European Patent Convention or the Patent Co-operation Treaty for registered designs and there is, it is fair to say, some considerable divergence in design law and practice internationally. Local enquiry using either a local or United Kingdom patent agent will almost invariably be necessary.

European legislation has extended the protection of medicinal products beyond the usual 20 year life of a patent and it is now possible to apply for supplementary protection certificates throughout the Union. The maximum extension is for five years and certificates are granted by individual member states.

Design

There is no single unified approach to design law issues as yet in the European Union and the international divergence of design law is not significantly less at the level of the Union. The European Commission did publish in 1991 a green paper consultative document on the legal protection of industrial design and more recently has published further proposals. The document incorporated a draft directive on the harmonization of European Community design law and a draft regulation introducing Union wide right protection for designs both registered and unregistered. The European Commission's view is that it regards the diversity of national design law as unacceptable given that national design rights can in many circumstances be exercised to prevent free movement of goods, contrary to a fundamental principle of the single market.

Copyright

Subsequent to the European Commission's consultative green paper on copyright and the challenge of technology (1988), and a follow up green paper (1990), there has been vigorous discussion on the impact of new technologies on copyright and neighbouring rights, and considerable legislative activity. At least six directives have reached one stage or another in the Union's legislative process. Those not yet adopted or implemented include: a proposed draft directive dealing with home copying (a proposal for a blank tape levy at Union level which has run into considerable opposition); an amended draft directive on copyright and satellite broadcasting and cable re-transmission (which is proposed for implementation by member states by 1 January

Licensing in Specific Countries and Regions

1995); an amended draft directive on harmonization of the term of protection of copyright (likely to be for the life of the author plus 70 years and thus controversial as it will serve to divide the Union period of copyright protection from that applicable in most of the rest of the world); and a draft directive on the legal protection of databases (unlikely to be adopted prior to 1994 with implementation planned for 1996). Of those adopted the first is the directive on the legal protection of computer programmes. It has also been implemented in the United Kingdom. This confirms that computer software should be protected as a species of copyright (as a literary work) and permits reverse engineering for testing and study purposes and limited reproduction of code for a programme where it is indispensable to achieve the interoperability (working together) of an independently created computer programme with an earlier programme. The other directive is one on rental rights, lending rights and certain rights relating to copyrights. This has been adopted and is to be implemented by July 1994 in the member states. It will require that exclusive lending and rental rights be included as part of copyright in a work, including sound recordings and films and giving the same rights to performers.

The distinction between adoption and implementation is that adoption relates to the conclusion of the European Union legislative process and implementation refers to the date by which time the directive should have become law in the member state.

EUROPEAN ECONOMIC AREA

There are currently plans to set up a European Economic Area which would see the European Union and the European Free Trade Area joining to form a wider European organization concerned with economic and trade issues including intellectual property.

The delay in these developments is partly due to an unfavourable referendum which was held in Switzerland.

5

GROUP POLICY

The European Economic Area will harmonize legislation on intellectual property, licensing and the free movement of goods.

Members will be required to be signatories to the European Patent Convention, the Patent Co-operation Treaty and the Madrid Protocol on Trade Marks.

5.1.2 INDUSTRIALIZED COUNTRIES

CANADA

INTELLECTUAL PROPERTY INFRASTRUCTURE, LAW ON PATENTS, TRADEMARKS AND COPYRIGHTS

Provision for protection is similar to that in the United States and the European Community.

Legislation: Patent Act (1935, 1970); Trademarks Act (1953, 1970); Industrial Design and Union Label Act (1952, 1970).

Patents are granted by the Patent Office. Foreign manufacturers have priority over any application for the registration of a patent if the patent is already registered in the manufacturer's own country which is a signatory of the Paris Convention. Registration in Canada must be within 12 months of application for registration in country of origin.

Life of a patent is 20 years from date of application; after that time, the patent is in the public domain.

An application for a patent by a non-resident must be made by a representative who is resident in Canada.

Licensing in Specific Countries and Regions

The patent must be worked either directly or through a licensing agreement within three years of being granted. Failure to do so may lead to the patent rights being revoked or other applications being accepted for the same invention.

Trademarks cannot be registered until they are actually used (unless they have been registered and used in a country which is a signatory to the Paris Convention).

The holder of a registered trademark has exclusive rights for a term of 15 years which can be extended.

Designs and industrial models can be protected for a five year period which may be extended for a further five years.

The Patent Act requires the registration of exclusive patent licences. In practice, most agreements are not recorded and there is no penalty for non-compliance.

Compulsory licences cover the manufacture and export of patented products.

MEMBERSHIP OF OTHER MAJOR GROUPING

The North American Free Trade Area has been established with the United States and Mexico.

GOVERNMENT MINISTRY OR OTHER ORGANIZATION FOR TECHNOLOGY TRANSFER

The Department of Consumer and Corporate Affairs deals with all applications for registration of patents, trademarks, copyright and matters concerning industrial property.

Exchange control problems

None at present.

Taxation of royalties and knowhow payments including any problems

Royalties are subject to income tax and a withholding tax of 25 per cent if payable abroad.

Taxation of licensing agreements: exclusive patent licences and trademark registered users are subject to a fee of 100 Canadian dollars on recording of agreement.

Italy

Italy, with its long history of membership of the European Union, has largely adapted its systems for the registration and exploitation of different forms of intellectual property to the relevant European regulations. Profits and royalties can be remitted freely, although particular attention should be paid to the position on taxation. The authorities are wary of the payment of royalties, knowhow fees and management fees as methods of tax avoidance rather than as the results of genuine commercial requirements. On the other hand, there are tax incentives for innovation by small enterprises which may be considered in relation to technology transfer. The transfer pricing of raw materials, semi-finished components and finished products is also subject to particular regulations.

With regard to anti-trust law, Italy has substantially adopted the relevant European Community law, and Law No 287 of 10 October 1990 only applies to agreements and situations not covered by the appropriate European legislation (Articles 85 and 86 of the then European Community Treaty and related regulations). Prohibited agreements involve market distortions by means of fixing purchasing or selling

Licensing in Specific Countries and Regions

prices and other trading conditions, restricting production volumes and technical development, and the sharing of markets or sources of supply. These latter are all points which could affect various forms of licence and knowhow agreement, although the size and scope of economic activity is also taken into account in assessing the effect on the Italian market.

SPAIN

Spain is a good example of a country which has increasingly liberalized its trading position since entry into the European Community. It is a signatory of the European Patent Convention and the 1883 Paris Union Convention in the Stockholm version. Spain is reviewing its position under the Patent Co-operation Treaty and, for example, chemical and pharmaceutical products are now patentable but forms and methods of medical treatment are not.

Spain adopted the European Union trademark law with effect from 1 January 1993. The duration of a trademark has been reduced from twenty years to ten in line with European practice. The 1988 Spanish trade mark law updates the view of the economic importance of trademarks and strengthens possibilities for action against infringement and unfair competition. The 1987 Copyright Law also includes considerable attention to computer programmes, including their look and feel, their sequence, structure and organization. Micro codes are protectable. The position of knowhow and trade secrets is being reviewed but currently they are only protected by contract; licensing partners should ensure that the scope and nature of the knowhow to be transferred under an agreement is fully defined (where possible by means of drawings, diagrams and manuals) and that suitable secrecy provisions are included in the agreement binding both the company and (insofar as employment law permits) its employees.

We have described elsewhere the constant tension between protectionism and free trade which seems to be a permanent feature of world economic development. While subscribing to the general principles of free trade and free competition as outlined in the Treaty of Rome, Spain in its 1989 competition law has retained the possibility of distortions of trade where these would improve the competitiveness of a certain industry or where they would strengthen the position of small companies. This means that it may be possible to obtain authorization for licences and knowhow agreements which have restrictions on geographical markets or other commercial aspects.

Exchange control has also been one of the slowest aspects of the Spanish economy to be harmonized with European Union practice. In most cases, companies intending to transfer monies out of Spain must obtain prior authorization and verification through the DGTE (Direccion General de Transacciones Exteriores) on behalf of the Ministry of Economy and Finance through the medium of the Bank of Spain and other authorized banks.

The notification to the DGTE on Form TE-30 must include a full outline of the proposed deal and the parties; any supporting documentation must be available in Spanish.

This regulation applies to transfers by residents to non-residents (companies and individuals) in respect of royalties on, for instance, patents and trademarks, services provided by non-residents to residents and payments made by residents to non-resident organizations in respect of research and development in which the resident company may have a share or interest.

Similar regulations apply to payments in respect of the use of copyright although the lowest limit for notification is rather less than in the case of patents, trademarks and the rest.

It should be noted that payments from a Spanish subsidiary to a foreign parent company may be treated differently to payments to third parties since transfers between related companies may be regarded as transfers of profit. The question of taxation of remittances of royalties, knowhow fees and management fees should be investigated carefully before the agreement is submitted to the authorities, since the basis

Licensing in Specific Countries and Regions

for taxation may change according to how a particular payment is viewed.

Spain enjoys agreements on double taxation relief in line with the OECD model treaty with most of the main trading nations in the West and in Eastern Europe although, surprisingly, an agreement with China is still under negotiation.

TURKEY

CASE EXAMPLE: EUROPEAN LICENSING INSTRUMENT

A private Turkish company had imported products from foreign Company A for over 19 years and the relationship had proved to be very successful.

Company A were very happy with the Turkish company and the relationship which they had developed and identified the Turkish company as a key strategic player in their Mediterranean marketing plan. In addition, Company A also thought that, in the long term, the Turkish company would make a good subsidiary. This had been raised with the Turkish company, which had not really pursued the idea further.

The Turkish company subsequently decided to become involved in manufacturing, however it had virtually no experience in this area. To this end, it decided to licence one of Company A's products which they had sold and which had demonstrated a high level of sales.

Licensing negotiations were undertaken with relative ease on both sides, assisted greatly by the discussions and cooperation which took place between engineers from each of the companies. These engineers were the product champions and although the initial drive originated from Company A's engineer, it was quickly matched by that of the Turkish company. Both were committed to making the relationship work and succeeded in doing so, despite the fact that conditions in the Turkish manufacturing industry were primitive at that time.

The licence itself was structured to allow the Turkish company to enter the manufacturing of the product in various stages from importing full assemblies down to eventually manufacturing their own die-castings and most other parts.

Several years, and a successful licence relationship, later the Turkish company did indeed became a full subsidiary of Company A.

This case example was supplied by the Licensing Centre Ltd, Glasgow.

The United States

As the initiator of a high proportion of new patents and a leading operator in international technology transfer, the United States is also developing measures for a high level of protection for intellectual property. The existence of a higher court specializing in patent issues is frequently mentioned as an example.

The following are special characteristics of this country.

Intellectual property infrastructure, law on patents, trademarks and copyrights

Foreign companies and individuals are advised to protect intellectual property rights before licensing the manufacture of process or product abroad.

An application for a patent in one's own country should be made before making an application in the United States.

Life of a patent is usually for 17 years and is not renewable.

Licensing in Specific Countries and Regions

Trademarks can be protected for a ten year period which is renewable.

Copyright and mask work (the photographic image used to photo-etch printed circuits) is protected by the United States Semiconductor Chip Protection Act of 1984 and is renewable for a term of life plus 50 years.

It should be noted that in the United States the use of the copyright symbol and registration of copyright is a pre-requisite for protection, but the registration can be carried out at any time including just before the issuing of infringement proceedings.

Plants have been patentable since 1985. Since 1980, an application for a certificate for plants reproduced by seed allows exclusive rights over plants and any new varieties.

Life of protection is 18 years from the issue of certificate date.

Animal Welfare Act allows transgenic animals to be patented (excludes farm animals).

Manufacturing under Licence (MUL) arrangements can be established, covering technology, the manufacturing process and any products. MUL is defined as a contractual agreement between licensor and licensee. It allows the licensee the right to manufacture and sell or represent the patented product or process for a specified period.

An MUL agreement is enforceable under law, but United States Government approval is not necessary for such agreements with a foreign business. A Manufacturing under Licence agreement usually covers all the States, but licences can cover a limited area. The term of the licence is not set, agreements can run for an extended number of years.

Agreement should set out details of patent or trademark process which is covered by the licence. The licensee is usually able to determine how the product will be worked. Foreign companies need to negotiate for greater consultation by making provisions in the agreement.

A licensor can also inspect a product to ensure that it is of satisfactory quality and adheres to the terms of agreement.

MEMBERSHIP OF OTHER MAJOR GROUPING

The United States, Canada and Mexico are planning to establish a North American Free Trade Area (NAFTA) which will harmonize member states' intellectual property rights.

GOVERNMENT MINISTRY OR OTHER ORGANIZATION FOR TECHNOLOGY TRANSFER

Patents, trademarks and copyrights are issued by: the United States Patent and Trade Marks Office and the Copyright Office.

Registered trademarks and copyrights can be recorded with the United States Customs Service which ensures protection.

EXCHANGE CONTROL PROBLEMS

There are no exchange control problems as such but, due to the sheer size and diversity of the United States, companies are advised to research the potential market for patented products or processes and to check carefully the suitability and financial status of the partner before an exchange of technology or knowhow. Good knowledge of selling into the United States market is also necessary.

TAXATION OF ROYALTIES AND KNOWHOW PAYMENTS INCLUDING ANY PROBLEMS

Royalties are generally based on a percentage of net sales – usually

Licensing in Specific Countries and Regions

from five per cent of annual net sales to 0.5%, although they can be as high as ten per cent.

The licence may stipulate payment of a minimum annual royalty, to be paid by the licensee, irrespective of net sales.

The foreign licensor may be required to contribute part of its royalty for the marketing of the product in the United States.

Royalties may be based on output or use of licensing rights.

There are several possible sources of revenue for a foreign licensor: a lump sum payment as compensation for the transfer of licensed rights and technology; fees for any technical assistance provided to the licensee or work such as construction and engineering. There may also be an agreement of reciprocal licence rights on a royalty free basis.

Restrictions on the Kinds of Deals Permitted

The following cannot be patented: any invention which is contrary to public morality or health; any method of conducting business; computer related inventions; any invention whose sole use is to utilize nuclear material or atomic energy.

Both hardware and software computer technology are eligible for the same legal protections as other intellectual property. Because the development of computer technology is still in its early stages, however, application of existing legal protections is not yet well defined. A mask work is a new type of intellectual property, protected by the US Semiconductor Chip Protection Act of 1984. It is, in essence, the design of an electrical circuit, the pattern of which is transferred and fixed in a semiconductor chip during the manufacturing process. Mask works may be registered with the Copyright Office for a non-renewable term of 10 years.

The vast majority of valuable technology is not patented. In fact, nearly all technology transfer agreements contain provisions for the transfer of non-patented knowhow. However, knowhow is recognized as a property right that may be transferred under contract and protected in court, subject to the same general prohibition against anti-competitive practices that apply to patents.

For further information foreign companies may write as appropriate to US Patent and Trademark Office, or the US Copyright Office, both in Washington.

Owners of registered trade marks and of registered copyrights can record these rights with the US Customs Service. This is relatively inexpensive, and provides the protection that imports of violative items will be liable to seizure and forfeiture as prescribed by the US Customs Regulations.

At the present time, the only protection US Customs can give a mask work is by means of an US International Trade Commission exclusion order, or court order directing denial of entry of violative items. However, regulations are currently in preparation which will permit the recordation of registered mask works with US Customs, thus giving them protection similar to that given to copyrights and trademarks.

5.2 Some regional and international organizations

A small selection of other regional trading organizations with a special interest in intellectual property are discussed here.

Table 5.2.1 gives details of membership of relevant regional and international organizations.

Table 5.2.1 Membership of regional and international organizations

This table sets out the principal members of some of the regional organizations and of countries which are not currently members. In both cases, membership of relevant international organizations is also given.

The following abbreviations are used.

ALADI: the Latin American Integration Assocation
ARIPO: the African Regional Industrial Property Organization
CARICOM: the Caribbean Community and Common Market
NAFTA: the North American Free Trade Area
OAPI: the African Intellectual Property Organization

The conventions or agreements are as follows.

Paris: the Paris Convention (1883) for the Protection of Industrial Property. General protection.

GATT: the General Agreement on Tariffs and Trade (a United Nations affiliate). Liberating trade.

Berne: the Berne Convention (1886) for the Protection of Literary and Artistic Works. Copyright.

Hague: the Hague Agreement (1925) concerning the International Deposit of Industrial Designs. Design.

Madrid: the Madrid Union (1891) concerning the International Registration of Marks. Trademarks.

Licensing in Specific Countries and Regions

Table 5.2.1 continued

Countries European Union	Paris	Convention/Agreement GATT	Berne	Hague	Madrid
Belgium	x	x	x	x	x
Denmark	x	x	x		
France	x	x	x	x	x
Germany	x	x	x	x	x
Greece	x	x	x	x	
Ireland	x	x	x		
Italy	x	x	x	x	x
Luxembourg	x	x	x	x	x
Netherlands	x	x	x	x	x
Portugal	x	x	x	x	x
Spain	x	x	x	x	x
United Kingdom	x	x	x	x	
Former COMECON					
Czech and Slovak Republics	x	x	x		x
Hungary	x	x	x	x	x
Poland	x	x	x		x
Romania	x	x			x
Yugoslavia	x	x	x	x	x
Australasia					
Australia	x	x	x		
New Zealand	x	x	x		
NAFTA					
Canada	x	x	x		
Mexico	x	x	x		
United States	x	x		x	
OAPI					
Benin	x	x	x	x	
Burkina Faso	x	x	x		
Cameroon	x	x	x		
Central African Republic	x	x	x		
Congo	x	x	x		
Gabon	x	x	x		

Table 5.2.1 continued

Guinea	x		x		
Ivory Coast	x		x		
Mali	x		x		
Mauritania	x	x	x		
Niger	x	x	x		
Senegal	x	x	x	x	
Tchad	x	x	x		
Togo	x	x	x		
ARIPO					
Botswana		x		x	
Gambia	x	x			
Ghana	x	x	x		
Kenya	x	x			
Lesotho	x	x	x	x	
Malawi	x	x	x	x	
Sierre Leone		x			
Somalia					
Sudan	x				x
Swaziland	x			x	
Tanzania	x	x			
Uganda	x	x			
Zambia	x	x	x		
Zimbabwe	x	x	x		
ALADI					
Argentina	x	x	x	x	
Brazil	x	x	x		
Paraguay					
Uruguay	x	x	x		
ANDEAN Pact					
Bolivia					
Colombia			x		
Ecuador			x		
Peru			x		
CARICOM					
Antigua and Barbuda		x		x	
Bahamas	x		x	x	

Licensing in Specific Countries and Regions

Table 5.2.1 continued

Barbados	x	x	x		
Belize		x		x	
Dominica					
Grenada					
Guyana		x			
Jamaica		x			
Montserrat					
St Kitts-Nevis					
St Lucia					
St Vincent & The Grenadines					
Trinidad & Tobago	x	x			
Turks & Caico Islands					
British Virgin Islands					
Others					
China	x				x
Indonesia	x	x	x	x	
Israel	x	x	x	x	
Japan	x	x	x	x	
Korea (North)	x				x
Korea (South)	x	x			
Malaysia	x	x			
Nigeria	x	x			
South Africa	x	x	x		
Taiwan					
Turkey	x	x	x	x	

5.2.1 NORTH AMERICAN FREE TRADE ASSOCIATION (NAFTA)

The NAFTA Agreement was signed in December 1992 by Canada, the United States of America and Mexico. The harmonization of national laws in the member states is to take effect by January 1994.

Members must meet the requirement of the Paris Convention, although greater protection than that laid out in this agreement is permitted.

Article 1709 of NAFTA states that patents shall be available and rights secured regardless of the field of technology or territory where the invention originally came from and whether the product was imported or locally produced.

Limited exceptions to this ruling include inventions which contravene public morality, plants, animals and other microorganisms and primarily biological processes for the production of plants or animals.

Competition

Inventions may not be excluded from patentability if exclusion is: 'based solely on the grounds that the party prohibits commercial exploitation in its territory of the subject matter of the patent'. (Paragraph 2, Article 1709). Paragraph 10 includes reference to anti-competitive practices including, for example, that a party is not obliged to apply the agreed conditions of article 1709 where the use of a patent is deemed to be anti-competitive.

5.2.2 The Association of South East Asian Nations (ASEAN)

ASEAN was formed in 1967 when Indonesia, the Philippines, Singapore, Thailand, Malaysia and later (in 1984), Brunei, signed the ASEAN Declaration.

In practice, there is little regional cooperation between the member states. The ASEAN Plan of Action on Science and Technology is a joint research body engaging in research in science, technology, agriculture, energy, manufacture and infrastructure development. ASEAN is still a long way from making significant moves to lift restrictions on the free movement of trade and intellectual property within the territory.

However, member states have signed the Manila Declaration which reads that:

Licensing in Specific Countries and Regions

member states shall further emphasize market access, trade and tourism promotion, investments, flow of resources, industrial development, transfer of technology, human resources development and support for Asean positions in international fora.

The Association seems to be concerned about economic development and the progress made by individual countries in this direction which makes greater cooperation possible.

5.2.3 THE ANDEAN PACT (ANCOM)

Member states of the Andean Pact are Bolivia, Colombia, Ecuador, Peru and Venezuela, who all signed the Cartegena Agreement in 1969. Agreement 85 sets out the rules on intellectual property. Decision 20 refers to technological transfer.

Common regulations on intellectual property cover patents, trademarks and designs and licensing agreements.

The various regulations are generally considered to be somewhat dated. They do not, for example, include discussions on intellectual property in the GATT Uruguay Round.

The Andean Technological Information Network (SAIT) collects information on direct foreign investment technology transfer contracts and the registration of patents and trade marks.

The relationship between the Andean Pact and the European Union (which is an important aid donor) has led to several economic and commercial agreements and considerable trade and technical assistance.

5.3 Developing and former communist countries

Country X is approaching take off; at this stage in its development, it has high tariff barriers – which have already led to arguments with officials of the GATT and the World Bank – to protect its infant industries. The barriers are likely to be reduced when the country at last finds its niche in world markets.

The country's present stage of economic development provides an incentive for foreign licences – both as a means of market entry for the licensor and as a route to a new business for the local licensee. The story also illustrates the attraction of a rapidly expanding economy – you need to be there, but you cannot export into it across the tariff barriers and periodical import bans. Investment may be too risky; even the rapid development may have increased political and economic instability. Licensing, as a policy, may also be risky which makes for an additional incentive to arrange licences in many countries to ensure that a disaster in one is balanced by a success in another. Uncertain but expanding economies are tailor-made for licensing deals for all companies with technology they need to sell but especially for those which cannot contemplate raising the capital needed for investment.

Developing countries tend to have paternalistic governments often imbued with the need to protect their citizens against foreign companies, considered over-greedy, by imposing constraints on the terms that can be negotiated. There is a widespread belief that these constraints are achieving different results from those intended. Instead of making life easier for local negotiators, the constraints remove some of their bargaining counters and with them the emergence of the skilled body of negotiators the developing country so badly needs.

Another feature of many developing countries is that the government appears as almost a third party in the negotiations. In particular, government officials are concerned with the implementation of policies on technology transfer which include training programmes for local engineers and technicians.

Licensing in Specific Countries and Regions

After these introductory comments, the rest of this chapter details the policies and practices of selected countries.

UNBUNDLING THE TECHNOLOGY

Developing country governments have one special interest which is not necessarily in common with the way licensors or licensees see things.

Governments may well feel that it is necessary to compel foreign licensors to offer parts of a technology package even though it is normally regarded as inseparable. This is to ensure that technology relevant to the country is being bought and that the licensee is not committing itself to a task that will eventually turn out to be beyond its capacity in the present stage of the industrialization of the country.

5.3.1 THE LICENSOR'S VIEWPOINT

The negotiation of a licensing agreement in a developing country is likely to be conditioned by local rules about the transfer of saleable knowledge and payment for it. The rules vary from country to country and over time, hence it is always necessary to check the current state of the legislation before entering into negotiations, but a general understanding of the local situation will always be helpful and the following are general questions from which current or future policies can usually be deduced.

1. What is the trading policy of the country: is it, on principle, restrictive?
2. Does the country protect patents?
3. Are there other forms of protection for intellectual property?
4. Are there restrictions on licensing arrangements and the payment of royalties or knowhow fees?
5. Are there incentives for licensing agreements and the payment of royalties and fees?

6 Are there other developments in the national economy which would affect the project?
7 Do the development policies of the licensee's country improve the chances of the project's success?

Whatever the policies of the government, local firms are likely to be offered government contracts; but their chances improve when they can offer advanced foreign technology.

While firms frequently hesitate to reveal technical knowhow because of fears about security or doubts about the enforcement of local patent legislation, it remains generally true that devices in use are better protected than those not in use which may not be protected at all. This provides another incentive for the licensor. In spite of all these incentives for licensing, a review of the early 1980s (reported in L.T. Wells (1983), *Third World Multinationals*, Massachusetts Institute of Technology) showed that none of the firms surveyed themselves operated licensing agreements.

5.3.2 THE LICENSEE'S STANDPOINT

'The use of licensing agreements has grown markedly over the past decade as one favoured approach to foreign expansion' (quoted from a United Nations report, *Licence Agreements in Developing Countries* published as long ago as 1987). The report goes on to list the advantages for developing countries of such agreements. From the licensee's standpoint they include the acquisition of technology, the ability to profit from the licensor's reputation and expertise and a reduced need for costly research and development. These are also advantages from the government's point of view; there is the added advantage that the benefits can be gained without appearing to compromise the country's independence. Against this, there is a parallel disadvantage. In African developing countries, there is no tradition of interest in science and technology and this contributes to a lack of interest among local businesses in seeking foreign licences; this lack of interest is increased by a tradition of discouragement to business on the part of governments

Licensing in Specific Countries and Regions

(especially the military governments that took over in several countries in the last quarter of the century). As a result, many of those with money either emigrated or lodged their money in a foreign bank.

As governments concentrate more on growth and on reducing the strings attached, they are at the same time providing a climate more favourable to local entrepreneurs and to foreign investors. These two processes are likely to have opposite effects on the use of licensing. Budding local entrepreneurs will be seeking licences to develop their businesses at the same time as foreign investors will be promoting licensing arrangements within the company (these latter come outside the scope of this book). The United Nations Report already quoted refers to steep increases in income from royalties both between independent firms and within a company.

The same report emphasizes that restrictions on the transfer of technology are intended to do for the developing countries what competition policies do for the industrialized namely: 'increase competition and development and create greater access to goods and services.'

One special incentive for developing countries to promote licensing agreements occurs when a lack of ability or technology makes it impossible for national projects to be completed and a licensing agreement turns out to be the most cost effective and acceptable way of achieving a national ambition.

Incentives provided for foreign licensors vary from country to country but may include preferential taxes and import duties for components that cannot be produced locally.

One country's efforts to foster and guide foreign licensing agreements – that of the Philippines – was described in an article (in *Les Nouvelles*, September 1988) which also listed 812 agreements registered during the first ten years of the incentives.

In spite of the incentives, most countries do (like the Philippines) also have restrictions on foreign licensors. Some of these (such as competition rules) are common in industrial countries as well.

Where countries have developed anti-trust legislation (like South Africa between 1979 and 1986), this legislation usually covers licensing agreements which include exclusive or other clauses held to be in restraint of trade. This is not thought to weaken a country's patent legislation unless there is legislation on this subject as well.

Other government intervention commonly found is a code or set of guidelines which provide criteria for regulating licensing agreements. These may include the use of the local law in interpreting the agreements. They may also include restrictions on royalty rates.

A common restriction (often in conflict with competition policies) is a prohibition on limiting the licensee's own foreign market.

5.3.3 THE GOVERNMENT VIEWPOINT AND COMPULSORY LICENCES

A number of disillusioning experiences have led developing countries to restrict companies' handling of technology transfer. For instance patents have sometimes been used to exclude competitors but not to develop business; as a result compulsory licensing (or the similar licences of right) have developed in some legal codes to ensure that the right to use a patent is not prevented in a particular country. It has been remarked (and is quoted above) that transfer of technology laws in developing countries are designed to increase competition and improve access to products and profits, the role performed by competition laws in industrial countries.

Global companies have been accused of using patents to block the emergence of a national industry and to ensure that the market is serviced by imports of their products from elsewhere. As against this, companies argue that lack of patent protection might leave the country without the product altogether.

Other measures to ensure that the technology patented is actually

Licensing in Specific Countries and Regions

transferred to a country are sometimes employed when compulsory licensing appears to take too long. These include a condition attached to the patent that it becomes inoperative if not used within a certain time. This prevents the use of the patent to safeguard imports to the country without any local manufacture.

Needless to say, all restrictive measures by developing country governments are bitterly criticized by executives of technologically innovative companies, and the governments find themselves faced with a dilemma here. It is hard to believe that the absence of any restriction can be beneficial except in the very long-term – a term that appears to be so long that all kinds of incalculable handicaps may appear before it is reached. The country needs to relax regulations to release the creative energies of its own entrepreneurial citizens. The most efficient way of operating this relaxation would seem to be on a case by case basis, but this lays the government service open to a temptation to corruption and a charge that it is corrupt. Sometimes this still remains the preferred option. The local company will know that it must sort out its bargaining counters with officialdom before embarking on negotiations while the would-be licensor will frame its policy on the basis of current practices (not necessarily the same as current regulations) in an industrializing country subject to rapid change.

The other pressure on the developing country government is the need to import a **suitable** technology. The dilemma is expressed by the word **suitable**. Not even the most industrialized nation has developed forecasting methods sufficiently sophisticated to predict technology needed even in the medium term future. The developing country may well decide that the import of a technology that cannot be exported in the teeth of world competition should be refused a licence but there must be many borderline cases. If the licensor is seeking only a lump sum payment this may be a warning sign to regulators; on the other hand the licensor may see opportunities for export not easily noticed if, for instance, the local licensee has a skilled and low cost labour force readily available. Where the government does not wish to hinder the licensing arrangement, there is another possible cause for dispute in the price. It is widely believed that prices charged for foreign technology are too high and this belief leads to an almost inevitable conflict. The government is looking at the benefits to the foreign concern while the would-be licensor sees mainly the risks and the losses that the deal may incur. It is likely that the company puts a higher price on the negotiating and managing of a project than the government.

Another influence on patent legislation is the opinion, held in some industrialized countries as well, that some products (such as food and pharmaceuticals) should not be protected by patent. This legislation does not necessarily prevent an application for licences by companies who cannot find any other means of using the technology.

IMPLICATIONS OF GOVERNMENT INTERVENTION FOR THE LICENSING PARTNERS

The implications of government intervention add an extra complication to licensing negotiations.

During negotiations in Romania, before the revolution, the West European and Romanian partners agreed to set up heads of agreement covering most major aspects of a deal on the provision of knowhow, training and machinery for the production of electrical goods.

The agreement was then vetted by the appropriate ministry, which sought to expand the scope of the knowhow provided, while reducing the price both of the knowhow and of the machinery to be imported. Strong recommendations also came from the ministry that local tools and equipment should be used in the project wherever possible.

Although the licensee and the licensor had known from the start that the ministry would be involved, and had indeed followed written guidelines from the Romanian government, this degree of intervention put both parties into a situation where the negotiations had to start again. The modifications stipulated by the ministry seriously reduced the profitability of the venture for the licensor, while the licensee was not at all confident that the requirements for increasing the local

Licensing in Specific Countries and Regions

content in the investment could be achieved.

The power situation in the negotiations changed radically, with the licensor and the licensee having to join forces to rework the deal to the satisfaction of the ministry officials. The officials, although part of the ruling technocracy, had no detailed understanding of the technology in the project and an inadequate understanding of the capabilities of their own factories.

After some nine months of haggling and additional studies, a new version of the project was presented which was technically acceptable to the ministry.

At this point, the officials who had been dealing with the original pricing of the deal handed over the baton to the next level of management above them.

This new group then subjected the licensor to further pressure on the price of the knowhow and equipment. Other potential licensors were still bidding for the project, and the ministry was clearly trying to play one off against another.

In this particular case, the Western European licensor objected in the strongest terms to the manner of the repeated interference by the officials. Part of the reason given was that foreign currency to pay for the deal was no longer available. In the end, a contract was signed but on a considerably restricted one-off plant and training basis, without ongoing collaboration or entitlement to further improvements in the licensor's technology and with only rudimentary quality guarantees.

Although the history of government supervision and control of licensing shows that in some cases (notably with MITI in Japan but also in Korea and India) a satisfactory balance may be found between the interests of licensor, licensee and licensee's government, some developing and former socialist bloc countries have suffered from the over-involvement of government departments, frequently acting at the wrong level.

Indian regulations have defined suitable subjects for technology transfer and have governed the availability of foreign currency for the payment of fees and the purchase of machinery but have not gone so far as to determine which machines should be purchased or how many hours training should be provided.

If governments in knowhow purchasing countries make too many restrictions, commercial considerations may even extend to companies making illegal extra-territorial agreements to ensure that the licensee receives the appropriate technology and equipment and that the licensor is appropriately remunerated – albeit through a circuitous route.

Over-regulation frustrates the free flow of ideas and funds, and it is noticeable that countries with interventionist policies eventually adopt a freer approach, either through experience or under the pressure of the world trading community through agreements such as the General Agreement on Tariffs and Trade.

Another disadvantage of an interventionist policy by governments in knowhow purchasing countries is the problem of corruption. Any dinner table discussion among licensing practitioners will feature both authenticated and apocryphal stories of slush funds built into the licensing budget and luxury cars finding their way into the ownership of the families of government officials.

A further complication imposed by the governments of developing countries short of foreign exchange is the need for countertrade.

The economics of countertrade are heavily influenced by the immediate saleability of the countertrade product. Where countertrade is offered in perishable foodstuffs or fashion goods which may become obsolete, additional safety margins must be allowed to insure against part of the countertrade articles becoming unsaleable.

In such cases it is usual to persuade the licensor's government to discount the cost of the countertrade product to safeguard the licensor against its possible deterioration.

Licensing in Specific Countries and Regions

Fortunately, this is not always the case, and there are many examples of countertrade with the People's Republic of China where this has been successfully arranged in metal ores or minerals and to the advantage of all concerned. The subject of countertrade has been considered in Chapter 4.3.

As against these problems of government intervention, the International Trade Ministry (MITI) in Japan and the Technology Ministry in Korea are examples of successful government interventions that have been beneficial to their countries' industrial development.

In those developing countries where government intervention in industry is normal (such as Taiwan, Malaysia, Singapore, Nigeria and others), this intervention is often helpful to both parties. Examples are the changing of import restrictions and tariffs to favour a particular project; other industrial regulations are sometimes altered when a would-be licensee in the country makes a convincing case that a proposed agreement would lead to the development of a new local industry; the case becomes extra convincing when the possibility of exports is included.

5.3.4 SPECIFIC COUNTRIES

THE FORMER COMMUNIST STATES OF EUROPE AND CENTRAL ASIA

At the time of writing, the situation of former members of the USSR and the COMECON bloc is still very confusing: not only are there still considerable political upheavals, but the change of the economies from the tight controls of state planning to the relative freedom of a market system (with more or less state intervention from case to case) has led to high rates of inflation together with logistical and financial problems in the supply of raw materials and distribution of finished goods.

USSR patents and trademarks remain in force in Russia, but most other countries are still in the throws of establishing their own systems for the protection of intellectual property. Countries such as Belarus, Estonia, Kazakhstan, Latvia, Lithuania, Moldavia, Ukraine and Uzbekistan are re-registering USSR patents and trademarks within their own systems. The new Czech and Slovak Republics are also setting up their own administrations for intellectual property; each recognize separately rights carried over from the former Czechoslovakia, and are setting up independent systems for registering new patents and trademarks. Croatia and Slovenia are carrying out similar processes to re-register the intellectual property rights from the former Yugoslavia.

Under the influence of the growing trade with the United States and the European Union, states such as the Czech and Slovak Republics and Romania are re-aligning their patents legislation along the lines of new European Union laws. Bulgaria, Hungary and Poland are also developing increased protection for pharmaceutical and chemical products and foodstuffs.

The laws on unfair competition in Bulgaria, the Czech and Slovak Republics, Hungary and Romania also include fairly comprehensive recognition of knowhow and trade secrets which may be protected by civil and criminal remedies. As we have stated elsewhere, the situation is not yet so clear in Poland, although better protection is included in a new draft law.

New licensing deals are reported from Poland and the Czech Republic while Hungary, which had already gone a considerable way towards re-orienting itself towards a western market economy, shows considerable potential. With the demise of the various forms of state control, the new regulations represent a difficult and constantly changing background to commercial activities. Companies proposing to carry out licensing and knowhow ventures with the former communist states should ascertain in advance the degree of protection afforded to their technology as well as the exchange control and taxation regulations, which will affect the way in which they are paid. Sources of convertible currency for licence and knowhow payments will be a problem for many years to come. Great care should be taken to obtain up to date

Licensing in Specific Countries and Regions

information on the financial resources of the partner company and on the management qualifications of the individuals representing it. If an agreement should go wrong, there are considerable doubts about how the courts in the new states would interpret the (often new) laws concerning technology transfer agreements. Hence, particular attention should be paid to the possibility for contractually agreed damages in the event of certain types of default, and on the enforcement of arbitration clauses.

OTHER DEVELOPING COUNTRIES

While many countries such as Chile or Thailand already have patent registration systems, other states, such as those of the United Arab Emirates are only now hastening to introduce modern systems for the registration and protection of intellectual property. With the tremendous weight of trade dependent on such agreements as the GATT, the establishment of an internationally recognized infrastructure for the trade in intellectual property is seen by many developing states as a prerequisite for full participation in world trade.

At the same time, the developed nations tend to expect such means of protecting and defending their interests before venturing into the production of goods or the provision of services under knowhow or franchise agreements.

Such trends are often counterbalanced by the wish, shared by many states, to control the technology being introduced into their economy and the flows of goods and currency used to pay for it. Some countries, such as Korea, have introduced organizations for vetting and channelling the import of foreign technology, as did MITI in Japan or INPI in Brazil. In Korea, this function is carried out by the Ministry of Finance which has the power to review proposed technical knowhow agreements. Other countries which have no exchange controls, such as Indonesia, have a relatively uncomplicated approach, and principally seek to protect particular local industries.

It is therefore surprising that a number of relatively well developed economies such as Thailand, Singapore and Nigeria do not fully conform to the international systems for the protection of intellectual property. For example: Thailand is a long standing member of the Berne Convention for the Protection of Literary and Artistic works but it is not a party to any international patent treaty. Singapore has laws on trademarks and copyright based broadly on United Kingdom models, but does not yet grant patents; it merely registers patents already obtained in certain other countries.

Although Nigeria has a rudimentary patent registration system, and is a signatory to the Paris Convention, it is not yet a signatory of the Patent Cooperation Treaty. Nigerian patent law does not require examination of a patent application for its innovative content, but only with regard to certain formal matters of an administrative nature.

In the case of Nigeria, there is a feeling that a full scale patent protection legislation might work against local industries who might wish to produce in Nigeria goods not protected under Nigerian law but subject to foreign patents. There is a feeling that countries such as Japan and Taiwan have grown strong on the basis of judicious copying of foreign technology and that, therefore, Nigeria should not restrict its own freedom without considerable incentives to do so.

A counter-argument is that Japan and later Taiwan have only been able to develop credible home technologies after companies from the developed economies felt sufficiently confident to make full licence and technology transfer agreements, involving the training of engineers, technicians and managers both in the licensee's premises and in the factories of the licensor. Only then did the recipient countries develop a credible technological infrastructure. It may be that the free-for-all approach is short sighted.

Licensing in Specific Countries and Regions

ARGENTINA

INTELLECTUAL PROPERTY INFRASTRUCTURE, LAW ON PATENTS, TRADEMARKS AND COPYRIGHTS

Comprehensive legislation introduced in 1991 to reform intellectual property law. Like Brazil, improving international relations are leading to more market based reforms and liberalization of trade.

Many restrictive licensing practices have been lifted.

Technology transfer is regulated by Law No. 22 426 (due to be replaced by a new law).

'Technology' is defined as any form of technical knowhow for manufacturing a product or performing a service.

Trademark legislation is regulated by Law No. 22 363.

Trademarks are protected for a maximum of ten years and can be renewed indefinitely.

Applications for approval of an agreement for technology transfer may be filed by any party involved. Information must include name(s) of parties, any participation in the capital of the licensee by the licensor, description of technology, number of employees of licensee and estimation of payments to be made under licence.

Three copies of application must be translated into Spanish and signed by a sworn public translator.

Foreigners and other applicants living abroad must appoint an agent in Argentina to patent an invention.

Foreign patents which have been granted abroad can be protected in Argentina. For revalidation, foreign patents should not have been manufactured in Argentina. A certified copy of the foreign grant patent must be filed within a 90-day period from the filing date of an Argentine application. Failure to do so after a ten day call by the Patent Office will result in the application for revalidation being abandoned.

MEMBERSHIP OF OTHER MAJOR GROUPING

Irrelevant at present.

GOVERNMENT MINISTRY OR OTHER ORGANIZATION FOR TECHNOLOGY TRANSFER

The National Institute for Industrial Technology must authorize any contracts for technology transfer by a foreign-owned local firm from the foreign company.

The National Register of Industrial Property supervizes the granting of patents and trademarks.

The National Register of Intellectual Property supervizes copyright.

EXCHANGE CONTROL PROBLEMS

None at present.

TAXATION OF ROYALTIES AND KNOWHOW PAYMENTS INCLUDING ANY PROBLEMS

Import licences are required, but the process has been simplified. Import duties have decreased from an average of 50 per cent in the mid-1980s to an average of 14.2 per cent (1993).

Remittances of royalties abroad are subject to income tax at 45 per

Licensing in Specific Countries and Regions

cent (Law No. 20 628) or 18 per cent for contracts which have been approved and registered.

There is a ten per cent tax on income from copyrights.

The National Institute for Industrial Technology supervizes the terms and conditions to ensure contracts are in line with usual market practices. Remuneration must be reasonable – not exceeding five per cent of net sales price (factory price minus discounts, refunds, excise duties and VAT) of goods and services provided by technology transfer.

RESTRICTIONS ON THE KINDS OF DEALS PERMITTED

Intellectual property legislation does not apply to contracts with security or the armed forces which are military secrets.

Processes for obtaining pharmaceutical compositions can be patented but the actual composition cannot.

Drug formulations, financial plans, any invention contrary to morality are unpatentable.

(New plant varieties are protected under a 1973 Law on Seeds and Phytogenetic Creations.)

BRAZIL

INTELLECTUAL PROPERTY INFRASTRUCTURE, LAW ON PATENTS, TRADEMARKS AND COPYRIGHTS

Brazil is currently in the process of introducing new legislation which will remove more trade barriers, but this is not yet confirmed (see 'exchange control problems').

Current conditions:

1 foreigners applying for a patent must appoint an assigned agent for the life of the patent;
2 foreign manufacturers or traders are advised to patent information, invention and register trademarks in Brazil for protection;
3 a foreign trademark which is registered and worked in the country of origin can be protected in Brazil if reciprocal rights are provided for Brazilian trademarks;
4 filing for applications in Brazil cannot be accepted until a period of six weeks has lapsed if an application has also been made in Britain to patent the same invention;
5 the title to patents is transferable but no restrictive measures can be taken against a patent within the first three years of life;
6 the life of a patent or invention is 15 years (subject to payment of annual renewal fees);
7 patents must be worked in Brazil within three years of the grant of a patent, and at least one year of continued use;
8 trademarks are valid for ten years and renewed indefinitely – all rights may be cancelled if there is non-use within two years of registration date or two consecutive years of non-use;
9 a new patent law is being prepared to make foods, chemicals and medical products patentable.

MEMBERSHIP OF OTHER MAJOR GROUPING

Irrelevant at present.

GOVERNMENT MINISTRY OR OTHER ORGANIZATION FOR TECHNOLOGY TRANSFER

All agreements must be approved by and registered with the National Institute for Industrial Property – INPI (Brazilian Patent Office).

Agreements must be submitted to the Patent Office for consultation

Licensing in Specific Countries and Regions

before registering, stating object of agreement, remunerations to be paid and relevant information about parties concerned. These must be in Portuguese with a foreign translation if necessary.

Remittance of royalties must be recorded with the Central Bank of Brazil.

EXCHANGE CONTROL PROBLEMS

Proposals to relax legislation on patents and greater intellectual property protection were presented to Congress in 1991 but had still not been voted on by March 1993.

The new government is seen as more protectionist than the previous Collor administration.

There are plans to force foreign drug companies to seek licences if they are found to be charging excessive prices.

TAXATION OF ROYALTIES AND KNOWHOW PAYMENTS INCLUDING ANY PROBLEMS

Royalties are calculated on net sales price of licensed products. If payment is by a 'running royalty' in a lump sum, the Patent Office usually request an estimate for the first 15 years to ensure that the lump sum and running royalty is not greater than the maximum percentage allowed over a five year period.

A withholding tax of 25 per cent on all payments or credits going to a foreign party or outside Brazil.

Minimum royalties on a licence agreement are not permitted but a minimum production and sales figure is acceptable.

The National Institute for Industrial Property (INPI) states the maximum royalties which can be remitted abroad – generally, five per cent of net sales for patent and knowhow licences; one per cent for trade mark licences.

All information about royalties and other remunerations must be registered with the Central Bank of Brazil.

Restrictions on the kinds of deals permitted

The following are unpatentable:

1. inventions contrary to law, accepted morality, health, public safety, religious doctrines;
2. substances and products obtained by chemical means or processes (but actual process can be patented);
3. foodstuffs, pharmaceuticals, micro-organisms, products of microbiological processes;
5. operating technology, theoretical ideas;
6. computer programmes are not patentable but can be protected by copyright;
7. plant varieties.

China: The People's Republic

Although space does not permit the treatment of every single country, we cannot ignore the nation which contains one quarter of the world's population and which has projected rates of economic growth of over six per cent per annum, far outstripping those of industrialized nations. Wogen Technology Limited, a London-based group with a long history of trading with China describes it as 'a complex and confusing amalgam of a centrally planned and a free market economy'.

China is working hard to align its laws to those of the rest of the world, and is a member of the Paris Convention for the Protection of Industrial Property. A new patent law came into force on 1 January

Licensing in Specific Countries and Regions

1993, offering 20 years' protection for patents and ten years' for designs. In addition, bilateral agreements have been entered into with such countries as the United States, Japan, Switzerland and those of the European Union granting protection in China to the foreign owners of patents in pharmaceuticals and agricultural chemicals wishing to make or sell a patented product in China. The government issues administrative protection certificates with a life of seven and a half years. China joined the Madrid Agreement for the International Registration of Marks in 1989. Trademarks can be registered for a period of ten years, and are renewable for further ten year periods. Service marks can be registered in China from 1 July 1993.

A new law on Copyright (China's first) came into effect on 1 June 1991, with regulations on the protection of computer software following in October 1991. China acceded to the Universal Copyright Convention and the Berne Convention for the Protection of Literary and Artistic Works in June 1992, with regulations for implementing international copyright treaties being promulgated in September 1992.

In its five year plan ending in 1990, China set priorities in developing and expanding science and technology associated with the primary needs of the country: food, agriculture, clothing, consumer durables, energy, transport and communications; together with some more advanced industries, such as production equipment and computer technology.

Within the framework of the 20 year plan to the year 2000, these trends are being maintained within the ambit of state control. However, there is a slow development towards a market system in which prices will gradually reflect supply and demand (although some commodity prices will be controlled by the government). Under the new Sixteen Point Plan, the government has tightened up on credit for Chinese companies, to such a degree that many enterprises are finding it difficult to buy raw materials and spare parts.

All these developments bode well for the field of technology transfer in general. The main difficulty is that the Chinese authorities prefer joint ventures and the establishment of wholly owned subsidiaries of foreign companies to straight licensing and knowhow deals. This is clearly due to the problems encountered in obtaining convertible currency for purchasing foreign technology and equipment. In these circumstances, projects with export potential, or paid for by countertrade are very popular. A survey of 50 technology transfer projects with China between 1983 and 1992 covers technology for mineral exploitation (coal and oil), power generation, civil engineering, food production, agriculture (animal breeding), refrigeration, telephone and communications technology, electronic components, aircraft production, glass production, chemicals, plastics, automotive components, boat building, steel making, pumps and compressors, cigarette manufacture, and machine tools.

Although the projects from the eighties included a number dealing with the supply of machinery and technology for particular processes, the contracts signed from 1990 onwards have all included an element of foreign finance and or payment by means of exports of the licensed goods or related products to the licensor.

For example, a joint venture agreement was made on 6 October 1993 between the French automotive manufacturer Renault S.A. and the Chinese Sanjang Space Group for the assembly of 40,000 minibuses per annum in Xiaogan, Hubei Province. By 1995, the partners will develop a new type of minibus for export to France and Brazil. The joint venture company will be 55 per cent owned by Sanjang and 45 per cent by Renault, who are investing $100m in the project.

Due to the relatively recent development of the infrastructure for the registration and protection of intellectual property in China, some foreign companies prefer the establishment of a WFOE (wholly foreign owned enterprise) which gives entire control of the Chinese operating company and its knowhow to the foreign owner. Once again, this means that the foreign company has to finance the venture. This reduces one of the advantages of the licensing as far as the licensor is concerned: namely that it is able to expand its market without the need to find additional capital to fund production equipment or work in progress.

Licensing in Specific Countries and Regions

In view of the large number of foreign companies prepared to work in China on the basis of joint ventures and WFOEs it will be some years before pure licences and knowhow agreements come into vogue again and, even then, they are likely to be associated with provisions whereby the venture earns the foreign currency with which the deal is paid for. Hence it is likely that such licences and knowhow agreements will contain provisions for the export of a certain percentage of the output from the new technology, or that the royalties and knowhow payments will be covered by exports to the licensor of countertrade goods. Another problem will be that the Chinese partners will tend to evaluate the technology in terms of local prices, rather than in terms of international costs. When the need for a fair reward for the licensor is stressed, the Chinese partner still tends to argue that the wealthy Western partner can afford to let China have the technology at a lower price, as 'it is already paid for'. Such arguments also used to feature in negotiations with partners of the former COMECON countries.

Apart from the commercial difficulties of licensing in China, there are also problems for foreign companies in publicizing the availability of their technology. In a survey carried out in 1991 by the R & D Research Unit of Manchester Business School, it was reported that Chinese firms have difficulty in identifying potential suppliers of new technology. According to the report, foreign licensors should identify and try to build up a close relationship with the State Research Institute specializing in their particular industry, which have the responsibility of collecting information on foreign technology for dissemination within China.

From other contacts of the authors, we learn that it is also possible for foreign companies to identify the larger Chinese enterprises who may have a need for a particular technology and to approach them through a suitable intermediary, such as a foreign trading company, or a non-competitor, who has already done business with that enterprise or with similar enterprises. Chinese companies are still relatively unaccustomed to receiving direct contacts from abroad, and there is still a large element of bureaucracy, which makes it difficult to target information to the desk of the appropriate decision-maker or opinion former.

In spite of the undoubted potential, China is not a market for the beginner or the unwary: in recent years, the freeing up of the market has led to inflation rates of up to 20 per cent and problems of the convertibility of the Yuan. The new doctrine of private enterprise has also been associated with the re-emergence of racketeers and fraudsters. Although those of us who traded with China in the seventies and eighties knew it as a country of the highest standards of personal probity, it is not unknown in the nineties that foreign capital transmitted to China as part of a technology transfer project has been siphoned off for the private benefit of an enterprising local businessman.

Perhaps we should leave the last word to a Western businessman who recently returned from China and hailed it with rueful enthusiasm as 'a country with immense long-term potential, coupled with enormous present difficulties'.

CZECHOSLOVAKIA (CZECH AND SLOVAK REPUBLICS)

INTELLECTUAL PROPERTY INFRASTRUCTURE, LAW ON PATENTS, TRADEMARKS AND COPYRIGHTS

Current legislation is undergoing reform as centrally planned make way for market economies.

State Planning Commission officials have called for greater use of Western technology in local industry and more cooperation.

Since 1985 new regulations have removed many of the legal barriers to technology transfer, allowing companies in Czechoslovakia greater freedom to purchase technology. More opportunities now exist to fund research and development, purchasing of equipment and implementing of modern technology. Prior to the change in the law, inventions required an Inventors' Certificate; as from January 1991, certificates can no longer be obtained, but those issued before reform remain in force for 15 years from the date of application.

Licensing in Specific Countries and Regions

Life of patents: 20 years from date of application subject to payment of annual fees. No extensions. Patents granted before January 1991 are valid for a 15 year term.

Foreigners not residing or established in Czechoslovakia must appoint a patent attorney approved by the Federal Office for Inventions or an authorized commercial agent.

An employer in Czechoslovakia is entitled to patent an invention devised by an employee on an employment contract, unless there has been an agreement stating otherwise. The inventor is entitled to remuneration.

Foreign companies are advised to get a Czechoslovakian attorney or consultant with experience in licence sales involved in negotiations such as drafting a contract, technical matters and marketing.

All technology transfer is subject to Act No. 92/91 of Digest.

The Slovak National Agency for Foreign Investment and Development cites the following examples of unprotected intellectual property: knowhow, technology processes, computer databases, research, developing notices and production processes.

MEMBERSHIP OF OTHER MAJOR GROUPING

COMECON (Council for Mutual Economic Assistance) economic organization for (former) Soviet-bloc countries – becoming defunct.

GOVERNMENT MINISTRY OR OTHER ORGANIZATION FOR TECHNOLOGY TRANSFER

The State Commission for Scientific, Technical and Investment Development (SKVTIR) plays an important role.

It provides the State Planning Commission with long-term proposals for importing knowhow and approving the purchase of licences. At present the SKVTIR can block the transfer of technology as well as participating in negotiations.

Exchange control problems

Until 1987, licence purchases were decreasing due to the expense of purchasing the necessary equipment and raw materials in order to implement licensing projects.

The whole process of purchasing licences is long – approval is needed from state planning boards and various government ministries and departments.

Bureaucratic regulations often result in modern technology having little use by the time a licence has been finally agreed.

Taxation of royalties and knowhow payments including any problems

A 30-40 per cent withholding tax is usually levied on royalties and fees paid to foreign businesses for technology transfer, patents and similar transactions.

The republics have inherited treaties with several countries for the avoidance of double taxation, which may effectively lower tax on royalties to five or ten per cent.

Foreign licensors are advised to negotiate receipt of net lump sums and net royalties in order to avoid further unexpected tax deductions and possible disputes.

If an employer claims a right to a patent (see 'law on patents') the employee inventor is entitled to remuneration. The technical and

Licensing in Specific Countries and Regions

economic importance of the invention or process is taken into consideration; also, any contribution by an employer such as raw materials. Any additional remuneration is then proportionate to the benefits obtained from the use of the invention or process.

Restrictions on the kinds of deals permitted

Articles contrary to public morality are unpatentable.

Methods for the prevention, diagnosis and treatment of animal and human diseases cannot be protected but the products for implementing these methods can be patented.

Plant and animal varieties and biological processes used to produce or improve plants or animals may not be patented.

Since a new law in January 1991, pharmaceuticals, chemically produced substances, foodstuffs and industrially productive micro-organisms are all patentable.

Hungary

Intellectual property infrastructure, law on patents, trademarks and copyright

The restructuring of the Hungarian economy has led to a greater import of modern technology. Hungarian businesses are seeking Western knowhow in areas such as pharmaceuticals, agriculture and organizational knowhow.

Although there has been a liberalization of trade legislation, there are still risks for foreign companies engaging in technology transfer during a period of rapid change.

Foreign applicants applying for a patent must appoint a patent attorney or attorney-at-law domiciled in Hungary to act as a representative.

In Hungary, an employer has the right to patent an invention which has been devised by an employee. The employee will be entitled to remuneration. The employer must file an application within 90 days of being presented with the invention by the employee (who must notify the employer). Failure to do so allows the employee inventor the right to patent.

Life of patent: 20 years from date of application for most processes or products; 18 years for patents on vines or trees and 15 years for other plants. Processes for plant and animal breeding are patentable.

Hungarian individuals and enterprises can obtain foreign trading rights and undertake licensing transactions. However, they usually lack the resources and expertise to negotiate with the licensor and therefore often do so through a Hungarian organization which specializes in technology transfer (see below).

Proposals for all licences are evaluated in terms of how the product relates to the Hungarian economic restructuring programme and whether the process or product can be profitably exported to the West.

MEMBERSHIP OF OTHER MAJOR GROUPING

COMECON (Council for Mutual Economic Assistance), economic organization for (former) Soviet-bloc countries, now defunct.

GOVERNMENT MINISTRY OR OTHER ORGANIZATION FOR TECHNOLOGY TRANSFER

Applications for patents are presented to the National Office for Inventions.

Licensing in Specific Countries and Regions

The Ministry of Trade must approve the purchase of a licence by the licensee if the process or product is not on the 'liberalized import list'.

The National Bank of Hungary must approve all licence agreements and reserves the right to perform a consultancy role for contracts which are over 1-1.5 million US dollars.

Larger enterprises in Hungary may have in-house experts to negotiate deals, but approximately 90 per cent of licences, technology and other deals which are imported are through foreign trade organizations (licensing agencies) which specialize in the sale of licences and technology transfer.

Exchange control problems

The process for importing foreign licences or knowhow has been relaxed since 1989. The introduction of a 'liberalized import list' covers approximately 40 per cent of Hungary's import requirements which no longer require special approval from government ministries.

Although this allows for more licensing transactions which are registered with the Ministry of Trade, the risk is greater for foreign companies because there is no guarantee of protection from the state of Hungary.

Taxation of royalties and knowhow payments including any problems

The specialized licensing agencies are paid a commission based on the royalties paid by the licensee for the purchase of a licence. This can be as much as 20 per cent of the licensing fee, although some of the larger agencies may pay a lump sum on royalties.

VAT at a rate of 25 per cent is withheld on royalties for patent licences; there is no tax on royalties from knowhow licences.

Customs duties may be paid on any equipment which is part of the licensing agreement.

Restrictions on the kinds of deals permitted

The following are unpatentable: foodstuffs for human or animal consumption; medicines; chemically produced products; inventions whose subject matter is the same as a Hungarian patent with an earlier priority date; any inventions which contravene law and social morality.

Case example: Hungary, a licensing agreement with joint production

A private Hungarian company made overtures to foreign Company C, indicating that it was interested in licensing-in a range of electronic components which were the property of Company C.

The Hungarian company was already involved in the manufacture and sale of its own range of electronic components which were very similar to those made by Company C. However, Company C could offer a superior product in a particular product category and this is what the Hungarian company was interested in obtaining.

As part-payment for the licence, the Hungarian company offered access to a product which they had designed and patented worldwide but had not yet exploited.

This arrangement was very unusual for Company C and they were initially unwilling to pursue this route primarily due to the fact that it would mean committing resources to a product which was as yet unproven. However, further to an examination by their in-house licensing executive, the company decided to consider the proposal. Subsequently, considerable testing of the patented product in prototype form, was undertaken and Company C decided to pursue licensing negotiations.

Licensing in Specific Countries and Regions

The main product champions were the engineering designers from both companies who were involved in the discussions from an early stage. Their efforts facilitated the subsequent licensing negotiations, and the final licence agreement was successful due to their efforts.

The final agreement reached between both parties resulted in a complex licence agreement which provided for joint production of the Hungarian company's product to be undertaken by both companies, with the territory being divided into East and West. In addition, a licence was also granted to the Hungarian company to licence-in the original conventional product owned by Company C.

This case example was supplied by the Licensing Centre Ltd, Glasgow.

INDONESIA

INTELLECTUAL PROPERTY INFRASTRUCTURE, LAW ON PATENTS, TRADEMARKS AND COPYRIGHTS

Legislation in 1989 saw a development of a Patents' Law which had been delayed for 30 years. Although intellectual property infrastructure remains limited, there is now greater protection since the law came into effect in 1991.

Law No. 21 refers to protection of trademarks.

Foreign companies or individuals must appoint an authorized representative in Indonesia to register trademarks. The procedure is generally regarded by foreign companies as working only to the benefit of Indonesian firms.

Exclusive rights must be granted to the first user of the trademark (who is recognized as the first person to apply for registration of the trademark). Foreign companies are advised to provide strong evidence of the first use of a trademark in order to ensure protection.

Registered trademarks allow exclusive rights to its use for a ten year period, but the delay in registering – usually three to five years – offers little protection during that time.

Membership of other major grouping

ASEAN (see Chapter 5.2.).

Government ministry or other organization for technology transfer

The Directorate of Patents and Trademarks at the Ministry of Justice is the agency responsible for the enforcement of the intellectual property law.

Exchange control problems

The 1989 Patent Law is seen to have many weaknesses which make it a relatively ineffective guarantee of protection. Generally, the transfer of technology and licensing agreements are seen as a prolonged and risky undertaking.

Taxation of royalties and knowhow payments including any problems

Withholding taxes on royalties normally vary between ten and 30 per cent although some tax treaties provide for lower rates.

Restrictions on the kinds of deals permitted

The following cannot be patented: foodstuffs, beverages and the processes for the production of beverages and foodstuffs. Plant and animal

Licensing in Specific Countries and Regions

varieties, and the processes for the production of plants or breeding of animals and their products (although micro-biological processes may be patented). Any method of examination, medication or surgery and scientific theories are unpatentable.

Law No. 7 of 1987 revised the Copyright Act to secure better protection for copyrights as a result of events in the early 1980s which saw Indonesia emerge as a large exporter of pirated video, computer and pharmaceutical equipment.

KOREA: THE REPUBLIC OF (SOUTH KOREA)

Of the two Koreas, the Republic of Korea (South Korea) has developed much more along the lines of an industrialized western economy, following in the footsteps of Japan, while North Korea (the Democratic Republic of Korea) has many similarities with former socialist republics such as Romania.

We will concentrate on the business situation in South Korea, since this is the country with which it is most probable that our readers will deal.

South Korea exports substantial volumes of ships, motor vehicles, machinery, steel, electronic goods, textiles and footwear, with manufactured goods making up the vast majority of exports. Recently, South Korea has tried to counteract the image of the 'technology borrower' by strengthening the penalties against infringement of patents, trademarks and the copying of computer programmes. Other developing countries could learn much from South Korea's approach.

INTELLECTUAL PROPERTY INFRASTRUCTURE, LAW ON PATENTS, TRADEMARKS AND COPYRIGHT

In the field of patents, there is a strong bias towards patenting products to obtain initial protection, and ensuring that the patent is only economical to maintain if it is used. This is achieved by a dual tactic:

patents which have not been used for two years consecutively may be cancelled by the Korean Industrial Patent Office; and the scale of patent registration fees increases on a sliding scale by a factor of almost 20 throughout the life of the patent. This means that the patent cannot be simply used to block the market as is often the case in other countries.

Under the Design Law and the Utility Model Law, the Korean Industrial Patent Office also offers protection for industrial designs (duration eight years) and models (duration ten years).

As is the case with patents, the law on trademarks has been aligned to good international practice, although it is interesting to note that trademarks are considerably cheaper to register than patents, and the protection of a trademark is allowed to continue beyond the initial life of a technology transfer agreement. However the emphasis is once again on active usage rather than passive protection: trademarks may only be renewed for successive ten year periods if they have been used in the three years preceding the date of filing of the renewal.

Copyright legislation (including the Phonograms Law) protects the written word, records, videotapes, broadcasting rights and theatre performances, while computer programmes are the subject of the Computer Program Protection Law, containing many of the recent doctrines developed in the United States. Since 1990 this law also covers computer programmes which are already under copyright in a foreign country.

MEMBERSHIP OF OTHER MAJOR GROUPING

Not relevant at present.

Licensing in Specific Countries and Regions

GOVERNMENT MINISTRY OR OTHER ORGANIZATION FOR TECHNOLOGY TRANSFER

The Ministry of Finance exercises a degree of direct control over the technology which may be imported and over the price paid for it and, in general, the government takes an active role in guiding the development of the country, in a manner similar to that in Japan or India.

All imports of technology must be reported to the Ministry of Finance under the terms of the Foreign Capital Inducement Law, but not necessarily in advance.

The Institute for Technology and Information collects trade information in Korea and abroad for use in technology exchange.

The Technological Committee and Joint Technological Working Group (JTWG) were set up at the 1990 Korea-USA Business Conference to promote greater technology transfer.

The Working Group seeks to identify barriers, to look at methods of encouraging and to make recommendations for the further transfer of technology.

EXCHANGE CONTROL PROBLEMS

The Bank of Korea and the Ministry of Finance exercise strict controls over the remittance of funds abroad, including royalties, loan repayments, dividends and the repatriation of investment capital. However, approved remittances are guaranteed by the government.

Technology may be contributed in return for equity in a joint venture.

Taxation of Royalties and Knowhow Payments Including any Problems

The Ministry of Finance has to approve the level and payment basis of royalties (which are exempt from taxes for five years) and knowhow fees. Royalties and service fees are tax deductible if they are the subject of an agreement of technology inducement and approved by the government in advance.

The Ministry of Finance or the Bank of Korea must approve in advance research and development or technical service agreements between subsidiaries in Korea and their foreign parent companies. Transfer pricing between related concerns is also subject to government control.

It should be noted that the South Korean government offers a number of incentives favouring the development of small and medium sized enterprises, research and development and the import of advanced technologies.

Restrictions on Kinds of Deals Permitted

The government does not favour agreements which interfere with free trade (especially exports) and competition, although it is also likely to protect local Korean industries by restricting the import of technologies likely to cause too sharp a competition against indigenous sources. The government also prefers to import advanced technology rather than outdated or low quality products and techniques.

The relevant government ministers will not approve licensing agreements for technologies which have been placed on the protected list or which violate the Anti-trust and Fair Trade Act, or the main purpose of which is to sell raw materials. A licence which covers a design or brand which has monopoly sales rights is also prohibited.

The Ministry of Finance requires a full business plan for the licensed business and will scrutinize sources of raw materials, production and

Licensing in Specific Countries and Regions

sales plans as well as the pricing policy for the licensed product, compared to prices of comparable goods produced at home and abroad. A form of maximum price control is exercised in South Korea through the taxation system. The government also examines the terms of the agreement itself, and reserves the right to review it during its term. A patent licence may not last longer than the period of validity of the patent concerned, although the government prefers a link between the duration of the agreement and the likely product life cycle: shorter for consumer goods and longer for capital equipment or long term process technology.

Guidelines for approving agreements for technology transfer from abroad state that the level of royalties should not normally exceed five per cent on sales.

In general there are less restrictions on the duration and terms of trademark licences, presumably because their success is far more open to market forces than is the case with patents: it is not possible to block defensively a market for a particular product by means of a trademark.

KOREA: THE DEMOCRATIC PEOPLE'S REPUBLIC (NORTH KOREA)

In North Korea, applications can be made for invention certificates as well as for patents. The Invention Committee of the Democratic People's Republic of Korea examines applications and grants a certificate of invention if it is acceptable.

The life of an invention certificate is unlimited, the state having exclusive rights during 15 years from the application date.

The life of a patent is 15 years from the date of application, subject to annual payments.

All international applications must be translated into Korean, or a request made to the Invention Committee for a translation within 20 months of filing the application from the priority date.

Foreigners who are not resident in North Korea must appoint an agent from the Pyongyang Patent and Trademark Agency.

MALAYSIA

INTELLECTUAL PROPERTY INFRASTRUCTURE, LAW ON PATENTS, TRADEMARKS AND COPYRIGHTS

Foreigners may apply for and obtain patents on the same basis as nationals and residents. Applications are made through a registered patent agent in Malaysia.

Patents are registered under the Patents Act 1983, amended by the Patents (Amendment) Act of 1986.

Other legislation: Trade Marks Act 1976; Trade Mark Regulations 1983; UK Designs (Protection) Ordinance 1949-1978.

Life of a patent is 15 years, with annual renewal fees.

Adequate training for local personnel should be provided by licensee and clearly specified.

MEMBERSHIP OF OTHER MAJOR GROUPING

ASEAN.

GOVERNMENT MINISTRY OR OTHER ORGANIZATION FOR TECHNOLOGY TRANSFER

Any agreement for transfer of technology must obtain written approval from the Ministry of Trade and Industry in Malaysia. Patent applications are filed with the Patent Registration Office.

Licensing in Specific Countries and Regions

EXCHANGE CONTROL PROBLEMS

None at present.

TAXATION OF ROYALTIES AND KNOWHOW PAYMENTS INCLUDING ANY PROBLEMS

Payment for technology depends on the merit of each case, but is usually based on a rate of one to five per cent of net sales.

Preferred method of payment is a 'running royalty' based on net sales rather than a fixed lump sum fee where there is no guarantee of success for a local company.

A withholding tax of 15 per cent is levied on all royalty payments. A royalty payment is not allowed where assembly operations are involved (motor vehicle assembly and heavy construction machinery, for instance).

Double tax deduction for expenditure incurred when providing training is available if the training programme is approved by the Malaysian Industrial Development Authority (MIDA). Capitalization of knowhow is discouraged by the government.

RESTRICTIONS ON THE KINDS OF DEALS PERMITTED

To be patentable, an invention must be a new idea which can be applied industrially.

The following cannot be protected by law: discoveries; scientific and mathematical theories; species of plant or animals; and biological processes for the production of plants or animals (excluding manmade micro-organisms).

Micro-biological processes and computer programmes can be protected by law.

SOURCES OF INFORMATION

Manual for the Handling of Applications for Patents, Designs and Trademarks Throughout the World. Published by Manual Industrial Property B.V., The Netherlands.

Malaysia – Investment in The Manufacturing Sector, policies, incentives, procedures. Published by Malaysian Industrial Development Authority (MIDA), Kuala Lumpur.

Hints to Exporters Visiting Malaysia. Published by Foreign and Commonwealth Office and the Department of Trade and Industry, DTI Export Publications.

POLAND

Since the revolution in 1989, Poland is making great efforts to make its transition from a planned economy to a free market economy. The government, primary and secondary industries and the retail and service sectors are trying to open to foreign investment in addition to the privatization of the large state sector and the convertibility of the zloty. Although the opportunities are undoubtedly great, the main question is how the Polish partner is to pay for the goods and services required.

Belonging to a low wage rate economy does not guarantee that industrial and consumer products can be manufactured or marketed successfully. For instance, modern capital intensive automotive production technology may mean that there is little advantage in producing high volume components in Poland for local needs. In addition, distribution technology – whether in terms of road or rail transport or in terms of point-of-sale presentation of retail goods – leads to considerable problems in countries not accustomed to just-in-time delivery or the enhancement of shelf life by suitable packaging.

Licensing in Specific Countries and Regions

INTELLECTUAL PROPERTY INFRASTRUCTURE, LAW ON PATENTS, TRADEMARKS AND COPYRIGHTS

Foreign manufacturers and traders are advised to patent inventions and register trademarks in Poland for protection. Applications to register patents should be made through a patent agent in the United Kingdom or through a representative in Poland authorized by the Minister for International Economic Cooperation.

Full patents are granted for a 15 year term from the date of application and are subject to a complete examination and payment of annual renewal fees.

Provisional patents may also be granted for a five year term with a restricted examination.

The first applicant is entitled to register a trademark, but any prior user is entitled to specified rights. Trademarks are protected for ten years and may be renewed for a similar period.

There is only limited protection for copyrights.

The United Kingdom has an Investment Promotion and Protection Agreement (IPPA) with Poland which allows for protection of investments and effective payment of any compensation.

With regard to trademarks, Poland ratified the Madrid agreement of 1891 and the 1957 Nice agreement for the international classification of products and services for trademarks.

On copyright, Poland subscribes to the Berne Convention on Copyright, although in practice the protection is less comprehensive than in many of the countries with a longer tradition.

The nature and identification of knowhow is still rather unclear under Polish law and (as in the past) it should be ensured that the scope and nature of any knowhow transferred under a licensing or knowhow agreement is clearly defined in the agreement or its appendices, especially in the form of drawings, manuals, training documents and such like.

The licensing of all intellectual property should be registered at the Polish Patent Office.

Membership of other major grouping

Poland belongs to the World Intellectual Property Organization and has made efforts to ratify various international intellectual property agreements. These include the Paris Convention of Protection of Industrial Property, the Patent Co-operation Treaty, and the Leipzig Agreement on the Unification of Requirements for Preparing and Filing Applications and Inventions.

Government ministry or other organization for technology transfer

The Minister for International Economic Cooperation registers patents, trademarks and copyright.

Government funded Central Fund for the Development of Science and Technology is a foreign exchange fund which finances the import of Western technology and knowhow.

Exchange control problems

State Council Decree No. 184 of 1986 governs the law on licence imports and exports. The legislation has led to a prolonged negotiation process for foreign companies and the need to consult several Polish authorities when purchasing licences.

Imports of Western technology are subject to strict criteria.

Licensing in Specific Countries and Regions

The convertibility of the zloty has considerably simplified trade with Poland, and onerous countertrade obligations by means of which knowhow and machinery had to be paid for in terms of products of that particular venture, or indeed any other products which could earn foreign currency are now a thing of the past. Thankfully, it is no longer necessary to try to arrange payment for computers by bartering jam and sausages.

On the other hand, in view of the tremendous upheavals in Eastern Europe which are likely to continue until the end of this century, it is well to ensure that the Polish partner does indeed have the necessary funds to carry out the deal, and to secure the funds by means of suitable bank guarantees.

The remittance of royalties requires approval from the Ministry of Finance, and this should be obtained through the appropriate department before the agreement is signed.

Taxation of royalties and knowhow payments including any problems

Poland has withholding taxes on licence fees and royalties at a rate of up to 30 per cent.

Bilateral double taxation treaties with specified countries allow for a reduced tax on licence fees and royalties. Standard rate is reduced to ten per cent in the United Kingdom and the United States, for example, and eliminated completely in Germany.

Restrictions on the kinds of deals permitted

New plant varieties and animal breeds may not be patented. Also unpatentable: foodstuffs, pharmaceuticals and chemical products; products obtained by nuclear transformation; scientific principles, processes for curing diseases; computer programmes and any invention contrary to law or public order.

Legislation is expected to be introduced in the near future which will allow foodstuffs, pharmaceutical products, chemical products and products obtained by nuclear transformation to be protected by patent.

CASE EXAMPLE: POLAND, A LICENSING DECISION

Company B were very keen to enter the Polish market and increase their presence; however they had previously only been represented there via their Austrian subsidiary which handled sales and marketing.

The Polish company which had imported the products had been happy with Company B; however they were keen to increase their skills and capabilities with a view to becoming more competent in this market sector.

There was therefore a need to undertake a licence which would allow the Polish company to increase its competence in this sector, while providing Company B with the market presence which it sought in Poland.

However, as was usual for the time, negotiations could not be undertaken directly with the company and Company B had to deal with the Polish ministry responsible for this particular market sector. The ministry thoroughly evaluated Company B and agreed to pursue an agreement with it. This evaluation was time-consuming; when it had been completed and the ministry officials decided to pursue a deal with Company B, they did so whole-heartedly.

The licence which was negotiated allowed the Polish company to import initially high level assemblies, followed subsequently by importing sub-assemblies. The final stage of the license allowed the Polish company to manufacture most of the piece parts with the exception of those which were considered critical; such parts continued to be bought from Company B.

Licensing in Specific Countries and Regions

During the term of the agreement, the Polish company re-designed a major section of one of the products and, as required by the licence, offered it to the licensor as an improvement. Company B examined the design, decided that it was a valid and worthwhile improvement and subsequently incorporated it into the product. This resulted in increased sales of the product for both parties.

This case example was supplied by The Licensing Centre Ltd, Glasgow.

SAUDI ARABIA

An example of a country approaching take-off is Saudi Arabia which has developed a number of schemes for promoting new technology industries partly through joint ventures and partly through licensing. One scheme is the National Industrialization Company (NIC) which has entered into various arrangements with foreign companies for the transfer of technology in its selected products including chemicals, medical, nutrition, glass, paper technology, food processing, furniture and porcelain. A private sector company, NIC is heavily government supported (50 per cent of its capital comes from a 'Government soft loan'). A biotechnology company, Crescent Diagnostics, also operates in contract manufacture.

It is nearly ten years since the **National Industrialization Company (NIC)** was founded in 1985 (1405H) to establish industries in advanced technologies in the Kingdom of Saudi Arabia.

With its emphasis on chemicals, engineering and related industries, the NIC has been following a pattern that applies in many countries that are rapidly industrializing and the Kingdom certainly comes into this class.

The economy is reaching up towards that of an industrialized country by the usually accepted measure of national wealth. At the beginning of the decade the gross domestic product per head was well over US$1200 and it has since continued to increase (even if more slowly than in the past) in spite of world recession and uncertainties about the price of oil.

An important means of promoting industrialization is by licensing. Entrepreneurial individuals and companies can obtain licences from foreign concerns providing business conditions are satisfactory. The Kingdom fits most of the 'ideal conditions' including:

1. economic growth;
2. a reasonably stable government;
3. a satisfactory infrastructure including a communications system;
4. protection for knowhow (the Kingdom is a member of the World Intellectual Property Organization);
5. ability to remit royalties;
6. ability to tap resources in the licensee country.

NIC has already proved its ability to tap other resources since it has mobilized funding from the government for half its capital requirement (in the form of a soft loan). It is also widely diversified with operations in a variety of sectors, many of them joint ventures with local concerns, at its own research and development facility in Jeddah.

Another project in Saudi Arabia is an agreement between the British and Saudi governments as part of a deal for the sale of arms, known as the **Al Yamamah Economic Offset Programme**. The programme is designed to promote technological exchange between the two countries and specifically mentions support for licensing arrangements. The Programme also offers support for a wide range of deals that will bring new industries to the country. It need hardly be said that the promotion of licensing and other means of technical transfer only becomes worthwhile when a country has in place measures that are satisfactory to foreign licensors including protection for their knowledge and patents. Saudi Arabia is a member of the World Intellectual Property Organization (see Chapter 3.1) which provides the necessary guarantees. These two initiatives clearly demonstrate how a rapidly developing country sees licensing as a route to industrialization; they are also a reminder that such deals can only take place in countries

Licensing in Specific Countries and Regions

where intellectual property is perceived to have protection.

TAIWAN (REPUBLIC OF CHINA)

INTELLECTUAL PROPERTY INFRASTRUCTURE, LAW ON PATENTS, TRADEMARKS AND COPYRIGHTS

Patent, trademark and copyright protection is available to all foreign individuals and companies.

Pharmaceutical products can now be protected by a patent, and the revision of copyright laws since 1990 allows for wide-ranging protection.

The new copyright law, effective from June 1992, no longer requires nationals of countries which provide reciprocal copyright protection to register copyright in Taiwan.

Copyright is effective from date of creation; term is life plus 50 years.

Life of a patent is 15 years from the date of publication of the patent application, it cannot exceed 18 years from the date of filing the application.

Trademarks are protected for ten years from the date of application and may be extended for a further ten year period.

Fair Trade Law of 1992 provides protection for well-known foreign trademarks which are not registered with Taiwan authorities.

MEMBERSHIP OF OTHER MAJOR GROUPING

None.

5

GOVERNMENT MINISTRY OR OTHER ORGANIZATION FOR TECHNOLOGY TRANSFER

The National Bureau of Standards of the Ministry of Economic Affairs (MOEA) supervizes the registration of all licensing agreements and registers all patents and trademarks. The Ministry of the Interior registers all copyrights.

An action plan for enforcing intellectual property rights was announced in April 1992. An inter-agency Coordination Task Force for Intellectual Property Rights was established under the Public Prosecution Office.

EXCHANGE CONTROL PROBLEMS

Regulations governing the screening and handling of outward technical cooperation projects govern the export of technology. The regulations are directed at controlling foreign exchange and promoting the Taiwan economy. However, the relaxation of foreign exchange controls has resulted in much technology transfer occurring outside the legislation.

TAXATION OF ROYALTIES AND KNOWHOW PAYMENTS INCLUDING ANY PROBLEMS

Royalties on patents, trademarks and other licensing rights provided from abroad are subject to a withholding tax at the Taiwan source.

Tax on royalties is currently 20 per cent. However, royalties on knowhow may be exempt from income tax.

Royalties on technology services which come from abroad may qualify for a lower rate.

A stamp tax of 0.04 per cent is levied on receipts issued in Taiwan for royalty payments.

Licensing in Specific Countries and Regions

RESTRICTIONS ON THE KINDS OF DEALS PERMITTED

Foodstuffs and beverages cannot be patented (although the manufacturing process may be protected by patent).

Also unpatentable: plant or animal varieties; micro-organisms; methods of surgical or medical treatment of humans or animals; scientific theories and inventions which are contrary to law, public health or morality.

Part 6

Present and Future: The Professional Licensing Executive

This part provides a conclusion to the main themes of the book – the requirements of the professional licensing executive. It echoes Part 1, itself a summary, and takes the issues considered into the future along with a final look at the opportunities and difficulties that may be anticipated.

6

6.1 The state of the art

These pages have reviewed an activity once peripheral to business and now continually growing in size and scope, an increasingly common (although still minority) means of servicing foreign markets. The strategic reasons for licensing between independent companies have been followed from the background facts (Chapter 1.6) through to the business implications. To a global firm, whose strategy dictates that every possible market be serviced, licensing offers an entry into otherwise unpromising regions; for a small firm, whose inventiveness needs foreign sales, licensing may represent the only available route abroad.

At the same time as these positive aspects have been identified, it has also been made clear that licensing is, in practice, often undertaken as a defence to protect a company's technology in its various markets. A licence to a distributor may not mean local production, it may be designed to safeguard an export business – effectively preventing local manufacture. For the smaller firm with a saleable technology, a licensing project is likely to be the only viable route internationally. Once a licensing policy has been determined, the probable countries are likely to dictate themselves by asking the question: where in the world does this company require a new facility? This insight does not, however, make market research unnecessary. On the contrary, the would-be licensee needs further confirmation that there is a market in the selected countries – unless a business already exists and the purpose of the licensee is either to replace or support existing exports.

THE STATUS OF THE LICENSING EXECUTIVE

Times have changed from the days when licensing deals were undertaken in the spare time of a sales executive who was not otherwise fully employed to the days when deals are negotiated by a specialized licensing executive who is more than fully employed. Chapter 4.1 outlines the options for organization and career structure within which the licensing executive now operates. Greater specialization has meant enhanced status and recognition.

Present and Future: The Professional Licensing Executive

The licensing executive has to take, or to advise on, the decisions outlined in Chapter 2.2. These include the commissioning of market research and a feasibility study, a decision on the product and geographical areas to be included in the deal and an investigation of the sources of finance.

An additional decision, to be taken by the licensor company, is about the use of intermediaries. Only firms with inadequate resources are likely to want to pay fees to intermediaries although they may well use expert consultants.

The increasing demand for cross-licensing places additional demands on the licensing executive who has to develop a facility for negotiating these sensitive arrangements.

The subject of negotiation brings us naturally to the most crucial decision of all, the choice of a partner. Chapter 2.2 provides a list of stages for this which applies to both licensors and licensees and can be summarized as follows:

1 compile a short list (preferably your own); and
2 negotiate a draft agreement which will ensure that each partner achieves its objectives. If this proves impossible, another partner must be found.

Various decisions on the relationship between the partners follow; these include the degree of autonomy to be left to the licensee, and finally there is the preparatory work required to make a company ready for a licensing project.

6.2 Problems and errors

A number of the more common difficulties that licensing partners face have already been outlined (see Chapters 2.1 and 4.6). This chapter will concentrate on other difficulties, some of them less obvious, that are likely to have a place on the agenda. These include: competition, political risk and differences in size and culture between the companies as well as differences in time horizons.

6.2.1 COMPETITION

As competitive pressures increase, especially within the European Community, it will be necessary for the licensor to keep a closer eye on the licensee's market if only to look out for a fresh licensee if the present one goes out of business as a consequence of intense competition. At least the licensee may need to be alerted to changes among its competitors as well as customers – changes in relative market power while some drop out and others come in. All these developments have to be anticipated when competition increases as it will when more countries adopt their various forms of anti-competitive legislation. Agreements may have to be renegotiated when competition forces down prices which previously supported satisfactory royalty payments.

Another worry for the licensor under the heading of 'competition' is that of setting up a competitor if the licensee company becomes a rival in world markets. This is often given as a reason for turning down licensing proposals. The danger may be more perceived than real, but sufficient examples of one-time licensees developing strong competition with their former licensors are quoted to make the fear a real one. Short-term safeguards can be written into the agreement, but the only long-term safeguard is to keep ahead of the technology. This may ensure the future dependency of the licensee company but requires some subtlety in the face of international competition (see Chapter 2.1).

Present and Future: The Professional Licensing Executive

6.2.2 POLITICAL RISK

Many licensing arrangements come about because an area is considered too risky for direct investment. The risk can take many forms. Nationalization is out of fashion these days, even in countries that still call themselves socialist, while the opposite is in fashion with $69bn worth of state enterprises worldwide passing into the private sector last year. This information may be welcome to managers but it brings with it a new threat of instability while not necessarily reducing an old one. In Latin America (where the largest number of privatizations took place) the soldiers have not given up their political ambitions. A military coup is the old threat, long-established; the new threat is the uncertain future for the licensee and its market as the expanding private sector goes through a period of shake up. The licensee's customers may disappear or change their business when, for instance, a new generation of computers uses different peripherals (common products for licensing) or changes in the health system alter the pricing structure for pharmaceuticals – also products frequently licensed.

A style of government which produces high inflation is another long-established political risk which will not go away. An understanding of these risks may not prevent companies going in for licensing, on the contrary it may encourage them to think of licensing as the best option, but it should affect decisions about payment and other arrangements for the contract (see earlier chapters, especially 4.3). Where political risk is seen to exist, larger lump sum remuneration will be preferred even if accompanied by smaller percentage royalties. Normally political risk stimulates licensing as a safer means of entering a market.

THE FRENCH EXAMPLE

A report on French companies in the mid-1980s (see the book by Julien Savaret on *French Multinationals* in the publications list) emphasized that French companies were increasing their world coverage rapidly. In industrialized countries the spread would be by subsidiaries but, in certain developing countries where subsidiaries were prohibited or considered too risky, licensing arrangements were undertaken. This is an example of the use of licensing as a safeguard against political risk.

6.2.3 DIFFERENCES IN SIZE AND TIME HORIZONS

The large company culture of the licensor may not mesh easily with the more informal culture of a smaller licensee. The likelihood of this problem is so obvious that it is expected to be examined in the original negotiations. The introduction of a control system, taken for granted in the large company, will cause confusion in a small licensee. 'We intended this deal to manufacture products not paper' will be said by licensee executives and countered with 'these people seem incapable of taking any notice of our repeated requests for learning how to run a company'.

When the licensor is itself a small company, the position may be reversed.

In each case, there will be different opinions within each partner. One of the authors remembers meeting the business development manager of a large British multinational who was enthusing about his success in signing up a small, entrepreneurial family firm in the Philippines. Meanwhile the controller's department were having nightmares about the consequences of this deal for their systems.

Closely linked to the question of size is that of time. The global company setting up a licensing arrangement, either to protect a market or to enter one, is not looking for an immediate return but is thinking long term. The licensee, on the other hand, may be thinking very short term indeed. Its objective is to establish a viable business in the shortest possible time and profits are an urgent necessity.

Present and Future: The Professional Licensing Executive

6.2.4 Liability

An issue which especially concerns the large company with its greater visibility and – one should add – with its staff employed to worry about such issues is that of liability both for products and for staff. Normally the issues will be settled within the country and the licensee will be responsible for the items that are under its control. One advantage of a licensing agreement, as opposed to a direct investment, is that the licensor (investor) is not liable for damages under product liability or labour protection laws in the host country although, if there is likely to be any difficulty, it has a duty to inform the licensee and ensure that the problem is incorporated in the training.

A responsibility which will rest with the licensor is that of liability if the licensed product or machinery does not work in accordance with specification. This may well be harder to resolve especially with advanced technology licences.

6.2.5 Over-optimistic Forecasting and Inadequate Information

One of the authors has found that over-optimistic forecasting – including an assumption of returns higher than the product has achieved anywhere – are a source of problems when either one or both parties are disappointed that results fall short of expectations.

Inadequate information on the part of either partner is another source of problems. This can stem from inadequate market research.

One review of American licensing failures (see the book by R.D. Robinson in the publications list) illustrated lack of market knowledge among licensors who did not have adequate procedures for evaluation; lack of cost-benefit analysis was also cited.

6.2.6 Conclusion

The general experience is that it is commercial rather than technical issues that cause difficulties in licensing projects. In addition to the questions mentioned already in this chapter, licensors frequently complain about unsatisfactory marketing by the licensee. This complaint does also cover an alleged lack of understanding of the full implications of the technology and its possibilities in the market.

The following chapter (6.3) looks at the prospects for the licensing profession in the future. There is a possibility that the difficulties – combined with a belief that foreign business is more profitably conducted in other ways – may reduce the use of licensing in the future. This is called the 'pessimistic scenario'. On balance, the optimistic view seems more likely. Under this view, licensing is set to increase and means will be developed to overcome the difficulties.

6.3 Prospects

The profession of licensing has now been outlined and its main activities identified and explained. The authors are satisfied that most of the knowledge required by a licensing executive can be found on these pages; we now turn to an attempt to glimpse at the future.

Much of what is likely to come has already been suggested and two features that already exist can be expected to dominate the future.

6.3.1 THE LICENSING PROFESSION

One of the features is an increase in professionalism along with a greater increase in the amount of licensing activity. Two contemporary activities point towards this increase.

One is the drive for industrialization among the less developed nations. Much of that has to be met by licensing agreements. On no other basis can a viable private sector come into existence. This remains true even if industrialization is accompanied by greater political stability; some Latin American regimes have demonstrated that this is not (as is often assumed) an inevitable development. Greater stability may remove one of the motives for licensing but the parallel rise of an entrepreneurial or business class will provide other powerful reasons for seeking licences.

The other feature that will lead to an expansion of licensing activity is the pressure towards more small companies in the industrialized countries. This 'pressure' is, in fact, compounded of two drives both operating in the same direction – the force of competition (anti-trust) legislation and official support for emerging small companies. Naturally both drives may fizzle out, but policy-makers would be wise to assume that both will become increasingly effective. The small company is unlikely to possess the resources to realize the full potential of its technology at home even, still less abroad. Its markets will be increasingly international and will be increasingly serviced by licensing.

Present and Future: The Professional Licensing Executive

In a business world eager to market innovation, licensing will remain a main means of transferring technology.

NEW TECHNOLOGIES

The licensing profession will need to devise new techniques for meeting the demands of new technologies. The safeguarding of intellectual property rights has already adapted to technical change. Among the concerns of the World Intellectual Property Organization (see Chapter 3.2) are: 'the international recognition of the deposit of micro-organisms for the purposes of patent procedure' (the Budapest Treaty, 1977), 'the distribution of programme-carrying signals transmitted by satellite' (the Brussels Convention, 1974) and other similar agreements.

The licensing by governments of biodiversity became an issue when, as part of the 1992 Earth Summit Convention in Rio de Janeiro, mechanisms were sought for compensating countries rich in biodiversity (rain forests, game reserves and other unspoiled plant and animal domains) in order to encourage them to preserve such regions as a world resource, when the general weight of economic development is likely to destroy them. One model is akin to the exploitation of mineral rights, where the government of a protected region of biodiversity would control access to and exploitation of such regions, only permitting exploitation of the biological resources in return for lump sum or on-going royalty payments. The multinational pharmaceutical company Merck recently paid the government of a central American country a substantial sum for the right to prospect for new medicinal plants in its rain forests.

Pharmaceuticals are a product that is likely to feature even more in licensing deals in the future, as are computers and peripherals. Much inventiveness is already concentrated round the electronic (computers) and the chemical (pharmaceuticals) and this tendency is set to increase rapidly.

6

Possible scenarios

The logic of this chapter carrying on a main theme of the book is an **optimistic scenario** from the licensing point of view, a scenario which will be taken for granted in most of this chapter and in which the function and importance of licensing will increase and this will be assumed for the rest of the chapter.

A pessimistic scenario

An alternative scenario is, of course, possible. In this, licensing would revert to a small and minority activity to be avoided by ambitious individuals and thrusting companies. For this to come about, a number of other things would have to happen including the following; the public affairs' departments of high technology companies will be doing their best to prevent them happening.

1 A resolution by a number of countries to refuse to recognize foreign patents. This unlikely action would knock the bottom out of the licensing profession in the countries concerned; there would be little basis for negotiating agreements when the licensee would have to compete with companies using the same technology without paying for it.
2 Legislation by national governments to disallow licences under competition legislation. This would also have a devastating effect and is a possibility, however remote. A licensing agreement is a restraint of trade; it does establish a monopoly for the licensee. Currently this problem is overcome in the European Union by the block exemptions (see Chapter 5.1) which permit licensing agreements, but these exemptions are frequently criticized and their future is not assured. The current assumption is that every country benefits by the transfer of technology on the only terms under which it is likely to happen. There is also an assumption that if competition legislation should cause difficulties, the ingenuity of licensing advisers will find a way out.

Present and Future: The Professional Licensing Executive

The possible need for this ingenuity as well as the remote possibility that the pessimistic scenario will happen should be taken on board by planners.

PREPARING FOR THE FUTURE (ASSUMING AN OPTIMISTIC SCENARIO)

This book is designed to feed a profession that is growing in size, in importance and in confidence. One consequence of this is that the diagram in Chapter 4.1 (Figure 4.1) will have to be redrawn to acknowledge the growth in importance even if the option that makes licensing part of the marketing department is always likely to be the most common. For the large multi-division company with a minimum of head office services, licensing will remain a divisional or subsidiary activity but licensing issues will find more space on the agenda of the main executive body (the board or executive committee).

6.3.2 ADVANTAGES OF LICENSING AND KNOWHOW SELLING AS A BUSINESS DEVELOPMENT STRATEGY FOR THE NINETIES

Global considerations including the opportunities for trade in know-how are shaped by wider global trends: the changing pattern of trade flows to meet the needs of large population groups; the communications revolution; and the marketing revolution.

THE CHANGING PATTERN OF TRADE FLOWS

The volume of trade between North America and Europe is running at about $240 000m per year. Trade between North America and the countries of the Far East (including Australia and New Zealand) is already in excess of $400 000m. The countries of the Asia-Pacific Economic Cooperation Agreement (APEC) already account for 50 per cent of world production and 40 per cent of world trade. The country members of the Organization for Economic Cooperation and Development (OECD) are beginning to suffer the problems of mature economies with ageing populations (high health and social costs), slower growth rates and technologies based on the replacement of existing goods and services, rather than the establishment of basic new industries which have the highest profit expectations.

The major population groups of the world – the People's Republic of China, the new states of the former USSR and the countries of South America and Africa are still at the threshold of industrialization with its promise of fast economic growth due to the large-scale adoption of a technological lifestyle. At a time when many countries are trying to promote indigenous manufacture, the question for any producer is 'How do I obtain a share of this new activity?'

THE COMMUNICATIONS REVOLUTION

The major development of the twentieth century is the communications revolution. Transistor radios and satellite television are far greater enemies of ignorance and oppression than the written word. In the midst of the worst battles and natural disasters of recent years, reporters have managed to find a telephone to deliver the latest news. More efficient forms of transport allow us to send people and goods to the remotest corners of the world in days.

At the same time, the governments of developing nations have learnt the bitter lessons of cash-crop economies and dependence on world commodity prices. They wish to produce sophisticated goods for export: the means of production are also being democratized. This in turn brings a demand for access to the knowledge and skills necessary for production. GATT, APEC and NAFTA show that there is a marked interaction between the re-definition of markets and political boundaries.

Computerized production technology has largely outlawed the idea that developing markets need primitive technology for cottage industries. The cost of labour per unit produced is becoming less and less, even in high wage-rate economies. The costs of production space, storage

Present and Future: The Professional Licensing Executive

space, and the costs of transport of components to the producer or of the final product to the end-user are often more important factors which drive companies to produce beyond the borders of the industrialized nations.

Modern capital-intensive production techniques and improved transport and logistics mean that automobile components or micro-chips are cheapest to produce in single sites which may be located almost anywhere. This raises the difficulty for small and medium companies that, unless they attack the world market, they may actually lose their home market.

THE MARKETING REVOLUTION

The communications revolution has its economic counterpart in the marketing revolution. The emblems of major producers of cars and consumer electronics and the logos of fast food chains and clothing stores are now as widely recognized as the symbols of ancient world religions. The developing nations see their progress not only in terms of better health and improved food production but in access to worldwide information flows, participation in global cultural developments and even in the possession of the totems of consumerism. The worldwide rural scene now features portable generators, the village television set, personal stereo players, jeans and sports shoes. The world's largest fast food restaurant is said to be the Kentucky Fried Chicken restaurant in Beijing.

An example which has long interested the present authors is the case of the Proton car manufactured in Malaysia. Thanks to the design and production knowhow of Mitsubishi, the first of the Proton range of cars to be marketed in Europe was in no way a simplified or bottom of the range product, as had been the case with some of the earlier cars produced under European licences in the USSR, Poland or Yugoslavia. It was a fully-fledged model with acceptable looks and a good name. It was targeted at a particular market identified by Japanese market research. Sales are going well and new follow-on models are being introduced. Issues of distribution, dealers, servicing (for many years a bane to foreign importers of high priced British cars) have been professionally structured from the start: this fledgling flew from its first hour.

By means of the Proton project, Mitsubishi gains an off-shore production base, and Malaysia gains valuable knowhow and experience in modern design and production technology with a product suitable for both the home and neighbouring markets and with a proven export potential.

Such developments indicate that unless the suppliers of components and services are themselves active on a global scale, they even stand to lose their home markets as the products of their traditional customers are replaced by imports. This is why even powerful companies such as GKN are entering into knowhow-based joint ventures in Malaysia and other countries of South East Asia. If they do not get a share of the business in this way, they will certainly not succeed by exporting from the United Kingdom.

If Malaysia can carry out such a project, there is no reason why any other country should not be able to succeed. Modern production technology no longer depends on arduously acquired craft skills; we no longer need craftsmen who forge red-hot iron with sharp eye and rippling muscles. Nor is the new labour force necessarily male, as we have described elsewhere with examples from India. What is needed are willing and malleable minds of which there is a universal supply.

IMPLICATIONS FOR A LICENSING STRATEGY

The above global trends affect the individual company and strengthen the case for a licensing strategy for each size of company and throughout the whole company life cycle.

When discussing licensing, managers tend to talk about technology transfer but we should be careful not to confuse the licensing process with its aim: the aim of licensing is to optimize the profit a company

Present and Future: The Professional Licensing Executive

makes on its intangible assets. The aim is viewed in terms of marketing, even if the means is a question of technology.

Small and medium-sized companies therefore should either concentrate on local niche markets which are not at risk from global competition, or they must seek to supply their products or technologies to players on the global field who benefit from the enormous power of modern marketing. The licensor has to consider whether he has the time and resources to supply his products or services throughout the world.

If you cannot sell your hot cakes fast enough, why not sell the recipe?

A positive response to that question is a key strategy for established industries and the argument is even more compelling if one can thereby climb onto one of the powerful bandwagons associated with the global marketing effort of a company like Mitsubishi.

Just as managers are confronted with make or buy decisions in obtaining components or office services, a licensee has to consider whether it is most profitable to develop knowhow in-house or to purchase it from a tried and tested source. This is an argument against pirating and product copying which seem to be condoned by some countries with inadequate systems for protecting intellectual property. Those who copy products are lucky if they understand half the generating process. Purchasing knowhow and the associated training and quality provisions is better for companies and nations than piracy or counterfeiting.

In the sixties, it was still possible for a relatively small company to export to most industrially active countries – at that time they were more or less the present members of the Organisation for Economic Cooperation and Development. Nowadays, though the trend towards the liberalization of trade has reduced many of the administrative obstacles to exporting, the sheer complexity of marketing in a large number of countries places severe stresses on the organizations of all but the largest or most export-oriented companies. A company selling a consumer product to South East Asia has to prepare literature in around one hundred languages, most of which are completely unrelated.

The information revolution also means that a dedicated researcher can find out about any published new development in a matter of days and few inventions are so novel that there is no alternative means of meeting the need they fulfil. It is therefore increasingly difficult for a company to make a comfortable niche for itself in a particular technology or geographical market.

Nowadays there is often a greater sense of urgency in new product development: if the inventor does not market the product, other versions will soon be brought onto the market to take away the prize. In the United Kingdom, the efforts of Clive Sinclair around 1980 to develop an affordable home computer failed in spite of his undoubted technical genius. The product need was filled five years or so later by a technically less innovative but better marketed product from Amstrad.

Hence a company which develops new technology would be well advised to consider whether it will manufacture and market its products to the whole of the global market or adopt a mixed strategy, supplying its home market from its own resources and serving the rest of the world via licensees or knowhow-based joint ventures.

SELLING THE FAMILY SILVER

Some opponents of licensing say that selling one's technology only strengthens the competition in return for a short term gain. Indeed, if a company is living well off a niche product which is difficult to copy, one might advise against licensing the idea to a third party. On the other hand, in a field where it is relatively easy for competitors to pirate or adapt a design, it might be better to bow to the inevitable and sell part of the family silver, if it enables one to survive into the next product cycle.

When looking at British companies such as Pilkington or The Glacier

Present and Future: The Professional Licensing Executive

Metal Company, one does not feel that they have become weaker because of their knowhow selling strategy – indeed there is strong evidence to suggest that the extra income and market penetration have helped them to outlast their competitors. In the mid eighties, Glacier took over Vandervell Products, a former rival against whom they had competed for forty years.

THE DEVELOPMENT LIFE-CYCLE OF A COMPANY

In examining a licensing strategy, it is also important to recognize that companies themselves are subject to something resembling a life cycle. Licensing may play a role in different phases of a company's development and the strategy appropriate at one stage may no longer be profitable as the company changes in size or market. Growth and diversification bring changes in approach to licensing.

A new company may begin life in order to market a new invention. If it can build up a profitable business and achieve adequate market penetration, it may not be appropriate to licence out its technology at this stage. On the other hand, it may be able to serve only part of the market, or it may only be able to exploit one part of a patent. In such circumstances, it might produce and market a core product and gain extra income by licensing peripheral technologies or products.

A company in the field of home decoration obtained two patents for new methods of fixing decorative wall profiles. It produced and marketed one version, but found that it could not itself exploit the other version made under the same patent, as the two products were seen to be mutually exclusive. However, the company saw that there was a market for both versions, and accepted that it would never reach 100 per cent market penetration with its preferred product. It therefore licensed the second version to a competitor who was well introduced into the market, but less innovative. The company then enjoyed a modest profit from the activities of the competitor as well as from its own preferred product.

As we emphasized in the section on training, one of the main problems of licensing for the smaller company is the amount of top management time and effort needed to negotiate the licence in the first place, and to make it work properly during its life.

THE ESTABLISHED COMPANY

Once a company is established with a good product portfolio and has generated a fund of in-house knowledge and experience, there may be a case for its management to concentrate its efforts on the production and marketing of these products, enhancing their value by means of various forms of legal protection and the bounds of secrecy. In such cases, it may be better to concentrate on the skills one knows than to branch out into the unknown. The question to pose is: What activity brings the best long-term profit per dollar investment or per hour of management time?

In our analysis of national and company statistics (Chapter 1.6), we established that the majority of licensing income is transferred between related concerns. This indicates that as companies grow and expand, licensing should remain an alternative alongside overseas investment and the establishment of foreign subsidiaries.

Another possibility for knowhow-based companies is to retreat from production altogether and to earn profits from the sale of ideas and consultancy. Since the marketing problems experienced by Clive Sinclair, this appears to be the direction he has taken. In the field of metallurgy, there are a number of companies which appear to run profitable businesses in providing processes and additives for various alloying and refining processes.

Cross-licensing is especially a feature of mature, research oriented industries. In the car industry, the aerospace industry and in the production of oil, chemicals and pharmaceuticals, where a large proportion of a company's income may be spent on research, cross-licensing is a common strategy to allow competitors to reduce costs or exploit new

Present and Future: The Professional Licensing Executive

markets. In such cases two or more companies benefit from a technological innovation which might be too costly to develop if it were later only used by a single company.

Considering the money spent on protecting knowhow and goodwill in the form of patents, registered designs and trademarks, it should be part of the business planning programme of every established company to examine whether it is getting an adequate return on these invisible assets. Many of the large fashion houses such as Dior make more profit from licensing their name than from the design and manufacture of clothes. The fact that only one sixth of patents are licensed out would indicate that there is considerable dormant potential. What is often lacking is the imagination and the will to exploit the potential.

THE ROLE OF INVESTMENT AND DISINVESTMENT

Finally, to complete the cycle, licensing is also a means of controlled disinvestment and should be taken more seriously as a way in which shareholders or liquidators can gain a return on the assets of companies which have come to the end of their lives. In the mid-eighties, one of the authors was indirectly associated with the liquidation of a small family-owned chemical company. The liquidators valued the company on the basis of the sale of its tangible assets and discounted this to account for the element of duress in the sale. A family shareholder who had been made redundant as a result of the closure asked to buy the company's portfolio of product recipes and one or two process patents for purifying and converting vegetable oils. The liquidators consulted another chemical engineer and put a value of 1000 deutschmarks on the company's entire knowhow.

The purchaser took the recipe books and some items of laboratory equipment and set up in his garage at home. By writing to a number of the former firm's competitors and others in similar fields throughout the world, he was able to secure an income of several hundred thousand deutschmarks over the next five years.

This example can be magnified in the case of larger companies, which should be looked at department by department for valuable knowhow before being closed down: in some cases the customer address list alone can be worth hundreds of thousands of dollars.

It is therefore clear that the option of licensing and knowhow selling has not only been a valuable part of the marketing strategies of many successful companies, but that it is a form of business development well adapted to the requirements of the next decades of global economic development, which will be moulded by the continuing emergence of information technology.

6.3.3 TRENDS IN THE EXPLOITATION OF INTELLECTUAL PROPERTY

THE IMPACT OF WORLD TRADE AGREEMENTS

The General Agreements on Tariffs and Trade and the European Union have already legislated for the inclusion of trade in intellectual property as well as in tangible goods. Other trade agreements such as the Asia Pacific Economic Cooperation Agreement (APEC) and the North American Free Trade Area (NAFTA) will also contain provisions on the protection and exploitation of intellectual property.

This will bring about a convergence in national laws governing the protection and sale or licensing of intellectual property. As more small and medium sized enterprises buy, sell and licence various aspects of intellectual property, the legal framework, and the agreements governing these processes will also converge. Over the years, there has been a convergence in the law and agreements governing the trade in various forms of tangible property; conditions of sale and purchases, or agreements governing the sale or leasing of buildings for instance. The role of solicitors and patent attorneys is likely to change to advising on the legal policy issues rather than in drafting agreements.

In the United Kingdom and in a number of other countries, there is a

Present and Future: The Professional Licensing Executive

movement to de-mystify legal proceedings for upholding intellectual property protection – for instance, the United Kingdom has introduced the Patents County Court to make legal proceedings in patent matters simpler and less expensive, and is looking at a reform of the trademark laws to simplify the registration of trade names and trademarks.

Countries refusing to align with world trends in the protection of intellectual property may well find themselves excluded from various types of trade. Developing countries, including the People's Republic of China, feel that capitalist states are also the knowledge-producing states. They resent intellectual property as much as they resent the power of the bankers.

Since the People's Republic of China is making a bid to replace the Soviet Union as a super-power, it could be that China will lead a movement for softening up international patents or reducing their lifetime at least as far as developing nations are concerned. Equally it may be that the People's Republic, after the absorption of Hong Kong and watching the success of Taiwan and South Korea, may decide that it is more responsible (and profitable in the long term) to conform than to dissent.

Whichever way developing countries evolve, the most energetic will found organizations similar to Japan's MITI, or Brazil's INPI to control or supervize the subject matter, the terms and the exchange control implications of intellectual property agreements with foreign companies and individuals.

THE IMPACT OF THE WORLDWIDE CONSUMER MOVEMENT ON INTELLECTUAL PROPERTY

As a countervailing trend to the information revolution, there is a mounting consumer pressure against certain aspects of the patent system, especially against the extension of the life of patents for medicinal drugs and equipment. There is a feeling among consumer groups that drug companies exploit the patent position in order to maintain prices at an artificially high level. The drug companies claim that on average it may cost over $200m to develop and test a new drug, which may then take over five years to pass approval and safety tests in any particular country. If competitors were allowed to introduce generic copies of new drugs before the inventor had had time to recoup his losses, many pharmaceutical companies would be very loath to continue their research programmes. It is said that less than two per cent of the price of a patented drug is represented by production costs.

Similar arguments apply to patented automobile components and copyright computer software: consumers claim that the cost of both is held artificially high by the abuse of a monopoly.

With regard to automobile components, consumers say that parts which fit correctly and function properly can be made and sold by competitors (often in developing countries) at half the price of the authentic manufacturers' spares.

It is claimed that intellectual property rights are being abused to enforce an artificial price maintenance system, which also increases the costs of car repairs, and consequently of insurance premiums.

The manufacturers reply that they try to keep the initial price of vehicles as low as possible and rarely recoup the development costs of vehicles from the selling price of the new vehicle; they are therefore forced to recoup some of the costs from the sale of genuine spare parts. There is also the point that (except in a few cases such as that of the VW Beetle), the actual life cycle of a vehicle may be only seven to ten years, whereas substantial numbers of spares may be sold for a period of 20 years or more.

It is interesting to note that some automobile producers such as Volvo have responded by reducing the price of their spares and offering a fair deal on repairs in their workshops.

There are moves afoot to permit the adaptation of designs for spare parts from the point of view of copyright, providing the copied spares

Present and Future: The Professional Licensing Executive

function correctly and do not actually infringe any process or other patent used in production. In this sense, consumers make a fine distinction between **copying** (which means producing a technically and visually equivalent product but not disguising the fact that it is not an original spare part) and **counterfeiting**, which means that a competitor will try to produce a copy of the product and sell it under the original name, or under a confusingly similar name. It is interesting to note that the United Kingdom (among others) is in the process of reforming the laws against counterfeiting.

Apart from the originator of a counterfeiting product losing considerable sums of money, it should also be noted that the governments of countries where counterfeiting goes unchecked lose large sums in sales tax, value added tax and corporation tax. Governments strengthening anti-counterfeiting legislation do not only have the interests of the inventors at heart.

Another application of the patent system which is slowly being eliminated from major unified markets such as the European Union (at least as far as large companies are concerned) is the abuse of a patent or trademark monopoly to enforce retail price maintenance upon third parties, after a product has been sold by the original manufacturer; this doctrine is called the exhaustion of rights. Basically it means that the restrictive rights of an inventor or manufacturer are exhausted after the first sale: if A sells a patented product to B, and B wishes to sell it at prices lower than the prices recommended or practised by A, A should not have any right to interfere with B's pricing policy. In spite of this general trend, there are particular cases such as the retail price maintenance of perfumes, where arguments to the contrary appear to be finding favour in the courts – this applies especially where the producer of the original product has substantial advertising costs, from which the retailer benefits without himself having to make a similar advertising investment.

Similar issues arise with computer software over the ability to use various standard programmes with a copyright operating system or with other standard programmes. In order to ensure that the two or more systems can operate properly together, it is necessary that the new system contains some features of the older system – much as two gears which mesh properly will have to have similar features. There have been a number of contentious cases between the manufacturers of hardware and of software, and also between different software houses to try to stop new software designs using reversed engineered features of an older system which may be subject to copyright or even patents.

There is a growing train of thought that such reverse engineering should be allowed, to such an extent as may be necessary to allow two systems to work together, while it would still be forbidden to make a straight copy of a whole system. Indeed consumers claim that the ability to use one system with several others in fact widens the scope of application of the original system, and is in the interests of the original inventor.

One danger in permitting the copying of spares is in the product liability risks. A producer of a road vehicle, an aircraft or a computer system may refuse to accept liability for breakdowns and failures unless approved spares or computer software are used. Hence the guarantees on a machine or system may expire if companies seek to cut corners in the specification of critical aspects of the system.

In addition, if a product from a small company were to fail, the company might not carry adequate product liability insurance to meet the (probably very high) claims for damages. Hence, insurers have to balance the costs of cheaper spares or software against the risks of suing potentially negligent companies with inadequate cover.

Over all patents, industrial designs and copyright, there hangs the question of authorship: as in the case of the author of works of fiction, there are movements to ensure that if inventors of a new product, process or design are individuals, they are fairly rewarded for the creative aspects of their work. In some cases, the rights of authors to receive some of the fruits of their inventiveness are seen as a basic human right and may go beyond the terms of their employment or consultancy contract. This trend towards strengthening and making

Present and Future: The Professional Licensing Executive

more automatic the remuneration of the inventor will continue, and there will be greater pressure to introduce such reward systems in countries where they are not yet accepted.

THE FUTURE IMPORTANCE OF TRADEMARKS AND REGISTERED DESIGNS

In the light of the above developments, it is conceivable that patents will become a system for the initial protection of a new technical development, to allow the inventor to recoup some of the development cost before the invention enters into the public domain. Licensing practitioners point out that the advertising and marketing budgets of most firms (especially in the consumer field and including pharmaceuticals) far exceed the research budgets. Therefore the long term protection of the goodwill of all but special research companies should come from trademarks as well as from patents.

Software companies, producers of automobiles and aircraft or of components for them, and companies producing or marketing pharmaceuticals or agro-chemicals would be well advised to take seriously the question of trademarks in their business planning; a patent usually lasts for a maximum of 20 years and gets weaker the longer it lasts. If a trademark is supported by advertising, it can be renewed indefinitely and gets stronger with increased use. This may be a way forward for companies trying to reap a long-term reward from marketing genetically engineered seeds, animal strains or biotechnology products; a powerful trademark subject to stringent quality assurance provisions could be licensed to the purchaser of the products, much as a computer user buys a software licence.

For similar reasons, movements are under way to increase the protection afforded by registered designs, especially for non-technical products.

THE FUTURE ECONOMIC ROLE OF INTELLECTUAL PROPERTY

If our pessimistic scenario applies, then intellectual property management will remain as a largely defensive activity, with financial and taxation implications, usually to be found in the international trade between related concerns.

However, there is much to be said for the optimistic scenario: as the business process becomes better understood, business executives will pay more attention to the protection of the intellectual property and goodwill of their companies from the outset and it will be built up, maintained and managed as are other company assets.

The role of protecting intellectual property as a defensive strategy has been described at length but, once managers (especially in small and medium sized enterprises) become aware of the value of this asset, they will seek to use it more aggressively, not merely to protect a profit potential but as a source of profit in its own right.

In particular, how are (for example) smaller European companies to get any share in the development of remoter markets such as those of the Pacific Rim, or how are countries such as Poland or Hungary to turn their well-developed educational and research facilities into sources of income if not through licensing?

The importance of licensing in the economic life of developing countries will also continue: the tides of protectionism and free trade will ebb and flow but, as a result of the information revolution, developing countries will reach a compromise between their own need to protect new industries and the need to provide a fair remuneration to suppliers of expertise.

To overcome difficulties of payment, there will be a continuing call for creative accounting, countertrade, and bartering. It is only a matter of time before services as well as raw materials and products will be offered by governments or licensees in developing companies as sources of revenue for foreign licensors. Countertrade with payment in airline tickets or holiday vouchers has already been suggested.

Present and Future: The Professional Licensing Executive

KNOWHOW EXCHANGES

Already there are a number of possibilities for bringing buyers and sellers together:

1. knowhow brokers who will carry out a specific search on the basis of a detailed brief;
2. shows (exhibitions) for inventors and inventions; and
3. magazines which publish information on new patents, products and processes in printed form.

In 1997, the *Salon International des Inventions* in Geneva will celebrate its quarter century. In April 1993, it publicized over 1000 inventions from 33 countries to over 110 000 visitors. Some 450 inventions were eventually involved in deals worth over $20m (over $40 000 per deal on average).

Another impact of the information revolution has been the establishment of patent and trademark data bases, both by the national organizations responsible for their registration and by private concerns.

In the next five years it is likely that the first on-line computer knowhow exchange will be set up, using technology not unlike that used for computerized real estate auctions. The owner of the data base will build up a store of information on technology available worldwide, using key-word systems already in use in searching through scientific literature. The knowhow sellers and buyers will probably have to pay the equivalent of an advertising fee to have their data published under a code number. To help small companies and developing countries, an alternative way of payment will be a basic appearance fee and a larger sum payable if a deal is successfully arranged.

Institutions and companies in search of partners will subscribe for a code number to gain access to the data base, and will pay a further brokerage fee to gain an introduction to the owner or potential purchaser of any knowhow they may find to be of interest.

As has been the case in the brokerage of other products, standardized forms of agreement will probably begin to find acceptance for the simpler deals.

Product liability and insurance

One difficulty remaining for smaller companies supplying technology for any product with implications for public safety – whether a domestic appliance, a vehicle or a piece of industrial machinery – is the responsibility of the inventor for any hidden defects inherent in the design (as distinct from faults arising out of incorrect manufacture). There is already a serious problem of liability insurance for companies trading with the United States. The costs of the litigation alone would be sufficient to break many small companies.

Some inventor's liability insurance will have to be developed for small companies to cover such eventualities, probably with a limit on the maximum claim. This insurance would be available for inspection by the potential licensee who then could make its own judgment on the risk.

Education, training and career patterns

In such a multi-disciplinary field as technology transfer, which can appear as a hotch-potch of scientific, legal, commercial and regulatory matters it might appear that it would be difficult to design a suitable general training course for company executives, independent licensing practitioners and specialists from the professions. However, in most industrialized countries there are an increasing number of introductory courses lasting from two days to two weeks. In the United States there are longer courses, varying from summer schools to a one year Master of Intellectual Property programme, such as that offered by the Franklin Pierce Law Center in Concord, New Hampshire.

As in other fields, it is likely that pure disciplines will be subjected to modifications by the fuzzy logic of commercial necessity, so that (as in

Present and Future: The Professional Licensing Executive

the United States or Germany) more high school students will study a number of subjects from the sciences and humanities to a higher level before specializing. There will be an increasing number of graduate and postgraduate courses on topics such as law for engineers or intellectual property management for scientists.

In the industrialized countries, more mixed practices will emerge: firms of patent attorneys with their own solicitors, or firms of solicitors having special departments concerned with protecting and exploiting intellectual property. Young civil servants from some of the developing countries will be able to profit from such training facilities before specializing in the administration of intellectual property and licensing in their own countries.

The career of **intellectual property specialist**, both within commercial companies and as a profession, will emerge more clearly as the profit potential of intellectual property is better understood. On the other hand, such a career will not be a straight line career such as that of an accountant or solicitor is presumed to be. It will consist of obtaining training in a number of allied disciplines and obtaining training in a number of organizations and roles. Indeed, it might be of interest to large companies and large firms of patent and trademark agents to run schemes for exchanging young specialists in intellectual property in a joint training programme.

THE LAST WORD

In the writing of this book, the authors fulfilled an ambition which has lasted almost twenty years. In this period, the whole field of intellectual property protection and licensing has become at once globalized and simplified: it has become more complex in terms of the number of countries and scientific and commercial subject matters affected, but it has become less complicated in the sense that national laws and intra-organizational practices have been winnowed by years of experience and informed scrutiny. The information revolution and the globalization of trade and consumer culture have been powerful forces which have moulded the evolution of intellectual property.

There is no sign that these forces are abating so that, on balance, we must assume the positive scenario: that the future for licensing is at least as progressive as the past. The planned exploitation of intellectual property will receive more attention as part of the business strategy of all enterprises. This will be especially the case for technologically based companies, for small and medium sized enterprises and for those lacking the capital to make investments in a number of production facilities throughout the world. The licensing alternative will be especially attractive for products and processes having a short product life and requiring simultaneous exploitation on many geographical or technological fronts in order to optimize the income for their owner.

Any profitable business requires the management of people, physical resources and information. The next century will see the emergence of the post-industrial society in which wealth and well-being will depend to a significant extent on a global trade in ideas. The era of intellectual property has only just begun.

Part 7

Appendices

Part 7 contains a thesaurus explaining some of the words and phrases commonly used in negotiating licensing agreements (definitions of the Licensing Executives Society). Also provided is a list of useful publications and organizations that can provide assistance or information.

7

7.1 Definitions

This chapter consists of two parts. The following list of words and definitions was produced by the Licensing Executives Society's International Patent and Technology Licensing Committee, chaired by Cruzan Alexander. It was drafted with the intention of helping negotiators in international licensing to understand one another more clearly and to improve communications between them. It was not intended to be a dictionary. The second part provides some extra definitions for the interest of readers.

7.1.1 THESAURUS

The Thesaurus is reprinted with permission from *Les Nouvelles*, the Journal of the Licensing Executives Society International Volume XXIII, No.2, June 1988 and the permission of the compiler, Mr Alexander.

ACT OF GOD

An event beyond the reasonable control of the parties preventing the carrying out or delaying of an obligation. Words or phrases sometimes used for the same meaning: force majeure, catastrophic event or happening, event not under control of a party. Preferred phrase: force majeure.

AFFILIATE

See subsidiary.

AGREEMENT

A binding contract between parties such as a license, however some

Appendices

countries such as China interpret an agreement as nonbinding but a contract is considered binding. Preferred term: contract or license contract.

AGREEMENT DATE

See execution date and effective date.

AGREEMENT NOT TO LICENSE OTHERS

See sole license.

ARMS-LENGTH TRANSACTION

Idiomatic English, means a transaction between strangers who have no financial interest in each other or no ties. May present difficulties in translation.

ASSIGN, ASSIGNMENT

Used primarily in connection with the transfer of the tangible evidence of a right such as a patent or trademark or copyright. Words sometimes used for the same meaning: grant, transfer, convey. Preferred word: assign or assignment. See exclusive license.

AUTHORISE

See license.

AVAILABLE TO THE PUBLIC

See generally known to the public and public domain. Term is not equivalent to generally known to the public since something available to the public in a library may not be generally known.

BEST EFFORT

Means the degree of commitment to an obligation. Has been interpreted by some court decisions to mean surprisingly high degrees of effort, perhaps the highest degree of effort ever used even though such effort would be unreasonable under the circumstances. Preferred phrases: bona fide effort, reasonable effort or diligent effort as appropriate or set minimum performance standards.

BONA FIDE EFFORT

See best effort.

CANCEL OR CANCELLATION

See terminate.

CERTIFIED OR REGISTERED MAIL

Terms primarily used only in the USA. Do not use in international licenses unless each country has this kind of mail.

COMMENCEMENT DATE

See effective date.

COMPOSED OF

See consisting of.

Appendices

COMPRISING

Means a group of items which includes those named and others not named – open ended. Other words and phrases sometimes used for the same meaning: including, such as. Preferred phrase: including but not limited to. See consisting of and composed of which are sometimes erroneously used to mean comprising.

CONFIDENTIAL INFORMATION

See secrecy agreement.

CONFIDENTIAL INFORMATION

Means information not generally known to the public. Supplier may not necessarily own information. Other words and phrases sometimes used and in some instances erroneously for same meaning: proprietary information, secret information, trade secret, knowhow. Preferred phrase: confidential information.

CONSISTING OF

Means only those items mentioned – closed ended. Other phrase sometimes used for the same meaning: composed of. Preferred phrase: use the word 'only' in conjunction with the above. See comprising which is sometimes erroneously used to mean consisting of.

CONTRACT

See agreement.

Convey

Used in connection with real property and assignments, not often used in licensing. See grant and assign.

Corporate address

See place of business.

Covenant not to use

See nonexclusive license.

Cross license

Means when each party to an agreement grants a license to the other on the same subject matter. Term is used most often as a title and not as a technical licensing term in the body of the agreement.

Customer

Usually a purchaser of goods or services, term is generic in time – first purchaser such as distributor or last purchaser such as retail purchaser. Terms sometimes used for same meaning: end user, purchaser. Preferred phrase: final customer if end user is intended or intermediate customer or direct customer as appropriate.

Domicile

Means place of residence, used in connection with tax law, should not be used in licenses. Sometimes used to indicate place of incorporation. See place of business.

Appendices

DOWN PAYMENT

See lump sum.

DUE DILIGENCE

A term used by investment bankers. Means evaluating the situation or technology within a short period of time. Not used in licensing.

EFFECTIVE DATE

Means the date when an agreement comes into full force and effect. Date may be before or after date of signing of agreement by all parties. Words and phrases sometimes used and in some instances erroneously for same meaning: execution date, agreement date, commencement date, signing date. Preferred phrase: effective date. See execution date.

ELECTION

A requirement to make a choice. Word sometimes used for same meaning: option. Preferred word: election when appropriate. See option.

EMPLOYMENT AGREEMENT

An agreement between employer and employee usually including provisions setting forth obligations of employee regarding confidential information, assignment of inventions, and obligations after termination of employment. Normally does not deal with monetary matters. Words and phrases sometimes used for same meaning: technical agreement, secrecy agreement, confidentiality agreement, assignment agreement. Preferred phrase: employment agreement. See secrecy agreement.

End user

Means final customer or purchaser. Is an idiomatic English term and may be difficult to translate. Preferred phrase: final customer. See customer.

Exclusive license

Means licensor grants the licensee the sole right to practice the invention or use trademark to the exclusion of licensor and others; may be limited to territory, field, product or time; normally exclusive licensee has right to license others. Phrases sometimes used, and in some instances erroneously, for same meaning: sole license, single license, assignment, limited license. Preferred phrase: exclusive license. See sole license.

Execution date

Means the date all parties have signed the agreement. Sometimes means the date an executory obligation has been fulfilled. Words and phrases sometimes used, and in some instances erroneously, for same meaning: agreement date, signing date, effective date of agreement. Preferred phrase: agreement execution date. See effective date.

Expiration date

See term of agreement.

Field of use

Relates to the scope of license, such as a particular product for a particular use. Should define product and area of use.

Appendices

FIRST OPTION

See first refusal.

FIRST REFUSAL, RIGHT OF

Right of one party of an agreement to receive a right, commitment or a license from another party of the agreement prior to being offered to any third party. Usually coupled with a time limit or a payment or both. Term per se not usually used in agreements but instead the specific terms of right are written out. Phrases sometimes used for same meaning: first option, right to improvement inventions, right to expand scope or to select other fields. In communications, right should be clearly defined and specified.

FIXED FEE OR ROYALTY

See lump sum and minimum royalty.

FIRST-CLASS MAIL

Does not have meaning in most countries outside the USA. In international licensing use term regular mail or airmail as appropriate.

FORCE MAJEURE

An event beyond the reasonable control of the parties preventing the carrying out or delaying of an obligation. Words and phrases sometimes used for the same meaning: act of God, catastrophic event or happening, event not under control of party. Preferred phrase: force majeure.

FREEDOM

See license and right.

GENERALLY KNOWN TO THE PUBLIC

Means information not confidential or secret. Information may, however, be subject to proprietary rights, such as information described in a valid unexpired patent. Words and phrases sometimes used for same meaning: in the public domain, nonconfidential, not secret, available to public, publicly known. Preferred phrase: generally known to the public. See public domain.

GRANT

Used primarily in connection with a license, such as 'grant a license'. Sometimes misunderstood to mean a warranty by licensor that no other licenses are required from third parties. Words and phrases sometimes used for same meaning: convey, transfer, assign. Preferred word: grant.

GUARANTEE

See warranty and indemnification.

HOLD HARMLESS

See indemnification and nonexclusive license and warranty.

IMMUNITY FROM SUIT

See nonexclusive license.

Appendices

INCLUDING

See comprising.

INDEMNIFICATION

Usually the licensor agrees to pay specified liabilities, such as repay any court awarded monetary damages, to licensee if he infringes another's patent or trademark in practising licensed inventions or using licensed trademark. Words and phrases sometimes used for same meaning: hold harmless, guarantee, liability, warranty. Preferred phrase: indemnification. See warranty.

INDUSTRIAL PROPERTY

See intellectual property.

INITIAL PAYMENT

See lump sum.

INTELLECTUAL PROPERTY

Ownership rights given by law in intellectual information such as inventions, patents, trademarks, trade names, logos, copyrights, knowhow, trade secrets. Words and phrases sometimes used for same meaning: industrial property, proprietary information. Preferred phrase: intellectual property. See proprietary information.

KNOWHOW (INFORMATION)

Knowhow may be confidential or nonconfidential and it may be proprietary or nonproprietary (such as in a text book). It may be technical or nontechnical. See confidential information, trade secret and proprietary information.

LETTER OF INTENT

Has different meanings in different countries. In the USA merely an outline of objectives for negotiations, usually not binding. In Japan, usually a binding agreement with terms in letter of intent having been agreed upon – further negotiations only on other terms not set out in letter. Unless intended to be a binding agreement, use another term such as 'non-binding proposal'.

LIABILITY

See indemnification and warranty.

LICENSE

Means permission to practice all or a part of a proprietary right. Words and phrases sometimes used for same meaning: right, right and license, permission, authorize, freedom. Preferred word: license. See non-exclusive license and right.

LICENSE RIGHTS

See proprietary rights.

LIMITED LICENSE

See exclusive license.

Appendices

Logo

See trademarks.

Lump sum

Idiomatic English. Means a single monetary payment. Words and phrases sometimes used for same meaning; down payment, initial payment or fee, fixed fee. Preferred phrase: lump sum.

Minimum performance

See best effort and minimum royalty.

Minimum royalty

Obligation to pay certain amount periodically, otherwise the license may be changed or terminated automatically or at option of licensor. Words and phrases sometimes used for same meaning: promise to pay, promissory notes, fixed royalty. Preferred phrase: minimum royalty.

Nonconfidential

See generally known to the public.

Nonconfidential agreement

See secrecy agreement.

Nonexclusive license

A license that does not prohibit the licensor from licensing others in the same field, or on the same product, or same territory, etc. Words and phrases sometimes used for same meaning: license, sublicense, immunity from suit, holds harmless, covenant not to sue. Preferred phrase: nonexclusive license.

OPTION

Right to make a choice, not a requirement. Word sometimes used for same meaning: election. Preferred word: option. See election.

OWNED

See proprietary rights.

PAID-UP LICENSE

A license which does not require further royalties because some consideration has been given in advance including cash but not necessarily cash. Phrase sometimes used for same meaning: royalty free license. Preferred phrase: paid-up license with no future royalty payments.

PERMISSION

See license.

PERSONAL LICENSE

Idiomatic English, means a nonassignable, nontransferable license, usually license terminates on death of individual or dissolution or merger of corporation or firm.

Appendices

Place of business

Means principal place of business or corporate offices. Words and phrases sometimes used, and in some instances erroneously, for same meaning: domicile, corporate address, place of incorporation, location of corporate offices, principal place of business. Preferred phrase: place of business. See domicile.

Place of incorporation

Used primarily for identification purposes in license agreements. See place of business and domicile.

Principle place of business

See place of business.

Promise or promissory

See minimum royalty.

Proprietary information

Means information owned by supplier but not necessarily confidential. Misused to mean confidential information. Words and phrases sometimes used, and in some instances erroneously, for same meaning: confidential information, all rights and title in intellectual property, owned, controlled. Preferred phrase: proprietary information. See confidential information and intellectual property.

Proprietary rights

Rights conferred by law for ownership or control (generic). Words and phrases sometimes used for the same meaning: patent, trademark and copyright rights, license rights, intellectual property rights, right, proprietary information, title, confidential information. Preferred phrase: proprietary rights.

PUBLIC DOMAIN

Means free to use; free of patent, trademark and copyright rights. Misnomer for generally known to the public. Words and phrases sometimes used for same meaning: nonconfidential, not secret, publicly known, available to the public. In the context of nonconfidentiality, preferred phrase: generally known to the public or available to the public (something that is available to public may not be generally known to public).

PUBLICLY KNOWN

See generally known to the public.

RESCIND

See terminate.

RIGHT

Means permission to practice all or part of a proprietary right. Has different meanings in different countries. Sometimes broader than a license but with restrictions on grantor. Words and phrases sometimes used for same meaning: license, right and license, permission, authorize, freedom. Preferred word: license. See license.

Appendices

ROYALTY-FREE LICENSE

See paid-up license.

SCOPE

See field of use. Sometimes refers to territory, type of license (for example, nonexclusive), subject matter. When used, it should be clearly defined. Seldom used alone.

SECRECY AGREEMENT

An agreement between two or more parties setting forth conditions of accepting or not accepting confidential information. Words and phrases sometimes used for same meaning: confidential agreement, nonconfidential agreement, employment agreement, technical agreement. Preferred phrase: secrecy agreement, when accepting confidential information, nonconfidentiality agreement when not accepting confidential information.

SECRET INFORMATION

See confidential information and proprietary information.

SEMI-EXCLUSIVE LICENSE

See sole license.

SERVICE MARK

See trademark.

SIGNING DATE

See execution date and effective date.

SINGLE LICENSE

See exclusive license and sole license.

SOLE LICENSE

Means licensor grants licensee exclusive license except for retained nonexclusive license of licensor. Has different meanings in different countries and regions. Phrases sometimes used, and in some instances erroneously, for same meaning: single license, exclusive license, semi-exclusive license agreement not to license others. Preferred phrase: exclusive license except for a nonexclusive license retained by licensor. See exclusive license and nonexclusive license.

SUBLICENSE RIGHT

The right of a licensee to grant licenses to others. Phrase sometimes used for same meaning: exclusive license right, sub-contract right. Preferred phrase: right to grant licenses to others.

SUBSIDIARY

Means a company at least partially owned by another company, the parent company. Should be defined in the license agreement. Words and phrases sometimes used for same meaning: affiliate, related company, joint venture. Preferred word: subsidiary with definition.

387

Appendices

TECHNICAL AGREEMENT

See employment agreement.

TERMS OF AGREEMENT

Means length of agreement until it automatically terminates in toto by an event or date certain. Not to be confused with right to terminate or cancel agreement before term of license agreement is up or termination of a specific right or obligation under the agreement. Words and phrases sometimes used for same or similar meaning: expiration of agreement, expiration date, termination date. Preferred phrase: term of agreement or the termination of a specific right or obligation under the agreement.

TERMINATION DATE

See term of agreement.

TERMINATE OR TERMINATION

Termination of an agreement prior to its normal term as the result of an event or the option of one of the parties. Not to be confused with term of agreement. Words sometimes used for same meaning: cancel or cancellation, abrogate, default, rescind. Preferred word: terminate or termination.

TERRITORY

Refers to the geographical area covered by a license; may be territory of sale or territory of manufacture or both. Term must be defined in the agreement.

TRADE NAME

Usually the name of a business enterprise. May or may not be protected by law. See trademark.

TRADEMARK

A mark, word or phrase for which the law has given the owner a right to exclude others from using. Often confused with trade name. Words and phrases sometimes used, and in some instances erroneously for same meaning: trade name, logo, motto, service mark, character. Preferred word: trademark.

TRADE SECRET

Means confidential information which is protected by law. Has different meanings in different countries. Limited or no protection in some countries. Words and phrases sometimes used, and in some instances erroneously for same meaning: confidential information, proprietary information, secret information, knowhow. Preferred phrase: confidential information or trade secret depending on use of term and jurisdiction.

TRANSFER

Used in connection with real property and assignment of title, not often used in licensing. See grant, assign and convey.

WARRANTY, WARRANT

Licensor's guarantee of ownership of licensed proprietary rights, right to grant license, no conflict with other licenses granted by licensor, noninfringement of other patents in practising license, usefulness of

Appendices

information for purpose of agreement, practicability of information, operability, nontoxicity and nonhazardous. The guarantee or obligation of licensor must be defined by type, duration, and monetary or other obligations. Words and phrases used for same or similar meaning: guarantee, liability damages, indemnification. Preferred term: warrant with definition of scope and subject matter. See indemnification.

7.1.2 Additional definitions

The above list is definitive and provided by the Licensing Executives Society; the following list is of a few additions which should interest readers who should also note the statement by WIPO quoted in Chapter 3.1 that there are 'no universally accepted definitions of expressions like inventions and trademarks'.

Knowhow consists of data, drawings, control techniques and methods of organization, formulae, specially designed machinery or apparatus – information, in short, which explains how to do something or to do something better. The information does not form part of the invention itself and does not therefore fall under the protection of the patent's specification. The information clearly has the potential to be valuable: a patent licence might well be useless without the side information which makes it capable of exploitation. The implication is clear that the person desiring the knowhow does not possess the information already and although secrecy, the fact that no-one else knows, is not necessarily a part of the knowhow, most knowhow agreements include clauses insisting that the person to whom the knowhow is disclosed does not disclose to any other party. Knowhow may consist of rights to use other intellectual property, like a trademark or a design copyright, and the maintenance of secrecy in such cases will not be appropriate or necessary.

Copyright is concerned with originality rather than the uniqueness which characterizes a patent. To be worthy of copyright all that is needed is that the copyright work is the result of independent intellectual effort. Original literary, dramatic, musical and artistic works are the basic categories capable of copyright protection.

Aesthetic merit is not essential. Provided that a test of originality is satisfied copyright can subsist in books, pamphlets, brochures, any writing of more than minimal length, writing tables, compilations, published editions, technical descriptions, catalogues and engineering drawings. Computer programmes are also protected as literary works.

Artistic merit is not essential and copyright may subsist in graphic works, photographs, sculptures, collages, architectural works and models and craftsmanship.

Copyright also protects sound recordings, films (including video films) and broadcasts (including cable and satellite broadcasts).

Copyright is not a monopoly right in any strict sense because it is the expression rather than the idea which is protected. There is no copyright in a name or title either. The right in copyright is to prevent others from copying the expression of your idea without consent. A new act, The Copyright Designs and Patents Act 1988 ('the 1988 Act'), came into force for most purposes on 1st August 1988 ('the commencement date'). This commencement date is worthy of note because copyright created before that date will either be dealt with under an earlier Copyright Act or be treated differently under the 1988 Act. Unless otherwise stated, this section deals only with the situation post 1st August 1988.

The general rule is that the author of a work is the first owner of copyright. For computer generated work the author is the person who undertook the arrangements necessary for creating the work. The main exception relates to employment. Where the work is created as part of the normal duties of an employee the copyright belongs, subject to any agreement to the contrary, to the employer. The situation with academics, research students and sub-contractors will not necessarily follow the general rule but care should in any event be taken to ensure that contracts of employment are specific on the subject. The 1988 Act made certain changes as to the allocation of ownership. Whereas, before, an owner of film owned copyright in a photograph, the photographer is now treated as the 'author'.

Appendices

The 1988 Act (in Britain) structures the entitlement as an exclusive right to do various restricted acts in relation to the work which, for others, would constitute a prohibited act of 'copying'. The restricted acts are to reproduce the work, to store it electronically, to issue copies of it to the public, to make any adaptation of it, to translate (including converting a programme from one computer language to another) or to publish it, performing or showing the work in public, broadcasting it or including it in a cable programme service. Copying is given a broad definition to include reproducing a work in any material form.

Owners of copyright in sound recordings, films and computer programmes can control their rental. This includes, for example the renting of videos.

Moral rights The 1988 Act (in Britain) introduced protection for two rights, of 'paternity' and 'integrity' belonging to authors of copyright works. The paternity right is the right to be named as the author of a work and does not apply unless it has been asserted in writing at the signature of the author of the work. The integrity right is the right to object to derogatory treatment and distortions of the work which are prejudicial to the author's honour or reputation.

Neither of the moral rights are applicable to computer programmes or computer generated works and they do not generally apply to employees. An assignee of copyright on taking any assignment should ensure that any moral rights have been expressly waived by the author of the work, since the moral rights themselves cannot be assigned and failure to obtain the waiver risks the assignees' freedom to exploit the copyright works being interfered with.

Moral rights apply to all copyright works created after the commencement date of the 1988 Act and to existing literary, dramatic, musical and artistic works at that time, providing the author was alive.

Copyright arises automatically when a work takes physical form. There is no registration system and therefore no forms to fill in and no fees to pay. Proving the existence of copyright is another matter.

Invention Normally, an individual inventor working for an organization will not own an invention if he creates it while performing his normal duties, though in certain economic sectors custom dictates the opposite (academics and research students usually own the inventions they create at universities). The contract of employment between inventor and employer should always make clear specification as to ownership. Where research work is sub-contracted too, the sub-contract should specify who is to own the patent for any invention which results from the sub-contracted research work.

Passing off Unlike in infringement proceedings, the person who brings an action for passing off will need to show a substantial reputation in the trademark and that there has been, or that there is likelihood of confusion in the market place, and that the confusion has caused damage. Evidence is normally assembled in the form of market surveys which ask consumers whether they were in practice confused by the similar product. The exercise will probably be expensive and the impression market survey evidence is likely to create with the judge is difficult to gauge. If the case is made out then remedies are available.

7.2 Publications

This chapter lists publications consulted in the production of this book. In this list, an (L) before the title means of immediate interest to licensing people, an (R) means useful for reference purposes, and an (A) means suitable for more in-depth studies.

Books are arranged alphabetically by name of author. The name is followed by the date of publication which is followed by the title and the publisher. If a later edition is available, this is shown after the title. In a dynamic subject such as this one, it is important to consult the most recent edition of a particular book. Some entries have a note about the use or usefulness of the publication at the end of the entry.

PERIODICALS

Copyright World, published by IPP Ltd, Parson's Green, London SW6 4TH, England

In-House Lawyer

Intellectual Property Journal, a new journal concentrating on developing countries, especially those of Africa and the Middle East

International Business Lawyer

(L) *Les Nouvelles*, published by the Licensing Executives Society (LES) which is a veritable mine of information (for further information, contact Licensing Executives Society, 71 East Avenue, Norwalk, CT 06851-4903, USA)

Managing Intellectual Property, published by Euromoney Publications Plc, Nestor House, Playhouse Yard, London EC4V 5EX

Patent World, published by IPP Ltd, Parson's Green, London SW6 4TH, England

(A) *R and D Management*, a prestigious periodical edited by Alan Pearson of the Manchester Business School (Booth Street West, Manchester M15 6PB) concerned with the origination and transfer of technology

Appendices

BOOKS

(R) *1991 Annual Report and Accounts of the UK Patent Office*, Her Majesty's Stationery Office, Publications Centre, PO Box 276, London SW8 5DT

(R) *Annual Abstract of Statistics* for the United Kingdom of Great Britain and Northern Ireland, Her Majesty's Stationery Office, PO Box 276, London SW8 5DT

(A) Ball, D.A. and McCulloch (1988), *International Business*, 2nd edn, Business Publications (Texas)

(R) Brooke, M.Z. and Buckley, P.J. (1988), *Handbook of International Trade*, new edition, Macmillan 1988

(L) Brooke, M.Z. (1992), *International Management*, 2nd edn, Stanley Thornes

(R) Brooke, M.Z. (1990), *Handbook of International Financial Management*, Macmillan

(R) Brooke, M.Z. (1985), *Selling Management Services Contracts in International Business*, Holt, Rinehart and Winston (now distributed by Cassell)

(R) Buchan, David, *Europe, the Strange Superpower*, Pitman (includes a chapter on licensing)

(R) Buckley, P.J. (1992), *Studies in International Business*, Macmillan

(A) Channon, D.F. (1978), *Multinational Strategic Planning*, Macmillan

(R) Clarke, B.W. (1993, updated annually), *International Trade Finance*, Chiltern Publishing

(R) Crawford, Nicholas K. and Morgan, Eleanor T., *The Innovators' Handbook*

(R) *Doing Business in ...* series, published by the international accounting and management consulting firm Ernst and Young, giving valuable advice on business conditions in over 30 key countries. Contact address: Ernst and Young International, 787 Seventh

Avenue, New York, NY 10019, United States

(R) European Commission, (1987), *Supporting Structure for Innovation, Technology Transfer and Enterprise Creation in Spain and Portugal*

(R) Fowlston, Brendan (1984 edn), *Understanding Commercial and Industrial Licensing*, Waterlow

(R) *Franchise Handbook 1993*, (ed Lynne Lister), Blenheim

(R) Hearn, Patrick (1986), *The Business of Industrial Licensing – A Practical Guide to Patents, Knowhow, Trademarks and Industrial Designs*, new edition, Gower

(A) Hofstede, G. (1980), *Cultures Consequences: International Differences in Work-related Values*, Sage

(A) Hughes, Helen (1988), *Achieving Industrialization in East Asia*, Cambridge

(R) *Increasing your Profit Potential through Licensing*, a booklet published by the Royal Bank of Scotland, Business Information Service.

(L) International Chamber of Commerce, a series of booklets on arbitration and related issues, including:
ICSID Basic Documents
ICSID Model Clauses
ICSID Additional Facility
Arbitration under the ICSID Convention (by Aran Brockes)
Towards a Greater Depoliticization of Investment Disputes:
The Roles of ICSID and MIGA
Also published is a quarterly periodical, the *ICSID Review*

(A) 'International trade in intellectual property: the emerging GATT regime', *University of Toronto Faculty of Law Review*, 49 (Winter 1993) pp. 106-151

(A) Kinsey, Joanne (1988), *Marketing in Developing Countries*, Macmillan

(R) Larkin, Kay (ed) (1993), *World Insurance Year Book 1993*, Longman

Appendices

(R) Leaffa, Marshall A. (1990), *International Treaties on Intellectual Property*, BNA Books (Washington D.C.)

(R) Liston, Lynne (1993), *Franchise Handbook 1993*, Blenheim

(R) Melville, L.W. (3rd edn 1979, revised 1990), *Forms and Agreements on Intellectual Property and International Licensing*, Sweet and Maxwell (London) and Clark Boardman (New York)

(A) Millman, A.E., 'Licensing Technology', *Management Decision*, 21 March 1983

(R) *Mining 1994,*(1993), Longman (Financial Times International Yearbook Series)

(R) *Oil and Gas 1994*, (1993), Longman (Financial Times International Yearbook Series)

ORGALIME Publications, Orgalime (the liaison group of the European mechanical, electrical, electronic and metalworking industries associations, for address see Chapter 7.3) produces a number of publications, including:
Model form of international patent licence contract
Model form of international knowhow licence contract
Product Liability in Europe – A practical guide for industry
Practical guide for preparing a knowhow contract
Drawings and technical documents – Ownership and protection against improper use

(L) Price Waterhouse (1993), *Corporate Taxes* (published annually).

(A) Robinson, R.D. (1978), *International Business Management*, 2nd edn, Dryden

(A) Rugman, Alan M. et al. (1986), *International Business: Firm and Environment*, McGraw-Hill. See index for passages on licensing

(A) Savary, Julien (1984), *French Multinationals*, English translation, Frances Pinter

(L) Scott, Bill (1986), *The Skills of Negotiating*, Gower

(L) Singleton, E. Susan, 'Intellectual property disputes: settlement agreements and ancillary licences under EC and UK competition law'

(R) Spilker, Bert (1989), *Multinational Drug Companies*, Raven Press (New York)

(R) *Statistisches Jahrbuch (Statistical Annual) of the Federal Republic of Germany*, the Statistisches Bundesamt (Federal Statistical Office), Metzler-Poeschel Verlag Verlagsauslieferung Hermann Leins, Postfach 7, 7400 Kusterdingen, Germany

(A) Stobaugh, Robert and Wells, Louis T. (eds) (1984), *Technology Crossing Borders*, Harvard Business School

(R) Swain, Christopher and Buckley Andrew (1981), *World Directory of Energy Information*, Gower

(L) Telesio, Piero, 'Foreign licensing in multinational enterprises' (see above, the book by Stobaugh and Wells in which this is Chapter 9 – a stimulating and well-researched chapter on licensing arrangements)

(A) United Nations (1987), *Licence Agreements in Developing Countries*, United Nations Centre on Transnational Corporations

(R) United Nations, *Draft International Code of Conduct on the Transfer of Technology*

(R) *World Energy CD-ROM 1994* (1993), Longman (Financial Times International Yearbook Series)

(R) *World Insurance 1993* (1993), Larkin, Kay (ed), Longman (Financial Times International Yearbook Series)

(L) World Intellectual Property Organization, *WIPO: General Information 1993*. A booklet on the work of the Organization

(L) World Intellectual Property Organization (1977), *Licensing Guide for Developing Countries*, Geneva

7.3 Organizations

The following is a selected list of organizations that can offer assistance to licensing partners.

Chambers of Commerce, to be found in almost every major business centre, are not listed here but can usually be discovered quite easily through local telephone directories. For many purposes they are to be regarded as the most valuable sources of information and assistance.

Both licensing partners need legal advisers (a solicitor in Britain and most Commonwealth countries, a lawyer or attorney in the United States and most other parts of the world) to draft the agreement but will need to be clear about the conditions that the agreement must enshrine – this book is designed to help in the preparatory process. Firms of solicitors and accountants active in international business are not included on this list but they exist in most commercial centres (including Gide Loyrette Nouel whose offices in Paris at 26 cours Albert Premier are near those of the International Chamber of Commerce). Names and addresses of those who specialize in licensing matters and in particular regions can be found by enquiring among other firms with licensing agreements. Many of the organizations listed below (such as WIPO – the World Intellectual Property Organization) are, however, capable of providing advice on legal matters.

Also possibly required, if counterfeiting is suspected, is a firm of private detectives. Once again these exist in most business centres (including Hoffmann Investigations of Van Leijenberghlaan 199a, 1082 GG Amsterdam, The Netherlands) and are best tracked down locally and are not included on this list apart from the Anti-Counterfeiting Group (ACG) which has much information on counterfeiting along with the US Anti-Counterfeiting Coalition.

The Commonwealth secretariat (which is also on this list) can provide information on counterfeiting. In Britain, trading standards officers in each local authority can be very helpful.

Appendices

Academy of International Business, School of Business Administration, Wayne State University, Detroit, MI 48202, USA

Advanced Technology Alert System (ATAS) c/o UNCSTD, One United Nations Plaza, New York, NY 10017, USA (a United Nations organization)

Advisory Committee for the Coordination of Information Systems (ACCIS), Palais des nations, CH-1211 Geneva 10, Switzerland (a United Nations organization)

Advisory Group for Aerospace Research and Development (AGARD), 7 rue Ancelle, Neuilly-sur-Seine, France (part of NATO)

African Academy of Sciences (AAS), PO Box 14798, Nairobi, Kenya

African Centre for Technology Studies, PO Box 45917, Nairobi, Kenya

African Development Bank (ADB), 01 BP 1387, Abidjan 01, Ivory Coast

African Intellectual Property Organization (OAPI), BP 887, Yaoundé, Cameroon

African Regional Centre for Technology, Avenue Cheikh Anta Diop, BP 2345, Dakar, Senegal

Agence Latinoaméricaine de'Information (ALAI) Casilla 17-12-877 Ecuador

AIM International, 634 Alpha Drive, Pittsburgh, PA 15238, USA

American Management Association International (AMA), Rue Caroly 15, B-1040 Brussels, Belgium

Andean Development Corporation (ADC), EdifTorre Central 5-10, Urb

Anti-Counterfeiting Group (ACG)

Altamira Apart Correos 69011Y 69012, Caracas, Venezuela

Aslib: The Association for Information Management, 20-24 Old Street, London EC1V 9AP

Association of Consulting Scientists, c/o Analysis for Industry, Factories

2-3 Bosworth House, High Street, Thorpe-le-Soken, Essex CO16 0EA

Association of Independent Research and Technology Organisations (AIRTO)

Association of the Electronics, Telecommunications and Business Equipment Industries (EEA), 10-12 Russell Square, London WC1B 5AE

Authors Licensing and Collecting Society (ALCS), 33-34 Alfred Place, London WC1E 7DP

BEAMA Ltd (Federation of British Electronical and Allied Manufacturer's Associations), Leicester House 8, Leicester Street, London WC2H 7BN. BEAMA is the British member association of ORGALIME, Brussels (see below)

British Institute of Management, Management House, Cottingham Rd, Corby Northants NN17 1TT

British Institute of Inventors, 38 Alma Street, Eccles, Manchester M30 0EX

British Library Science Reference and Information Service, 25 Southampton Buildings, London WC2A 1AW (this address is expected to change soon)

Business Equipment Industries, 10-12 Russell Square, London WC1B 5AE

Centre for International Briefing, Farnham Castle, Farnham, Surrey

Chartered Institute of Arbitrators (CIArb), International Arbitration Centre, 24 Angel Gate, City Road, London EC1V 2RS

Chartered Institute of Patent Agents (CIPA), Staple Inn Buildings, High Holborn, London WC1V 7PZ

China-Britain Trade Group, 5th Floor, Abford House, 15 Wilton Road, London SW1V 1LT

Common Law Institute of Intellectual Property, 17 Russell Square, London WC1B 5DR

403

Appendices

Commonwealth Commercial Crime Unit (CCU), Marlborough House, Pall Mall, London SW1Y 5HX

Commonwealth Consultative Group on Technology Management (CCGTM), Marlborough House, Pall Mall, London SW1Y 5HX

Commonwealth Development Corporation (CDC), 1 Bessborough Gardens, London SW1V 2JQ

Commonwealth Legal Advisory Service, c/o BIICL, Charles Clore House, 17 Russell Square, London WC1B 5DR

Commonwealth Secretariat, Marlborough House, Pall Mall, London SW1Y 5HX

Confederation of Asia-Pacific Chambers of Commerce and Industry (CACCI) 10th Floor, 122 Tunkua N Road, Taipei 10590, Taiwan

Confédération européenne d'organismes de contrôle (CEOC) Rue de Commerce 20-22, B-1040 Brussels, Belgium

Confederation of International Contractors Associations (CICA) 128 rue de la Boétie, F75008 Paris, France

Coordination Committee on Multilateral Payments Arrangements and Monetary Cooperation among Developing Countries, Palais des Nations, CH-1211 Geneva 10, Switzerland

Copper Development Association BENELUX, Blvd Paepsem 22, B-1070 Brussels, Belgium

Council for Arab Economic Unity (CAEU), BD 925100, Amman, Jordan

Council of the Bars and Law Societies of the European Community, Rue Washington 40, B-1050 Brussels, Belgium

Council of the European Communities, Rue de la Loi 170, B-1048 Brussels, Belgium

Council of Mining and Metallurgical Institutions (MMI) 44 Portland Place, London W1N

Development Bank of the Great Lakes States, BP 3355, Goma, Zaire

Development Innovations and Networks, 3 rue de VarembÈ, Case 116, CH-1211 Geneva, Switzerland

East African Development Bank (EADB), 4 Nile Avenue, PO Box 7128, Kampala, Uganda

Eastern Caribbean Central Bank (ECCB), PO Box 89, Basseterre, St Kitts-Nevis

Economic Community of West African States (ECOWAS), 8 King George V Road, PMB 12745, Oniken, Lagos, Nigeria

ECU Banking Association (EBA), 4 rue de la Paix, F75002 Paris, France

EEC-EFTA Free Trade Zone, rue de la Loi 200, B 1049 Brussels, Belgium

Electric Components Quality Assurance Committee (ECQAC) Gartenstrasse 179, D-6000 Frankfurt-Main 70, Germany

Eurachem, Laboratory of the Government Chemist, Queens Rd, Teddington TW11 0LY

Euro-China Research Centre for Business Cooperation, Rue Général MacArthur 39, B-1180, Brussels, Belgium

European Association for the Transfer of Technologies, Innovation and Industrial Information, 3 rue des Capicins, L-1313 Luxembourg, Luxembourg

European Association of Manufacturers of Business Machines & Information Technology (EUROBIT), c/o VDMA Lyoner Strasse 18, D-600 Frankfurt-Main 71, Germany

European Bank for Reconstruction and Development, 122 Leadenhall Street, London EC3V 4EA

European Coal and Steel Community (ECSC), B,timent Jean Monnet, rue Alcide de Gasperi, Plateau de Kircherg, L-3424 Luxembourg, Luxembourg

European Committee for Electrotechnical Standardization, rue de Stassaert 35, B-1050 Brussels, Belgium

Appendices

European Committee for Standardization (CEN) rue de Stassaert 36, B-1050 Brussels, Belgium

European Union, rue de la Loi, 200, B-1049 Brussels, Belgium

European Economic Area, rue d'Arloon 118, B-1040 Brussels, Belgium

European Federation of Biotechnology c/o BECHEMA, Theodore-Hauss-Allee 25, Postfach 150 1004, D-600 Frankfurt-Main 15, Germany

European Free Trade Association (EFTA) 8-11 rue de Varembé, CH-1211 Geneva 20, Switzerland

European Investment Bank, Boulevard Konrad Adenauer 100, L2950 Luxembourg, Luxembourg

European Patent Office, Erhardtstrasse 27, D-8000, Munchen 2, Germany

European Rail Research Institute (ERRI), Oudenard 500, NL-3513 Utrecht, Netherlands

European Space Agency, 8-10 rue Mario Nikis, F-75738 Paris Cedex 15, France

General Agreement on Tariffs and Trade (GATT), Centre William Rappard, rue de Lausanne 154, CH-1211 Geneva 21, Switzerland

Group of 77, United Nations, UN Plaza, PO Box 20, New York, NY, USA

Industrial Copyright Reform Association (ICRA), Ribchester House, Lancaster Road, Preston PR1 2QL

Industrial Development Fund, c/o UNIDO, Vienna International Centre, PO Box 300, A-1400 Wien, Austria

Institute of Information Scientists (IIS), 44-45 Museum Street, London WC1A 1LY

Institute of International Licensing Practitioners, Suite 78, 87 Regent Street, London W1R 7HF

Institute of Investors, 19-21 and 32 Fosse Way, Ealing, London W13 0BZ

Institute of Materials Management, Cranfield Institute of Technology, Cranfield, Bedfordshire MK42 0AL

Institute of Patentees and Inventors (IPI), Suite 505a, 189 Regent Street, London WC1R 7WF

Institute of Scientific and Technical Communicators (ISTC), PO Box 479, Luton LV1 4QR

Institute of Trade Mark Agents (ITMA), 4th Floor, Canterbury House, 2-6 Sydenham Road, Croydon CR0 9KE

Inter-American Development Bank, 1300 New York Avenue, Washington, DC 20577, USA

International Association of Technological University Libraries, Herriot-Watt University Library, Riccarton, Currie, Edinburgh EH14 4AS

International Centre for the Settlement of Investment Disputes, 1818 H Street NW, Washington, DC 20433, USA

International Chamber of Commerce (ICC), 38 cours Albert premier, 75008 Paris, France

International Confederation of Associations of Experts and Consultants, 10 rue Débarcadére, F75852, Paris Cedex 17, France

International Copyright Information Centre, c/o Association of American Publishers, 17/18 Connecticut Avenue NW, Washington DC 20008, USA

International Copyright Society, Rosenheimer Strasse 11, D-8000 Munich 80, Germany

International Development Association, 1818, H St. NW, Washington DC 20433, USA

International Development Research Centre, PO Box 8500, Ottawa, Ontario K1G 3H9, Canada

International Federation of Investors' Associations, 3 rue Bellot, CH-1206 Geneva, Switzerland

Appendices

International Law Association (ILA), 17 Russell Square, London WC1B 5DR

International League of Competition Law, 85 Boulevard Malesherbes, F-75008 Paris, France

International Monetary Fund, 700 19th St NW, Washington, DC 20832, USA

International Organization for Standardization, CP 56, rue de Varembi 1, CH-1211 Geneva, Switzerland

International Trade Centre, Palais des Nations, CH-1211 Geneva 10, Switzerland

International Association of Technical Associations & Organizations, Maison de d'UNESCO, 1 rue Miollin, F-75732 Paris Cedex 25, France

Latin American Association for Science and Technology Policy, Apartado Postal 22016, 14000 Mexico DF, Mexico

Latin American Integration Association, Calle Cebollati 1461, Casilia de Correo 527, 1001 Montevideo, Uruguay

League of Arab States, 52 Green Street, London W1Y 3RH

Licensing Executives Society International, 71 East Avenue, Norwalk, CT 06851-4903, USA

Licensing Executives Society, 57 Makfield Road, Caterham, Surrey CA3 6RQ

London Court of International Arbitration, 2-5 Minories, London EC3N 1BJ

Network for Environment Technology Transfer, Ave Louise 207, Boîte 10, B-1050, Brussels, Belgium

North Atlantic Treaty Organization (NATO), B-1110, Brussels, Belgium

OPEC Fund for International Development, PO Box 995, A-1011 Wien, Austria

ORGALIME (Organisme de Liaison des Industries Métalliques

Européennes) is a group of 'central engineering and metalworking trade associations' in 13 western European countries. Address: rue de Stassaert 99, B-1050 Brussels, Belgium

Organisation for Economic Cooperation and Development, 2 rue André Pascal, F-75775 Paris Cedex 16, France

Organization of African Unity, PO Box 3243, Addis Ababa, Ethiopia

Organization of American States (OAS) 12th St. & Constitution Ave NW, Washington DC 20006, USA

Patent Solicitors' Association, c/o Taylor Joynson Garrett, 10 Maltravers Street, London WC2R 3BS

Technical Information Pilot System, TIPS, via Parisperma 203, 1-00184 Rome, Italy

Third World Network of Scientific Organizations, ICTP, PO Box 586, Strada Costiera 11, 1-34136 Trieste, Italy

United Nations, One United Nations Plaza, New York, NY 10017, USA

United Nations Centre on Transnational Corporations, One United Nations Plaza, New York, NY 10017, USA. This centre is now closed and its activities are being carried on under the auspices of UNCTAD (see next entry)

United Nations Conference on Trade and Development, Palais des Nations, CH-1211, Geneva 10, Switzerland

United Nations Development Programme, One United Nations Plaza, New York, NY 10017, USA

United Nations Industrial Development Organization, Vienna International Centre, PO Box 30, A-1400 Wien, Austria

US Anti-Counterfeiting Coalition

West African Development Bank, BP1172, 68 ave de la Libéralion Lomé, Togo

World Bank (IBRD), 1818 H St NW, Washington DC 20433, USA

Appendices

World Intellectual Property Organization (WIPO), 34 Chemin des Colombettes, 1211 Geneva 20, Switzerland

Acknowledgements: This list was originally compiled by the authors from existing knowledge and contacts and checked through correspondence and telephone directories. The entire list was then rechecked with *Whittaker's Almanack* and the *Directory of International Organizations*.

Part 8

Indexes

8.1 Index of subjects

Advertising, 224-225
Agent,
　patent, 102
　sales, 51-52
　trademark, 100
Agreement, see contract
Anti-trust law, 215
Anton Piller order, 114-115
Arbitration, 28, 119-127
Bayer order, 115-116
Biodiversity, 346
Chambers of commerce, 237
Communication(s), 159-171, 181
　revolution, 349
Communist countries
(former), 287-334
Competition, 16, 28, 49, 138, 273, 339
　policies, 24, 140, 164, 262-263, 264, 290-291
　see also Anti-Trust
Computer,
　programmes, 112, 268
　technology, 346
Conciliation, 121, 126
Confidentiality, 134
Conflict, 164-165, 250
　causes of, 293
Construction contracts, 86
Consultant,
　licensing, 71
Consumer movement, 358-362
Contract manufacture, 6-7, 86
Contract (agreement), 145-156
　negotiating, 70

Control system, 159, 173-191
Copyright, 94-110, 267-268, 272, 275
Cost(s), 17, 191-205
　benefit analysis, 48
　development, 197
　direct transfer, 197
　dissipation, 198
　indirect transfer, 197
　opportunity, 193, 197-198
　real, 193
Countertrade, 17, 200-203, 295-296, 363
Cross-licensing, 25, 68-69, 169, 185, 250
Culture, 186-187, 355
　background, 173, 249
　barrier, 51
Currency,
　regulations, 24
Data transfer, 169-170
Decision-making, 168-169
Design, 163, 267, 269
Developing
countries, 25, 52, 54-56, 91, 102-103, 117
　manufacturing skills, 140, 143
　objectives of licensing, 257
　restrictions on
　licensing, 133, 137
　role of licensing, 263, 374
Disinvestment, 27, 356-357
Disputes,
　settlement of, 119-130, 134
Dividends, 17, 56-57

413

Indexes

Dumping,
    anti-dumping legislation, 56
Duration (of agreements), 133
Education, 365-366
Equity, 17, 45
Exchange control, 259, 273, 277
Export, 7, 51-52
Fashion industry, 98
Feasibility studies, 67
Fees, 56, 199, 295
Finance, 191-205
    strategies, 39-40
Forecasting,
    over-optimistic, 16
Franchising, 3-7, 45-46, 83-87
Funds,
    sources of, 199
Future of licensing, 347-367
    assistance for licensing, 118-119
    guidelines, 23-28
Globalization, 91
Government,
    negotiations, 14
    regulation of
    licensing, 117-118, 141-142, 291-296
Incoterms, 123
Industrialization, 26, 103, 288
Information, 23, 246
Innovation, 12, 67, 118, 138, 209-212, 261
Intellectual property,
    protection, 35-41, 102, 109, 112-116, 117-118, 138, 196, 239, 288, 357-366
    rights, 91-92, 106, 236, 274

International
    organizations, 27, 142
Internationalization, 183
Investment,
    direct, 8, 52-54, 138, 356-357
Joint venture, 7, 52-53, 62-63
Knowhow, 104, 165
    safeguarding, 128-130
    selling, 3, 117
Knowledge,
    transfer, 76-175, 180-182
Legal adviser, 71, 131
    issues, 89-113
Legislation, 117
Liability,
    personal, 16
    product, 16, 80, 365
Licensee, 13, 289-296
    guidelines, 19-21
Licensing, 3
    agreements (contracts), 8-9, 14-15, 29-33, 53, 72, 117
    managing, 157-255
    updating, 170-171
    compulsory, 25
    defined, 45
    policies, 24
    problems, 3, 39-343
    profession, 337-338, 335-346
    prospects, 345-357
    route to world markets, 45-46
    stages, 174-188
    strategy, 5-7, 47, 351-353
    sub-licensing, 32
    summary, 337-338

Licensor,
   guidelines, 11-18
   point of view, 48-49, 288-289
   relationship with licensee, 249-255
Management contracts, 3, 45-46, 83, 105
Management services, 24
Manufacturing, 175, 182-183, 276
Mareva order, 115
Market,
   share, 62-63
Marketing, 12, 132-137, 207-255
   licensing, 163
   revolution, 350-351
Market research, 11-12, 210-211, 213-224
Mediation, 123
Monitoring, 27, 141, 159, 185-188
Negotiations,
   contract, 71, 73-81, 174-180
   government, 287
Objectives,
   national, 26-27
Organization, 159-171
Patent(s), 35-37, 91, 166, 347
   agent, 237, 239, 266
   European, 112-113
   laws, 25, 114, 269, 275
   protection of, 138, 270, 288, 299
   United Kingdom system, 110, 111
   use of, 29

Performance,
   monitoring, 15
Personnel,
   services, 235-247
Pharmaceuticals, 67, 111, 185, 272, 293, 346
Planning, 69, 166, 173-190
Pricing, 191-205
   policy, 59-64, 79-80, 228
Profits, 53, 59-65, 191-198
   repatriation of, 56-57
Quality, 135, 229-230
Raw materials, 229
Recruitment, 235-237
Regional organizations, 281-286
Remuneration, 17, 132, 191-198
Research and development, 160
Resource(s), 48, 160
   utilization, 161-162
Responsibility, 159-160
Risk, 160-161
   political, 16, 23, 52, 56, 132, 148-149, 340
Royalty(ies),
   rate, 201
   taxation, 277-278
Scope (of agreements), 133
Selling, 12, 226
   knowledge, 3-7
Staffing, 235-237
Strategy(ies),
   business, 43-58, 185
Subsidiary(ies), 7, 53-54, 62-63
Tariffs, 49, 287
Tax, Taxation, 26, 52, 56-57, 80, 118, 203-205
   agreements, 274

Indexes

efficiency, 200
withholding, 23, 26, 27, 277-278
Technology, 133, 261, 288
  acquisition of, 292
  new, 346
  selling, 173, 261
  transfer, 24, 26, 37, 138, 181, 255, 262, 295
  agreement, 145-156
Test marketing, 49
Trademarks, 3, 91, 100-101, 135, 150-155, 362-363
  law of, 264, 269-270, 272
Trade unions, 235
Training, 143, 235-247
Transfer see Technology
Turnkey agreements, 7, 86

8.2 Index of names

Adoutte, R., 208
Africa,
    developing countries, 289
    sub-Saharan, 120
African Intellectual Property Organization (OAPI), 94, 281-283
African Regional Industrial Property Organization (ARIPO), 94
ALADI, 143, 281-283
America, 62
    Central, 346
    Latin, 122
    North, 120, 258, 348
    (see also: United States)
    South, 62, 349
American Arbitration Association, 120
Andean Community and Common Market (ANCOM), 143, 284
Antigua and Barbuda, 282
Arbitral Tribunal, 122
Argentina, 125, 204, 300-302
Asia, 62, 120, 227
    South-East, 53, 258, 351-352
Asia-Pacific Economic Cooperation Agreement (APEC), 348, 357
Association of South East Asian Nations (ASEAN), 143, 285-286
Australia(n), 62, 125, 177, 282, 348

Avis, 85
Bahamas, 282
Bahrain,
    patents, 35
Bank of Spain, 273
Barbados, 282
BEAMA, 145
Beamish, P.W., 140
Beijing, 350
Belarus, 297
Belgium, 125, 214, 261, 282
Belize, 282
Benelux, 222
Benin, 282
Berne Convention (1986), 93-94, 102, 281-283, 299
Bolivia, 282
Botswana, 94, 282
Brazil(ian), 242, 258, 298, 302-305, 358
British Virgin Islands, 284
Brooke, M.Z., 45, 83
Brussels Convention (1974), 346
Buckley, P.J., 47
Budapest Treaty (1977), 346
Bulgaria, 297
Burkina Faso, 282
Cameroon, 282
Canada, 125, 258, 269-271, 277, 282
Caribbean Community and Common Market (CARICOM), 143, 281-283
Casson, Mark, 208
Caterpillar, 214

417

Indexes

Central African Republic, 282
Centre for International Briefing, 249
Chile, 298
China,
   People's Republic of, 108, 201, 258, 274, 284, 296, 305-309, 349-358
Coca-Cola, 52, 227
Colombia, 125, 282
COMECON (former), 258, 282, 296-374
Communauté économique de l'Afrique de l'Quest (CEAO), 143
Congo, 282
Contractor, Farouk J., 179
Copyright, Designs and Patents Act, 96
Copyright Office (US), 277, 279
Croatia, 297
Customs and Excise, 114
Customs Service (US), 277, 279
Cyprus, 35
Czech Republic, 112, 282, 297, 309-312
Denmark, 261, 282
Department of Commerce (United States), 118
Department of Consumer and Corporate Affairs (Canada), 270
Department of Trade and Industry (DTI), (Britain), 118
Dexion, 62
Direccion General de Transacciones Exteriores (DGTE), 273

Dominica, 282
Dun and Bradstreet, 220
Earth Summit Convention, 346
Economic Community of West African States (ECOWAS), 143
Ecuador, 282
Egypt, 125
Estonia, 297
Europe, 62, 75, 109, 120, 181, 227, 347, 348
   countries, 282
   Eastern, 228, 236, 258, 274
   licensing partners in, 214, 235
   licensors, 236
   trade, 297, 357
European Economic Area, 261-269
European Free Trade Area, 268
European Patent Convention (EPC), 265-266, 268, 272
European Patent Office, 93
European Union, 62, 93, 99, 111-112, 120, 258-269
Far East, 348
   block exemptions, 138, 264, 347
   patents, 166
   licensees, 236
   regulations, 264-265, 267-268, 271
Farnham Castle, 249
Ford, D., 247
France (French), 62, 125, 204, 282
   information, 215

licensees,	212, 243-244	Hofstede G.,	249
patents,	36-37	Hong Kong,	258, 358
Francovitch doctrine,	265	Hughes, Helen,	255
Franklin Pierce Law Center (Concord),	365	Hungary,	282, 297, 309-316, 363
Fry, Robin,	98	ICI plc,	38-39
Gabon,	282	India,	108, 119, 181, 201, 204, 258, 294-295
Gambia,	283		
General Agreement on Tariffs and Trade (GATT),	91-92, 251-258, 281-283, 287, 295, 298, 357	Indonesia,	214, 258, 284, 316-318
		Institute of Licensing Practitioners,	237
		International Centre for Settlement of Investment Disputes,	28, 124-126, 142
Uruguay round of,	113		
General Motors,	128-130		
Geneva,	364	International Chamber of Commerce,	28, 121-124, 154
Germany,	54, 128, 204, 282, 366		
companies,	238	International Council for the Settlement of Industrial Disputes (ICSID),	
information,	215		
licences,	212, 226		
licensees,	222	Court of Arbitration,	122
licensors,	229	International Court of Justice,	126
patents,	36-37		
Ghana,	283	Iran,	258
GKN,	351	Ireland,	261, 282
Glacier Metal Co Ltd,	163, 224, 353-354	Israel,	284
		Italy,	204, 222, 261, 271, 282
Gossilies,	214	patents,	37
Greece,	261, 282	Ivory Coast,	125, 282
Grenada,	284	Jamaica,	284
Guinea,	282	Japan(ese),	53, 54, 62, 107, 140, 236, 284
Guyana,	284		
Hague Agreement (1925),	94, 105, 281-283	licences,	212
		patents,	36-37
Hertz,	85	tax,	204
Hills, Carla,	92	Jordan,	125
Holiday Inn,	85	Kazakhstan,	297

419

Indexes

Kentucky Fried Chicken, 62, 350
Kenya, 35, 91, 282
Kodak, 109
Kompass, 220
Korea: The Democratic People's Republic (North), 284, 322-323
Korea: The Republic of South, 62, 91, 119, 255, 258, 284, 294, 298, 318-322, 358
KPMG, 129
Latin American Integration Association (ALADI), 143, 281-283
Latvia, 297
Lesotho, 94, 282
Licensing Executives Society, 237
Lisbon Agreement, 95
Lithuania, 297
London, 238
London Court of International Arbitration, 28, 120-121
Luxembourg, 282
Madrid Agreement for international trademark registration, 101, 105, 269, 281-283
Malawi, 282
Malaysia, 119, 204, 214, 258, 284, 296, 323-325, 350-357
Mali, 282
Mallott, Robert H., 92
Mauritania, 282
Melville, Leslie William, 145
Merck, 346

Mexico, 258, 270, 277, 282
Middle East, 122
Ministry of Economy and Finance (Spain), 273
Ministry of International Trade and Industry (Japan), 118-119, 294, 296, 298, 358
Mitsubishi, 350-351
Moldavia, 297
Monsoon, 98
Montserrat, 284
Mrs Field's Cookies, 85
Munich Convention, 93
National Research and Development Corporation (NRDC), 209
Netherlands, 204, 282
New Zealand, 282, 348
New York Agreement (International Chamber of Commerce), 122
Niger, 282
Nigeria, 35, 214, 243-244, 284, 296, 299
North American Free Trade Area (NAFTA), 143, 258, 270, 277, 281-285, 357
ORGALIME, 145
Organisation for Economic Cooperation and Development (OECD), 215, 274
   member countries, 37, 110, 348, 352
Ovshinsky, 211
Pacific Rim Countries, 120, 363

Pakistan, 62
Paris, 125
Paris Convention, 93-94, 102, 105, 113-114, 142, 269, 281-283
see also Stockholm
Patent and Trade Marks Office (US), 277, 279
Patent Co-operation Treaty (PCT), 95, 105, 265-268
Patents County Court (United Kingdom), 358
Patent Office (European Union), 112
Patent Office (United Kingdom), 31, 110-111
Patent Office (United States), 110
Pepsi Cola, 85-86
Peru, 282
Philippines, The, 125, 290
Pilkington Plc, 39-40, 62, 201, 353-354
Poland, 201, 282, 297, 325-330, 350, 363
Polaroid, 109
Portugal, 282
Proton car, 350-351
Price Waterhouse, 204
Research Corporation (United States), 209
Rio de Janeiro, 346
Romania, 53, 282, 293-294, 297
Russian Federation, 204, 296-297, 349, 350
St Kitts-Nevis, 284

St Lucia, 284
St Vincent & The Grenadines, 284
Salon International des Inventions (Geneva), 364
Saudi-Arabia, 330-334
Savaret, Julien, 340
Selina Knitwear, 97-99
Senegal, 282
Senel, Allen, 99
Sierra Leone, 282
Simon, Peter, 98, 99
Sinclair, Clive, 353
Singapore, 119, 204, 296, 299
Slovak Republic, 282, 309-312
Slovenia, 297
Somalia, 282
South Africa, 284, 291, 349
Soviet Union (former), 112, 258
Spain, 125, 204, 261, 266, 272-274, 282
Stephens Innocent, 98
Sterling, cycle engine, 211
Stockholm version of Paris Convention, 272
Strategic Programme for Innovation and Technology transfer (SPRINT), 261
Sudan, The, 94, 282
Sweden(ish), 110-111, 173, 177
patents, 37
Switzerland, 125, 204, 210, 268
Syria, 125
Taiwan (Republic of China), 113, 258, 284, 296, 358

421

Indexes

Tanzania,	282	studies,	366
Tchad,	282	taxation,	204
Technology Ministry (Korea),	296	United Kingdom Atomic Energy Authority,	52
Technology Performance Financing Scheme,	261	United Nations,	215
Telesio, Piero,	47, 138-139	Centre on Transnational Corporations,	27-28, 289-291
Thailand,	258, 298, 299	Conference on Trade and Development,	28
Thunman, Carl C.,	173	Industrial Development Organization (UNIDO),	12, 142
Togo,	282	United States (America),	73-81, 92, 109-114, 128, 282
Top Shop,	98		
Trademarks Registry (Britain),	100-101, 265		
Trade Related Aspects of Intellectual Property (TRIPS),	113	companies,	214
Treaty of Rome,	113, 262, 273	free trade,	257
Trinidad & Tobago,	284	information,	215
Tunisia,	125	jobs,	258
Turkey(ish),	54-55, 227, 258, 274, 289	liability insurance,	366
		licensees,	212, 235
Turks & Caico Islands,	284	licensing,	297, 262
Turner and Newall plc,	163	marketing,	226
Uganda,	282	membership of Free Trade Area,	270
Ukraine,	297	patents,	35-37, 266
United Arab Emirates,	298	regulations,	275-277
United Kingdom (Britain),	93, 282	technology,	139
companies,	353-354	trade,	297
exports,	351	Unusier, J.C.,	173
government,	39-40	UPI,	209
information,	215	Uppsala, University of,	173
inventions,	353	US Shoe Corporation,	97
legal proceedings,	358	Uzbekistan,	297
licensees,	21, 228, 229	Vinci, Leonardo da,	212
patents,	35-37	Volkswagen,	128-130, 242, 247
products,	226		

Wankel,
 engine, 212
Washington
 Convention, 125-126
Wells, L.T., 289
Wilkinson Sword, 201
World Bank, 12, 125-126, 142, 215, 287
World Intellectual Property Organization (WIPO), 27, 92-99, 102-103, 105, 109, 142, 346
Xerox, 212
Yugoslavia (former), 53, 11, 213, 282, 350
Zambia, 282
Zimbabwe, 282